Are We Not Foreigners Here?

Indigenous Nationalism in the
U.S.-Mexico Borderlands

. . . .

JEFFREY M. SCHULZE

University of North Carolina Press Chapel Hill

The University of North Carolina Press has been a member
of the Green Press Initiative since 2003.

Library of Congress Cataloging-in-Publication Data
Names: Schulze, Jeffrey M., author.
Title: Are we not foreigners here? : Indigenous nationalism in the
    U.S.-Mexico borderlands / Jeffrey M. Schulze.
Description: Chapel Hill : University of North Carolina Press, [2018] |
    Includes bibliographical references and index.
Identifiers: LCCN 2017044579| ISBN 9781469637105 (cloth : alk. paper) |
    ISBN 9781469637112 (pbk.: alk. paper) | ISBN 9781469637129 (ebook)
Subjects: LCSH: Yaqui Indians—Mexican-American Border Region—History. |
    Kickapoo Indians—Mexican-American Border Region—History. | Tohono
    O'odham Indians—Mexican-American Border Region—History. |
    Transborder ethnic groups—Politics and government. | Nationalism.
Classification: LCC F1221.Y3 S38 2018 | DDC 972/.1—dc23 LC record available
    at https://lccn.loc.gov/2017044579

Cover illustration: Photograph by John Malmin, originally captioned
"Easy Crossing—Two Papago Indians ride through one of the scores of
openings in the fence that marks the border between Sonora and Arizona.
There are no customs officials here." Copyright © 1977, *Los Angeles Times*.
Used with Permission.

Portions of chapter 3 were previously published in a different form as
" 'The Year of the Yaqui': Texas Tech's Sonoran Expeditions, 1934–1984,"
Journal of the West 48:3 (2009). Copyright © 2009 by *Journal of the West*,
an imprint of ABC-CLIO, LLC. All rights reserved. Reproduced with permission
of ABC-CLIO, LLC, Santa Barbara, California.

For my mom, Deborah Anita Pierce,

in loving memory

Contents

Illustrations and Map

Are We Not Foreigners Here?

Portrait of José María Leyva (Cajeme), taken while he was under arrest. National Anthropological Archives, Smithsonian Institution NAA: 81-7675.

Introduction

· ·

While traveling through Sonora in April 1887, a reporter from the *Tucson Daily Citizen* witnessed the public execution of Cajeme, one of Mexican history's great enigmas.[1] José María Leyva, as he was less commonly known, had been born to Yaqui Indian parents and raised in the Yaqui village of Ráum in southern Sonora, but lived much of his life in another world entirely. Shortly after the young Leyva and his father returned from Gold Rush–era California having failed to strike it rich, his parents made the no doubt difficult decision to entrust their son to Prefect Cayetano Navarro of nearby Guaymas. It was at this moment that Leyva left his Yaqui home for what appears to have been the last time. In Guaymas he began his education, supplementing the smattering of English he had learned in California by learning to read, write, and speak Spanish. He completed his studies at the age of eighteen and left Guaymas literate, trilingual, and well traveled— in other words, a very atypical Yaqui. At some point during his residence in Guaymas, however, he had evidently ceased to identify himself as such.

Rather than return to his village, Leyva entered into a period of aimlessness, joining, then abandoning, the military repeatedly, briefly apprenticing with a blacksmith, and working in a mine for a short period of time until drifting back to Sonora around 1861. Upon his return, he learned that the Mexican government was in the process of putting down the latest in a string of Yaqui uprisings. He immediately, and inexplicably, enlisted in the expeditionary force sent to quell the rebellion. They succeeded and then disbanded. From there, Leyva drifted around Sonora with no stable occupation until 1867, when he again enlisted in the military following reports of yet another Yaqui uprising. This latest campaign was especially violent, culminating in the so-called Bácum Massacre, in which 120 Yaquis lost their lives when a church Mexican soldiers were using as a makeshift prison for some 450 captives mysteriously went up in flames. It is remembered, to this day, as one of the darkest chapters in Yaqui history.[2]

Why Leyva took up arms against his own people during this period is an intriguing unknown, though it has been the subject of speculation. It has been argued, for example, that since he had had virtually no contact with the Yaquis since departing for Guaymas he probably no longer felt rooted in his Yaqui heritage, if he ever had in the first place.[3] Opportunism also cannot be discounted as a possibility. His acquaintance with the Yaqui language placed Leyva on the fast track within the Sonoran military establishment, providing opportunities available to few enlistees, opportunities that must have seemed attractive given his perpetual lack of occupational stability. Whatever his motivations may have been, Leyva quickly distinguished himself as a respected Indian fighter and a dependable member of the local militia. In 1874, Sonoran governor Ignacio Pesqueira handpicked Leyva for the post of *alcalde mayor* of the Yaqui River valley, charging him with the governorship of the lands encompassing the Yaquis' eight pueblos with the expectation that Leyva would help pacify his people.[4] Leyva apparently made quite a bit of progress in his new post, with the creation of a regional tax system, a commercial market that connected the Yaquis with outsiders, and a more refined system of local government on his list of accomplishments. But for reasons that are not entirely clear, Leyva ultimately vacated his government post and traded his Spanish name for Cajeme, which in the Yaqui language translates as "he who does not drink," a name attributable to his habit of drinking water only once a day, at four in the afternoon, as a form of self-discipline. He then seized control, through infamously violent means, of the eight Yaqui pueblos, and, from there, directed one of the largest indigenous uprisings in North American history. Cajeme's objective, put simply, was to win Yaqui independence from Mexico, and he had what the Mexican military estimated to be between 4,000 and 5,000 Yaqui soldiers—organized into cavalry, artillery, and infantry units and possessing some 12,000 firearms—backing him up as he attempted to establish control of the Yaqui River valley.[5]

Mexican soldiers sent to quell the rebellion found Cajeme to be surprisingly elusive. In fact, some Mexican authorities began to question whether he existed at all. As one Mexican soldier put it, "He seemed to be an imaginary being, invisible, a myth created by the fantasy of his people."[6] More pragmatic military officials, meanwhile, were predicting that the cunning and crafty Yaqui leader would most likely try to disguise himself and head for the U.S.-Mexico border.[7] Cajeme managed to remain at large until 1887, when an Indian spotted him just outside of Guaymas and notified the military. When finally ferreted out of hiding, he reportedly put up no struggle and, at least according to one account, appeared relieved. The Mexican military transported Cajeme by ship to the Yaqui River valley and paraded him through the streets of the tribe's various pueblos to erase any doubt that he had been apprehended and would be executed. His "tour" ended in Cócorit. Sonora's governor at the time, Ramón Corral, allowed Cajeme to visit with friends, family, and even the general public while awaiting execution. Corral was apparently so taken with Cajeme that he went on to become the Yaqui leader's first biographer. He would characterize him as not the stuff of myth, but "a man of medium height, slim but not skinny, with an astute smile on his wide mouth, friendly and good-natured and communicative as few Indians are."[8]

After Cajeme's execution, the aforementioned reporter from the *Tucson Daily Citizen* watched as a grieving Yaqui approached the tree against which Cajeme was felled and affixed to it a small cross containing the inscription "INR, aque [sic] fallecio General Cajeme, Abril 23, 1887, a los 11 y 5 la mañana." The abbreviation INR is Latin for Jesus of Nazareth, King. Among at least some of the Yaqui people, Cajeme was akin to a deity.[9] Among his enemies, however, he personified a disturbing conviction, one deeply held by indigenous peoples across the Americas: that only Indians should govern Indians. It is this conviction that forms the heart of the present study. A relentless insistence on political and cultural autonomy became a fundamental component of indigenous identity virtually from the moment of European contact, and this impulse remained just as acute even after geopolitical borders coalesced, gained international recognition, and gave rise to powerful, omnipresent nation-states. These nation-states had as their primary objective the smothering of any and all competing claims to sovereignty within their borders, and indigenous peoples, it turned out, tended to represent the biggest obstacle in these nationalizing projects. Stories of indigenous resistance in this context are extraordinarily common. Less common, however, are stories of indigenous resistance in a transnational context, or stories of Indian peoples challenging, subverting, capitalizing upon, or just plain ignoring any geopolitical border that sought to contain, neutralize, and ultimately extinguish their *own* nationalistic aspirations. And stories of Indian peoples *winning* these contests, as the Yaquis ultimately would, are even fewer and farther between.

Under Cajeme, or from roughly 1875 through 1887, the Yaquis entered into a bitter and violent bid for independence that displaced and nearly destroyed the tribe. It was akin to blowing on a dandelion clock: the Yaquis, like seed-bearing spores, scattered aimlessly in all directions, entering into a period of dormancy while awaiting the opportunity to flower. They became, in the words of the anthropologist Edward Spicer, "the most widely scattered people in North America," thinly and precariously settled from central and southern Arizona and California all the way down to the Yucatán Peninsula.[10] In hindsight, however, it appears that Cajeme did the Yaquis more of a service than many would have predicted during those tumultuous years. He helped reawaken and reinvigorate a once-powerful nationalist impulse that had waned somewhat among the Yaquis in the years leading up to the late nineteenth-century cycle of rebellion. And although the rebellion under Cajeme had wide-ranging consequences, when the dust finally settled the Yaquis were in a much better position to bargain with Mexican authorities in their push for the greatest degree of Yaqui autonomy possible, an opportunity they did not hesitate to seize. Once it was safe to come out of hiding, a portion of the tribe negotiated its return to the Yaqui River valley, and thereafter maintained at least a precarious peace with Mexican authorities. Other Yaquis, meanwhile, looked to the United States for refuge during and in the immediate wake of the tumultuous Cajeme years, founding what would become a series of vital transborder communities, one of which would ultimately gain official sanction as an "American" Indian reservation despite the fact that the tribe originated in Mexico. Over the course of the twentieth century, the tribal whole would work toward not only forging transborder ties in order to link these far-flung settlements, but also reconstituting the Yaqui nation. It was an unusual strategy for overcoming seemingly insurmountable obstacles in maintaining political cohesion and cultural continuity. Not surprisingly, other tribes inhabiting the border region hit upon a similar strategy, with some even enjoying a similar degree of success.

While the Mexican government waged war on the Yaquis during the latter years of the nineteenth century, the U.S. government waged a war of a different sort on Kickapoo Indians living in Oklahoma. They became one of many targets of the government's ill-fated 1887 General Allotment Act, designed to hasten the Indians' assimilation by undercutting their more traditional land use practices, or by dividing communally held reservation lands into private plots. As in the Yaqui case, many Kickapoos responded to this assault on their autonomy by simply crossing the border. Kickapoos had been migrating to Mexico since at least the 1820s, arriving in a succession of waves for a variety of reasons. The Mexican government, looking to bolster defenses along its northern periphery, typically welcomed these migrants, gave them land, and even guaranteed their right to speak their own language and maintain their distinctive culture. Still, the population of Kickapoos in Mexico fluctuated wildly for much of the nineteenth and twentieth centuries as Kickapoo bands traveled back and forth between

Mexico and Oklahoma. At one point Mexico boasted a Kickapoo population of several thousand, at another point less than twenty. Gradually, however, the tribe solidified and legitimized its transnational orientation. As in the Yaqui case, what began as a last-gasp effort to maintain tribal cohesion and cultural continuity evolved into an utterly new way of life, though not one without unique pitfalls.[11]

The U.S.-Mexico border has also profoundly affected the Tohono O'odham tribe of southern Arizona and northern Sonora, though in a different way. In contrast to the Yaqui and Kickapoo cases, the Tohono O'odham's division by the U.S.-Mexico border was not the result of either voluntary or forced migration, but of simple geographic orientation. Essentially, the 1853 Gadsden Purchase, which added the far southern portions of the present-day states of New Mexico and Arizona to U.S. territory, cut the Tohono O'odham in two, leaving a portion on the U.S. side and a portion on the Mexican side.[12] Like the Yaquis and Kickapoos, the O'odham often jumped at the chance to capitalize on borderlands dynamics. At the turn of the century, the O'odham entered the cash economy, laboring on both Mexican and American ranches, plantations, and mines. More long-standing subsistence patterns, however, gradually fell by the wayside. The O'odham quickly slid into a pattern of dependency on both sides of the border, with little holding the two halves of the tribal whole together. Then in 1916, concerned U.S. officials created a formal reservation for the tribe. While a protected land base might seem like a good thing, the reservation symbolized a kind of compartmentalization of the O'odham, or a tacit recognition that there were now two kinds of O'odham: "American" and "Mexican." In short, the reservation ultimately fostered a sense of displacement on both sides of the border despite the fact that the tribe had not actually moved. However, although the O'odham may appear to have come up short as nation builders when examined alongside the Yaquis and Kickapoos, the fact is that they emerged with their collective identity, many of their traditional lifeways, and a respectable (although vastly reduced) portion of their ancestral land base intact. Even O'odham residing south of the border who were being forced to endure what the historians Andrae Marak and Laura Tuennerman characterized as a "massive assault" on their ancestral lands by non-Indians could not be purged of their O'odham identity.[13] Regardless, for at least a few decades after the border's advent, the O'odham, like the Yaquis and Kickapoos, would successfully use it to at least their economic advantage. For a variety of reasons, however, the window of time in which they were able to do so would be frustratingly narrow. Put simply, it would not take long for the United States and Mexico to step up their bureaucratic presence in the border region and attempt to more meaningfully manage transborder traffic. While the Yaquis and Kickapoos proved to be remarkably adept at navigating these changes, the O'odham often seemed to be surviving in spite of, rather than because of, the existence of the international boundary.

Still, for much of the late nineteenth and early twentieth centuries, historical parallels between the three groups are easy to locate. Spurred to action by unremitting assaults on their sovereignty, each developed a counterstrategy that included, first and foremost, exploiting U.S.-Mexico borderlands dynamics, a strategy that they carefully expanded and refined over time. For these Indians, border crossings became acts of "creative defiance," as the historian Oscar Martínez phrased it in a more general discussion of what he termed "border people." Such crossings were a way to capitalize—economically, politically, and culturally—on a political line of demarcation created without their consent (and in some cases without their knowledge), but one that nonetheless held a tremendous amount of promise. Like Cajeme, these Indians gradually grew adept at moving between an array of individual and group identities and ethnic and cultural worlds, all the while maintaining a specific indigenous identity and a nationalistic agenda. Border crossings, then, enabled these Indians to strike a balance between asserting their sovereignty and maintaining their anonymity.[14]

Along the U.S.-Mexico border alone there are a host of indigenous groups that have assumed a transnational orientation in response to pressures at home, including the Mixtecos, Zapatecos, Triquis, Otomíes, Purépechas, Cocopahs, Kumeyaays, and Nahuas, among others.[15] Furthermore, similar processes continue to play themselves out not just along the U.S.-Canada border, but essentially anywhere tribal and nonstate peoples have challenged the authority of nation-states to restrict their movements and dictate their national loyalties. Formal international boundaries have historically been notorious for inviting the creation of transborder networks that enable and even encourage transnational interaction. Such was the case with, for example, the Baluchis, divided by the borders of Iran, Afghanistan, and Pakistan, or the Kurds, divided by the borders of Turkey, Iraq, and Iran. The Yaquis and Tohono O'odham, incidentally, could easily be added to this list in that while they technically belong to a nation-state, they nonetheless continue to harbor the sense of being a people apart.[16]

But the stories contained herein are not merely case studies of individuals, families, and/or communities struggling to adapt to the reality of geopolitical borders while also attempting to capitalize on those same borders.

Focusing primarily on the three groups of border Indians discussed above—the Yaquis of Sonora/Arizona, the Kickapoos of Texas/Coahuila, and the Tohono O'odham of Sonora/Arizona—this book highlights moments when these peoples began, in a sense, nation building in the U.S.-Mexico borderlands. Although their transnational orientation complicated this pursuit considerably, it also, serendipitously enough, made its realization far more likely. Near-constant movement on a transnational scale kept these indigenous groups beyond the political and cultural purview of each of the nation-states within which they resided (or to which they migrated), exempted them, in many cases, from detrimental Indian policy currents on both sides of the border, and, above all, helped them maintain a measure of anonymity, which allowed them both the physical and ideological space within which to enact their *own* vision of nationhood. The resultant trans-border settlements, some of which non-Indians initially viewed as little more than refugee camps or way stations, gradually became officially sanctioned, durable, and dynamic centers of indigenous life.

The use of the U.S.-Mexico border as a strategy for group survival, and ultimately group expansion, required the ability to identify and capitalize on holes in the immigration system (which these groups often had a penchant for locating) and the audacity and vigilance to confidently assert their legal privileges as indigenous peoples, privileges that both the United States and Mexico were morally obligated, if not treaty-bound, to respect. Doing so helped them carve out a unique (and uniquely legal) position for themselves within the borders of both the United States and Mexico, a position from which they negotiated, little by little, an almost staggering degree of autonomy. This is a remarkable feat even in the arena of transnational history, where stories of displacement and survival are the norm. One scholar defined "transnationalism" as "a process through which migrants cross international boundaries and synthesize two societies in a single social field, linking their country of origin with their country of immigration."[17] Far more improbable, however, is the endeavor of *nation building* across extant international boundaries.

Reorienting one's perspective within these *indigenous* nations, then, allows one to approach these three groups' histories as might a historian of foreign policy or international diplomacy. Native peoples were no strangers to external relations with European powers prior to the advent of the United States and Mexico. Add other indigenous groups to the mix, and Indian diplomacy assumes a complexity that would baffle even established nation-states as they attempted to navigate the world stage. However, the temptation has long been to regard Indian history as, in the words of the historian Donald Fixico, "a special or exotic subfield" or "a minority history of less importance." Yet even a cursory look at these three groups reveals that they were far from "internal subjects." Instead, they consistently displayed a determination to assert some form of control over foreign relations, often with surprising degrees of success.[18] Rather than present these Indians as variables moving within a larger transnational system, then, this book inverts this formulation and demonstrates that the Indian peoples examined herein envisioned their *own* system, a system within which both the U.S. and Mexican governments, and neighboring Indian nations for that matter, were but variables.

Thus, more than simply being a line on a map, the U.S.-Mexico border affected and still affects individual and group processes of identity construction and retention in profound ways. Traversing the physical border often meant traversing less tangible classification systems. The indigenous peoples discussed in this book experiment with countless combinations of identities—tribal versus pan-Indian, Mexican versus American, Mexican versus Indian, American versus Indian, along with a host of regional and intertribal identities—all the while maintaining an inherent and inalienable sense of Indianness fed by a desire for independent nationhood, one that was not often articulated but, as will be shown, was always deeply felt. Although they did not boast borders that marked the landscape in as formidable a fashion as that separating the United States and Mexico, the conception of themselves as distinct political and cultural entities was no less acute. Writing about the Yaquis in the 1950s, one anthropologist observed, "As present Yaqui leaders conceive it, their government is for Yaquis only and is one which exists by virtue of a divine, or supernatural, mandate."[19] It would prove difficult for both the United States and Mexico to argue with this brand of logic.

This book, then, examines in comparative fashion these Indians' experiences as they struggled to reconcile an indigenous vision of nationhood with that of two powerful, omnipresent nation-states. But it also highlights those moments when the realities of international coexistence forced these indigenous nations, like other transborder peoples, to forfeit some of their hard-won autonomy, or to learn to share power with surrounding nation-states. After all, maintaining one's political isolation and unqualified sovereignty in an increasingly interconnected world is no small task. Still, the surprising end to this story is that these three groups managed to force two powerful nation-states to essentially redraw their borders, or to at least rethink the real and imagined limits of their own nationhood.[20] What we are left with, then, is a distinctly different North American legal, political, and cultural milieu than those typically proffered by historians, one in which nations and nation-states not only abut one another, but also overlap and interact from varying positions of power and with varying degrees of consequence. It is one in which "borderlands" appear more multidimensional and less binary than the term "transnational" implies, since formal lines of demarcation, when viewed from the ground rather than on a map, all too often command little, if any, respect.[21] Finally, it is one in which "nationhood" is, more often than not, really in the eye of the beholder.

The larger U.S.-Mexico border region has long been a contested space and meeting place, even prior to the creation of the formal border. At different moments during the colonial period, Spain, France, and England all competed for control of the region with both one another and the indigenous peoples who called the region home. First explored by the Spanish during the sixteenth century, the arc that came to be known as the Spanish Borderlands, which reached from present-day Florida to present-day California, changed hands repeatedly as the fortunes of colonial powers and, later, nation-states rose and fell. Spanish, French, and British colonial powers came into increasingly regular contact in the region during the eighteenth century as the French expanded from the Great Lakes region into the Mississippi River valley and as the British began their own exploration of and expansion into parts west and south. Thus began the often violent process of staking territorial claims. The first to leave the region were the French, who, at the end of the French and Indian War, forfeited their claims to Louisiana, leaving the region temporarily in Spanish hands. The British continued pressing south and west, putting the Spanish on the defensive. After gaining its independence from England, the new United States continued the British tradition of contesting Spanish claims. Its efforts produced a slow but steady southward recession of the Spanish frontier. In the early nineteenth century, Louisiana changed hands yet again, passing from Spanish to French hands, only to be sold to the United States shortly thereafter. The fact that France failed to specify the Louisiana Purchase's exact boundaries, however, virtually assured continued conflict between the United States and Spain.[22]

The two nations settled the boundary dispute in 1819 by drawing a line of demarcation from the Sabine River in present-day Texas, north to the forty-second parallel, then west to the Pacific. Mexico's independence from Spain in 1821 meant that the task of defending the northern frontier from

U.S. expansionist designs now fell to the nascent Mexican government, a task it was largely unprepared to undertake. Chaos reigned in the region from the early 1830s through the 1840s as the new nation was unable to forge a lasting peace with area Indians, and soon the northern third of Mexico degenerated into what one historian called a "vast theater of hatred, terror, and staggering loss for independent Indians and Mexicans alike." Chaos and instability, in turn, left the region vulnerable to the United States' designs. Another blow for Mexico came in 1836, with Texas's independence, then another in 1845, with Texas's annexation by the United States. It was the U.S.-Mexican War of 1846–48 and the resultant Treaty of Guadalupe Hidalgo, however, that resulted in the most significant loss of land in Mexico's history (the present-day American Southwest, which amounted to about half of its territorial holdings). The United States and Mexico took the last step in formalizing their boundary in 1853 with the Gadsden Purchase. Because of worsening financial woes, coupled with a great deal of pressure and intimidation emanating from Washington, the Mexican government sold southern sections of present-day New Mexico and Arizona to the U.S. government, which was then envisioning a potential route for a transcontinental railroad.[23]

It is important to keep in mind that those Indian groups situated closest to the border were among those borderlanders (and there were many) who were not convinced that the retreat of Mexico's northern frontier was complete by 1853. Like everyone else in the region, they often contemplated how best to protect themselves and both their individual and collective agendas in such a volatile and unpredictable atmosphere, and were sometimes moved to action. For example, writing to an American military officer in 1873, Chief John Horse from the "Seminole Wildcat Party," which briefly lived alongside the Kickapoos in Nacimiento, Coahuila, implored, "The [U.S.] Government might take Mexico every hour or minute and of course will take all the land and General please let us know what we shall do to keep our own."[24] In the end, however, Chief John Horse's fears proved unfounded. Although rumors of annexation schemes emanating from north of the border persisted until the end of the nineteenth century, and although Mexican officials would go so far as to query the U.S. State Department about these rumors, the State Department would ultimately deny any hand in their fabrication and any knowledge of their origin. And although efforts to either seize or purchase additional Mexican lands by either filibusters or more formal agents of the U.S. government did not cease in 1853, the boundary between the two nation-states moved very little in subsequent years.[25]

With the formal border separating the United States and Mexico now drawn, the region entered into a new phase in its long history, one in which local populations began mounting challenges to the efforts of distant centers of power to dictate their national loyalties and confine them within seemingly arbitrary boundaries. After all, though the United States and Mexico claimed ownership of their respective sides of the border, much of the region was actively controlled by indigenous peoples. This new trend produced what one scholar called a "confusion of identities" in the borderlands. In other words, the border region had officially become a site where once-stable identities were being "deterritorialized and renegotiated," a process that challenged and even undermined "culture, class, and region, as well as gender and nation."[26] But although the "confusion of identities" characterization is apt, borders can and often do have the opposite effect. Some of the indigenous peoples in this study were drawn to the region only after the United States and Mexico delineated the boundary between their national domains. It has not been unusual for indigenous peoples living on the "periphery" of their *own* "core" to re-create and revitalize social and cultural norms in even far-flung and unfamiliar geographic contexts. In fact, those living farthest from the group's "traditional" core often prove the *most* determined to safeguard their indigenous identity, a trend that will be brought into sharp relief in subsequent chapters.[27]

Similarly, while the border may often divide peoples and places, it has also historically done the opposite. After all, national borders do not always deliver on the promise of national sovereignty. As the historians Elaine Carey and Andrae Marak observed, while borders are indeed "contested spaces that divide people, leading to the construction of seemingly distinct races, nationalities, genders, and cultural practices," they also tend to "act as barriers across which social, political, cultural, and economic networks function." Put simply, they very often create "nebulous spaces" that have the tendency to invite all manner of opportunism.[28] Indeed, since the U.S.-Mexico border's advent, peoples, processes, and phenomena have conspired to keep transnational channels open. Mines and military posts in Arizona, for example, relied on supplies and laborers from Sonora from the second half of the nineteenth century on. In fact, a railroad connecting Sonora to Mexico City was not completed until 1927. By that point a railroad had connected Sonora and Arizona for over four decades. Religious events, such as the annual fiesta of San Francisco in Magdalena, Sonora, drew an international crowd, including Indians from both sides of the border as well as Mexican migrant workers, for much of the nineteenth and twentieth centuries. Since mines and smelters on both sides of the border would often suspend operations for these occasions to allow workers to attend, some *Anglo-American* workers even joined in the festivities. Wayward cattle required transborder roundups, roundups in which local custom tended to trump the laws of the state. Law enforcement officials on both sides of the border often allowed one another to cross the border in the pursuit of alleged lawbreakers. To get around the illegality of such crossings, officials simply requested temporary leave prior to the transborder pursuit, thereby sidestepping international law. Thus, despite the efforts of distant policymakers to impose a national divide, borderlanders themselves gradually forged economic networks and local customs that defied all efforts to sever hard-won, and often surprisingly active, transnational networks. By the twentieth century, then, many of the indigenous peoples in this story were moving on well-worn paths, paths between mines and fields, between ranches and smelters, even refugee pathways, all of which, sometimes coincidentally and sometimes not so coincidentally, traversed the international boundary. In the process, as this book will demonstrate, many also managed to locate so-called regions of refuge within which to exercise individual and group autonomy in the state's shadows, acting in defiance of not only the geopolitical boundary, but also the sovereign authority of two looming nation-states.[29]

But Indians were not your ordinary border crossers. Scholarship on transnational peoples and phenomena has all too often either ignored the indigenous perspective or done little to differentiate their experiences from those of other immigrant groups and/or ethnic/cultural enclaves, and the result has been a diminution of their significance in these debates. Certainly historians need to pursue *all* manner of border crossers so that they might more fully appreciate how even ordinary individuals defied the authority of the state in shaping and reshaping the border region, but they also need to remain mindful that as far as Indian peoples are concerned, Indians belong to nations, not shadowy enclaves. Defining "nation," however, is no small task, as the rich body of literature devoted to this effort can readily attest. Crafting a definition that does not exclude those political entities whose borders are not as tangibly delineated as those of, for example, the United States and Mexico, has required a bit of scholarly creativity, and even scholarly license. Benedict Anderson, for one, famously defined the nation as an "imagined political community" that is imagined as both "inherently limited" and "sovereign." It is *imagined* in the sense that its members, although rarely personally acquainted with one another, still foster a sense of collective communion with fellow members. It is *limited* in the sense that it has, in Anderson's words, "finite, if elastic boundaries, beyond which lie other nations." It is *sovereign* in that the concept came of age in a postdynastic era in human, or at least Western, history. Finally, it is a *community* in the sense that its members tend to feel a kind of comradeship or fraternity that has made it possible, again in Anderson's words, "for so many millions of people, not so much to kill, as willingly to die for such limited imaginings." Anderson also acknowledges the increasingly visible phenomenon of what he calls "sub-nationalisms" within the borders of "old nations," political entities that not only challenge the dominant nationalistic impulse but also "dream of shedding [their] sub-ness one day."[30]

Historians of Native America, however, have tended to question the supposed "sub-ness" of competing nationalisms within "old nations." As the historian Jeffrey Shepherd reminds us in his study of the Hualapai, for example, "nations" need not "possess large populations, standing militaries, or bureaucratic states," as one might assume, but "they do include literal and figurative boundaries and cultural borders, common origin stories, a mother tongue, and the assertion of some superiority over surrounding groups." In fact, employment of the "rhetoric of the nation" alone goes a long way in "gaining control over the cultural, human, and natural resources of a people and using them in ways that further the survival of that nation." Similarly, in her history of Spanish colonial Texas, the historian Juliana Barr asserted that the "fluidity of native political configurations . . . does not negate their structural integrity or the aptness of characterizing them as 'nations.'" Networks of kinship, for example, often proved robust enough to provide "the infrastructure for native political and economic systems" and to codify "both domestic and foreign relations."[31] And as a 2008 study concluded, indigenous groups like the three discussed herein have had much in common with "other emergent and reemergent nations in the world" in that "they are trying to do everything at once—self-govern effectively, build economies, improve social conditions, and strengthen culture and identity. They are engaged in nation building."[32] Yet nations can be difficult to identify, at least for outsiders. The historian Thomas Holt argued that "nation" as a concept has much in common with "race" in that neither is "fixed in conceptual space"; both concepts are instead "in motion, their meanings constructed, their natures processual, their significance at any given moment shaped by their historical context." And it is not unusual for nations to go through a process of reinvention should the need arise to determine "who belongs and who does not, who defines the character of the nation and who is its antithesis."[33]

Challenging the "sub-ness" of indigenous nationalisms in the face of "old" nationalisms is not a new trend in American Indian scholarship. In 1976, for example, the Yaqui specialist Edward Spicer presented a paper at a conference on border studies, held in El Paso, Texas, in which he argued that the era of the nation-state "has passed its period of ascendancy" in both scholarship and on the world stage. Its dominance, he concluded, "is being threatened by new forms of organization." If one defines a nation on its most basic level, or, in Spicer's words, as a collection of people "who identify with one another on the basis of some degree of awareness of common historical experience," then indigenous groups easily qualify. Indian groups, like nation-states, share a unique, common experience, with their own set of symbols that "stand for and evoke . . . the sentiments which the people feel about their historical experience." Thus, every modern state could be said to contain several or many nations. Spicer counted at least fifty in Mexico alone. A glance at an ethnographic map of that particular nation-state makes his point, showing a vast array of linguistic and cultural distinctions. In fact, to this day Mexico is peppered throughout with peoples who speak neither Spanish nor English, instead still relying on indigenous languages such as Triqui, Mixtec, and Zapotec, which are among the 162 "living languages" recognized by the Mexican government.[34] In conceptualizing the history of the Yaqui tribe, one of his specialties, Spicer admitted to mistakenly conceiving of Indian tribes and nation-states as two different entities, both with fixed boundaries. "It only slowly dawned on me," he revealed, "that Yaqui boundaries were fluctuating and that the lines on the ethnographic maps were very misleading in many ways." Compounding this problem was the fact that many Yaquis "accepted no border defined by mestizos."[35]

Still, indigenous nationalism as a concept remains problematic. Utilizing a "borrowed" conceptual framework such as "nation," one collection of scholars warned, could send the message that American Indian studies "cannot independently develop a core assumption or construct a model or paradigm based solely on internally generated information," which could doom it to a life as a "tributary" field of history, sociology, political science, and so on. In short, it suggests that Indian studies "is not and probably cannot become a fully developed, autonomous discipline." But more seriously, it saddles indigenous peoples with a paradigm that fails to paint an accurate picture of "the ways in which [they] act, react, pass along knowledge, and connect with the ordinary as well as the supernatural worlds." Instead, it imagines Indians as being on a very specific, very narrow political trajectory, the destination of which cannot but be parity with non-Indian nations. It also supposes that Indians lacked that parity prior to contact with Europeans.[36]

"Peoplehood" exists as an alternative. It is a conceptual framework that emphasizes the centrality of language, religion, land, and sacred history (or where they came from in a collective sense) in attempting to account for sets of social, cultural, political, economic, and ecological behaviors among peoples who are indigenous to particular territories. By eschewing modern political constructs and emphasizing instead ethnic sameness, peoplehood helps us more fully understand why modern indigenous nations, such as they exist, are so often built on a foundation of kin networks and village-level government, and also why native spirituality often figures so prominently in indigenous notions of national belonging. Finally, peoplehood reminds us that, in the words of the aforementioned collection of scholars, "nations come and go, but peoples maintain identity even when undergoing profound cultural change."[37]

The fact remains, however, that the language of nationhood has been a constant in Indian-white relations virtually from the point of contact. The application of the word "nation" in an official capacity to describe Indian groups both within and on the perimeters of U.S. borders goes back at least to the 1830s, when Chief Justice John Marshall famously characterized Indians groups as "domestic dependent nations." Similarly, one can find similar references in Mexican government correspondence dating back to the earliest decades of Mexican independence.[38] In the twentieth century especially, Indians and non-Indians alike on both sides of the border freely used the term. It is not unreasonable, then, to assume that Indians have gradually internalized the concept, either adopting it wholesale or adapting it to fit their own realities. As will be shown, the indigenous peoples in this story found the term "nation" to be a rather comfortable fit when finally forced to articulate their own conception of themselves. And it could be argued that the aforementioned four factors of peoplehood—language, religion, land, and sacred history—help explain their determination to legitimize claims to sovereignty via terminology that might not wholly apply to their historical experience and/or precise sense of rootedness. Like the non-Indians on their peripheries and/or in their midst, these Indians' physical terrain was gradually made meaningful through a history of religious,

cultural, socioeconomic, political, and military engagement that very often arose from and revolved around a sacred attachment to place.[39]

A distinction should be made, however, between the "imagined" reality
of *nationhood* and the more tangible reality of *self-government*. Nationhood,
according to the historians Vine Deloria Jr. and Clifford Lytle, "implies a
process of decision making that is free and uninhibited within the community, a community that is in fact almost completely insulated from external
factors as it considers its possible options." Self-government, on the other
hand, "implies a recognition by the superior political power that some measure of local decision making is necessary but that this process must be
monitored very carefully so that its products are compatible with the goals
and policies of the larger political power."[40] For most Indian individuals and
groups, self-government has by and large become the contemporary reality, yet the conception of one's group as something akin to a nation remains
a central, transcendent component of indigenous identity. And while reducing the indigenous nationalistic impulse to something more "subnational"
in character may be appropriate in some circumstances, especially given
the reality and seeming durability of modern geopolitical borders, there are
also circumstances in which indigenous peoples have, in fact, managed to
shed their "sub-ness" in a more "official" capacity. The most notable of those
circumstances is federal recognition, which, as will be shown, the Yaquis
and Kickapoos both vigorously pursued in the mid- to late twentieth century
in an attempt to carve out something more substantial than a mere "subnational" existence.

Federally recognized status, at least north of the border, affords Indians
the opportunity to govern themselves in a more official capacity, with the
(sometimes reluctant) sanction of neighboring communities and the surrounding nation-state or states. Thus, federal recognition represents a substantial realization of the impulse toward nationhood that is so prevalent
in these tribes' histories. Yet it also involved making a difficult choice. While
recognition by the U.S. government meant an affirmation of at least semi-
sovereign status for Indian groups, the pursuit of this status also meant ac-
knowledging the United States as an arbiter of authenticity, and the *only*
arbiter at that. It also meant, by and large, a more constricted existence for
Indian groups that have historically resisted being bounded within such
narrow constructs. Federal recognition, then, could prove to be the prover-
bial double-edged sword, complicating, if not ending, hard-won patterns of
transnational migration, while effectively dividing indigenous peoples of
similar cultural affinities, religious persuasions, and nationalistic convic-

tions. But on the other hand, oftentimes the benefits of that status appeared worth the forfeiture of sovereignty, thus the dogged pursuit of a change in status under the U.S. government. In fact, federal recognition, as will be shown, was often a last resort, a strategy improvised at a moment of crisis and designed to meet a shorter-term goal.

In examining moments of transnational indigenous nation building, it is important to remain mindful of the strategies employed by both the U.S. and Mexican governments in their efforts to incorporate these Indians into their respective social, political, and economic arenas. Boasting remarkable parallels as well as notable differences, the policies enacted by both the U.S and Mexican governments to govern "their" indigenous peoples met with mixed results, to say the least. It will be prudent, then, to examine both those similarities and dissimilarities in order to contextualize the experiences of the Yaquis, Kickapoos, and Tohono O'odham in the late nineteenth century and throughout the twentieth. Both governments frequently changed direction with regard to those legislative measures designed to catalyze change in indigenous communities. Depending on the presidential administration, the ideological climate, and, especially, the availability of funding, Indian groups were sometimes celebrated and subsidized, sometimes maligned and marginalized, and sometimes ignored altogether. Yet they were fairly consistently considered social, cultural, and economic burdens and even impediments, and, in turn, were most often treated as such. Although policy climates on both sides of the border did not always directly affect the Yaquis, Kickapoos, and Tohono O'odham, they do often explain these groups' mobility, or their tendency to cross international borders and, thus, escape national prerogatives that usually proved detrimental to Indian peoples. Yet federal Indian policies could also serve as tools, or as a convenient means of pursuing either an immediate or a long-term agenda. Appealing to policymakers and/or submitting to prevailing Indian policies, as will be shown, could prove vital to the maintenance of a semiautonomous existence. However, it often did so at the expense of broader efforts at nation building. Some of these Indians were, in the end, forced to choose the lesser of the two evils when it came to U.S. and Mexican Indian policies, which meant finally severing the ties that bind at the increasingly formidable international boundary.

The stories contained herein all in some way highlight the efforts and degrees of success attained by the Yaquis, Kickapoos, and Tohono O'odham in negotiating and maintaining a measure of political, cultural, and religious autonomy given the increasingly pervasive federal presences. This book places particular emphasis on efforts at transnational movement and tribal reconsolidation over the course of the twentieth century, including land acquisition and protection, federal recognition, and economic development. The progress made by Indian peoples in these arenas, in turn, prompted the U.S. and Mexican governments to respond by making their presence, and especially the weight of their sovereign authority, known to these Indians, sometimes as their benefactors and at other times as their hated enemies. After all, as the historian Miguel Tinker Salas observed, the United States and Mexico were both well aware that the "location of the border divided [some] indigenous peoples" while providing all that called the borderlands home "the opportunity to mitigate their situation and seek better treatment."[41]

The task confronting both the United States and Mexico, then, became preventing the subversion of their authority by protecting the integrity of their borders, while also making sure that their efforts to do so meshed with broader, and ever-evolving, sentiment about what was and what was not acceptable behavior in Indian policy arenas. As for the Indians in this story, the lure of self-determination and group autonomy proved sufficiently strong to justify drastic measures, including nearly constant migration and deprivation, aggressive legal and political activism, and even violent rebellion. At the end of the day, however, these indigenous groups sought little more than a stable, secure existence in which their vision of nationhood was more real than imagined, a struggle that is just as relevant to the indigenous peoples of North America in the twenty-first century as it was in the sixteenth and seventeenth, and even before.

1 The White Man Came and Pretty Soon They Were All around Us

Yaqui, Kickapoo, and Tohono O'odham Migrations

• •

> The people came out of the earth somewhere in the east. There they
> spent the first night; and the chief said to them, "In the morning we
> will divide into many groups, so we can occupy the entire earth. Some
> of you will go to the sea, and others to the north and the west." . . . So
> in the morning they divided as the chief had instructed, and set out.
> All over the country they traveled.
>
> —Papago migration legend, 1919

In the waning years of the Yaquis' late nineteenth-century bid for independence from Mexico, the Los Angeles–based journalist John Kenneth Turner
traveled to Mexico to investigate the tribe's fate. The Yaquis had reportedly
become targets of a sweeping government-sponsored relocation campaign,
courtesy of Mexico's president/dictator, Porfirio Díaz, which government officials hoped would once and for all end the group's long history of violent
resistance to Mexican authority. The deportees' destination, according to
available accounts, was Yucatán, which many Mexican political refugees
often likened to Russia's Siberia. "Siberia," one told Turner, "is hell frozen
over; Yucatan is hell aflame."[1] The government sent the Yaquis to labor in
essentially slave-like conditions on plantations that produced henequen,
an agave plant grown extensively in southern Mexico whose fibers can be
used to produce rope, twine, coarse fabrics, and alcohol.

In order to gain access to the closely guarded plantations of the "henequen kings," Turner played the part of a wealthy American investor, complete with interpreter in tow. The ruse worked. His imaginary fortune served
as an "open sesame to their clubs, and to their farms." He was able to observe
thousands of Indian "slaves" laboring under everyday conditions, while
he slowly but surely won the confidence of the planters. Soon, they began
supplying Turner with what he must have considered journalistic gold.
For instance, Turner noted that although the planters referred to their

system of labor as "peonage," or enforced service for debt, and to their chattel as "people" or "laborers" in public, privately they did not mince words, admitting that they were, in fact, slaveholders. They freely spoke of employing corporal punishment on uncooperative field hands on a regular basis, and viewed their workers as little more than commodities. In fact, one planter offered to sell Turner "a man or a woman, a boy or a girl, or a thousand of any of them, to do with them exactly as I wished." Turner also learned that these powerful planters had similarly powerful friends. Local police, public prosecutors, and judges could all be counted on to protect this enterprise. Finally, the planters insisted that slavery was actually quite common in Mexico. "Slaves are not only used on the henequen plantations," Turner learned, "but in the city, as personal servants, as laborers, as household drudges, as prostitutes."[2] In explaining his particular interest in the Yaquis given such widespread abuse, Turner stated, "The Yaquis are exiles. They are dying in a strange land, they are dying faster, and they are dying alone, away from their families." He concluded, "I went to Yucatan in order to witness, if possible, the final act in the life drama of the Yaqui nation. And I witnessed it."[3]

Turner, however, was premature in his pronouncement. The "Yaqui nation" did not die during the early twentieth century, though one might say it entered into a period of dormancy. The Yaquis had been stretched too thin to function as a tribal whole. Aside from those who suffered through deportation, others managed to remain near the Yaqui River, masking their Yaqui identity so as not to attract official attention. Some used area mountain ranges as a base of operations, stubbornly perpetuating the tribe's rebellion against Mexico. Some moved to Sonora's larger cities—Guaymas, Hermosillo, Ciudad Obregón—and disappeared into the local labor force. And still others sought refuge in the United States, settling in or near cities such as Tucson, Phoenix, and even Los Angeles. Thus, while Turner was enjoying immense success with the publication of his "Barbarous Mexico" series, the Yaquis were testing out a variety of survival strategies.[4] And they were not alone. The Kickapoos and Tohono O'odham were also contending with the legacy of attacks on their autonomy, and their responses, as this chapter demonstrates, mirrored those of the Yaquis in significant ways. By the turn of the century, all three groups were in the unenviable position of having to rebuild their societies, cultures, and governments from the ground up. Geographic space, and even geopolitical boundaries, separated families and tribal members, interrupted kinship and land use patterns, and complicated efforts to maintain tribal cohesion and cultural continuity.

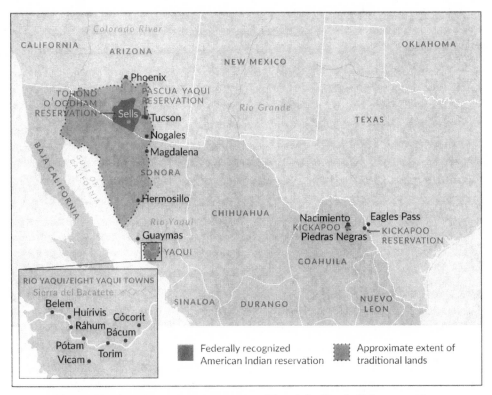

Traditional lands and contemporary communities of the Yaqui, Kickapoo, and Tohono O'odham. Original base map by Nakota Designs.

Yet in the process of confronting these new sets of challenges, physical movement on a transnational scale gradually became, for the Yaquis, Kickapoos, and Tohono O'odham, a tribal imperative, the most convenient and expedient strategy to regain lost autonomy. Further, it was a strategy which, although improvised in fits and starts under less than ideal circumstances, meshed well with tribal traditions of movement. The Tohono O'odham's migration legend, cited above, attests to the fact that tribal movement has a long history within O'odham culture. And the very name "Kickapoo" is Algonquian for "he moves about."[5] In fact, when asked in 1868 if he would prefer to live on a reservation in the United States or "become a Mexican," one Kickapoo reportedly replied, "God is my Captain—the world my Camping ground, and I am at liberty to go where I choose."[6] One scholar recently observed that the Yaquis' history of displacement and movement has come to define Yaqui identity, as evidenced, for example, by contemporary Yaquis' regular use of the word "nómada" in discussing tribal history.[7] Thus, those familiar with these groups would not be surprised by their assumption of a transnational orientation in the pursuit of a tribal agenda or agendas. After all, movement across boundaries that had been defined by outsiders was a common historical experience among these three indigenous groups. This chapter explores the myriad factors that forced these Indians to "go transnational," in a manner of speaking, beginning with their earliest contacts with Europeans and concluding early in the twentieth century. Though often viewed by outsiders as last-gasp strategies to postpone the "final act" in their various dramas, these groups' new patterns of spatial distribution ultimately evolved into broader strategies aimed at maintaining tribal cohesion and cultural continuity while negotiating the greatest possible degree of sovereignty.

The Yaqui Struggle for Autonomy

Attacks on Yaqui autonomy had become commonplace by the time Turner arrived on the scene, having occurred with a disquieting regularity since the beginning of the tribe's documented history. When first encountered by Europeans, the Yaquis lived in a cluster of pueblos along the Yaqui River delta region, which contained, and still contains, some of the most productive agricultural land in North America. Although their language and culture, according to the anthropologist and Yaqui specialist Edward Spicer, was "nearly identical" to that of the neighboring Mayos, their respective responses to the arrival of the Spanish immediately differentiated the two. The Mayos, in short, consistently sought to ally themselves with the newcomers, while the Yaquis did not. The earliest known conflict between the latter and invading Spaniards occurred in 1609, and resulted in the Spaniards' quick and easy defeat at the hands of an estimated 7,000 Yaqui soldiers. Rather than risk what would likely have been a long series of violent clashes with the invading Spanish, however, the Yaquis invited Jesuit missionaries into the Yaqui River valley in 1617, and were ultimately sent Fathers Andrés Pérez de Ribas and Tomás Basilio. Both reportedly received an enthusiastic welcome upon their arrival in the river valley. Jesuit occupation, the Yaquis wagered, would be preferable in the longer term to further warfare, military occupation, or worse. It was the first in a long series of inspired strategies to maintain group cohesion, a cohesion that as of the seventeenth century seemed contingent on proximity to the river and the modest bounty that it made possible. Accepting the Jesuits also meant reluctantly acquiescing in the invading Europeans' efforts to incorporate the Yaquis into what Spicer called "the great Spanish political leviathan." The Indians incorporated elements of Catholicism into their own belief system, learned Spanish, and accepted some strictures of colonial government. Unlike the great bulk of indigenous peoples who confronted European customs, institutions, and military might with trepidation (if not outright hostility), the Yaquis adapted surprisingly well. In the 150 years of Jesuit occupation, the Yaquis experienced a period of remarkable creativity, revitalization, and growth, while also managing to retain their fertile lands and avoid taxation. Scholars have gone so far as to question whether or not we can speak of the Yaquis as a tribal unit before the arrival of the Jesuits. Through tribal stories the Yaquis have hinted that their conversion to Catholicism helped unite disparate peoples under the umbrella of a single cultural and political entity. And as the historian Rafael Folsom pointed out, "The Jesuits agreed in some sense, claiming to have defined them as a distinct nation."[8]

But although the relationship between the Yaquis and the Jesuits appeared to be one of give-and-take, it would not be a stretch to argue that the Yaquis were bargaining from a position of strength, and that all involved knew it. In fact, Folsom describes those Jesuits who lived among the Yaquis as "marginal figures," "pawns," and "tools" that the Yaquis used "for the furtherance of their own political ambitions." Still, the Yaquis' experience with the Jesuits helped establish a tradition of advancing their agenda "within, not against, the structures of empire." He explains, "Throughout the colonial period the Yaquis pursued their interests through tough negotiation, offers of valuable aid, threats, and tactical violence. These acts were always enveloped in a shared understanding that reciprocal ties with the empire would be sustained." It was a diplomatic attitude and approach, as will be shown, that would outlive the colonial era. Under the Spanish, then, the Yaquis managed to maintain a remarkable degree of autonomy. As Folsom concludes, "The fragmentation of the colonial government and the swirling rivalries among the Jesuits, secular institutions, miners, parish priests, and Franciscans made it impossible to impose colonial rule on the Yaquis in a direct and intensive way."[9]

The Jesuit period came to a close in 1767, however, when the Spanish colonial government, acting on the orders of King Carlos III, called for their expulsion, likely in an attempt to remove a formidable obstacle to secular reform throughout Spain's empire.[10] Couple this development with Mexican independence early in the next century, and the Yaquis' situation began to appear increasingly precarious. Sonora evidently met the distant war for independence from Spain with a collective yawn. Although fighting did take place in New Spain's far northwest, Sonorans fought, in Spicer's words, "without much intensity, perhaps without much conviction." As for the Yaquis, the handful who participated in the conflict fought on the side of the royalists, perhaps fearing that a more invasive government might replace the mostly hands-off Spaniards. In fact, by war's end it would become clear that the Indians in the region interpreted the independence struggle quite differently from the rest of the new nation. Thereafter, periodic indigenous unrest would serve to indicate that these groups considered themselves independent of any and all political entities with European origins, even those directed by native-born descendants of the Spanish. In short, the Yaquis and their neighbors made clear that they would submit only to indigenous authority, an attitude held by the tribe long before Mexico's war for independence, and one that the birth of a new nation-state in their midst only reinforced.[11]

Thus, new patterns of violence among Sonora's indigenous communities accompanied the change in government, as Mexico's Indians continued to resist challenges to local autonomy. The Yaquis, especially, began resorting to armed resistance more frequently during the early Mexican national period. Their first major conflict with the Mexican government occurred in 1825, only four years after Mexico established its independence, and perhaps not coincidentally it happened at a time when the tribe was becoming more mobile. A series of famines during these years repeatedly forced many Yaquis out of their villages for seasonal employment in the regional economy. The Mexican government, meanwhile, came to view Yaqui mobility as a direct threat to internal security, since it had long equated mobile Indians with hostile Indians. At the same time, however, the Mexican government recognized Yaqui mobility as an opportunity to weaken the Yaquis' hold on the Yaqui River delta. While it appears that the Yaquis had hoped for even greater freedoms under the new government, including possibly a seat in the Mexican Congress, the arrival of tax assessors on Yaqui farms in 1825 dashed any such hopes. Rebellion soon followed. Led by Yaqui Juan Banderas, the uprising had as its primary goal the establishment of an Indian confederation in Mexico's Northwest. Banderas managed to unite not just the Yaqui people, but also members of the Opata, Lower Pima, and Mayo tribes. Since the federal government had its hands full with the Apaches on Mexico's northern border, responsibility for quelling the Yaqui rebellion fell to the state level, and the state was, at best, ill equipped for the task. The Banderas rebellion highlighted the fact that Sonora's Indian policy overall tended to be merely reactionary, confronting problems as they arose in lieu of devising a long-term plan. It also highlighted the fact that the disorganized and financially strapped state did not have the clout, military, political, or economic, to enforce any kind of policy measure anyway. Luckily for local officials, the Banderas rebellion ultimately fell apart. Although it failed to give rise to an Indian confederacy, other circumstances intervened to help stave off the physical encroachment of non-Indians, at least for the time being.[12]

This is not to say, however, that the Mexican government did not continue in its efforts to divest the Yaquis of their homeland. In 1828 the government announced that it was officially bestowing citizenship on the Yaquis and decreeing that Indians and whites be treated equally under Mexican law and in Mexican society. In so doing, the Mexican government appeared to be extending an olive branch of sorts. Yet, one historian argued, although these new laws "masqueraded as acts of generosity," they were, in reality, "attacks on everything the Yaquis held dear." Citizenship represented "an attack on the special rights, privileges, and cultural peculiarities the Yaquis had developed over the course of the colonial period," while the statement of equality essentially served as an invitation to non-Indians to settle on Yaqui lands. In fact, the Mexican government ultimately offered tax incentives to non-Indians to do just that. The Yaqui homeland was clearly under siege, and the situation would only deteriorate in the coming decades.[13]

Those who chose to leave the Yaqui homeland to participate in the broader Mexican economy, meanwhile, did not always fare well. At Chihuahua's mining center, La Villa de San Felipe El Real de Chihuahua, for example, the Yaquis had established a presence by the mid-1850s. They formed their own settlement complete with their own chapel on the outskirts of the primary Mexican settlement. Although historians have tended to laud such efforts on the part of the Yaquis to maintain their political and economic independence, this is one instance where at least some tribal members had clearly grown dependent on wage labor. As one scholar put it, "Yaquis used to be considered quite autonomous and resistant against colonization, but as shown in the case of the mining centers during colonial times they were the ones who suffered the most." Because of the back-breaking nature of the work, the lack of proper ventilation, and the constant contact with mercury, "nobody would be willing to work in the mines," with the exception of the Yaquis. Thus, many suffered a slow death due to lung disease. They remained bound to the mine owners by debts, and could face legal action if they attempted to abandon the mines.[14]

Part of their participation in the non-Indian economy, however, could also be explained by a well-documented propensity for travel. Writing in 1761, for example, a Spaniard described a group of Yaquis who had migrated to Chihuahua as being "of a hardworking spirit and inclination, very dedicated to mining, which they love, and for that reason, in distinction from other Indian nations, they are hardly rooted, if at all, in their home soil; and they are of a spirit so haughty and generous that it impels them to travel." Indeed, another Spaniard observed that although the Yaqui mission towns were more populous than any other mission towns in the region, roughly two-thirds of the population of each lived elsewhere, including nearby Soyopa, Chihuahua, Parral, and Santa Barbara. Put simply, the Yaquis had learned that mobility equaled freedom. Although that freedom had its unique pitfalls, it was but one of many strategies designed to help maintain their distinctive political and, especially, cultural identity.[15]

Then, with Vice Governor José T. Otero's 1879 announcement before the Sonoran Congress that "there is in this state an anomaly whose existence is shameful for Sonora," significant events in Yaqui history began unfolding at a dizzying pace. Otero was referring to Cajeme, the Yaquis, and their "separate nation within the state."[16] During the intense Cajeme period, from 1875 to 1887, a long tradition of Mexican expansion into Yaqui territory met an abrupt end as hopeful colonists suddenly found themselves unable to wrest lands granted to them by the Mexican government from the increasingly determined Yaquis. Aware of Cajeme and the Yaquis' growing stronghold, many colonists simply fled, forfeiting their claims rather than risk conflict. The Mexican government, perpetually embroiled in bitter factional struggles during these years, was unable to give top priority to confronting the Yaqui problem. All that changed, however, under President Porfirio Díaz.[17]

The Díaz regime had as its main objective national economic development, which, at least in the state of Sonora, first required the removal of "marauding" Apaches, followed by an increase in statewide mining and agricultural production, improvements in communication and transportation networks, and, lastly and most significantly, colonization of the fertile lands of the Yaquis and Mayos.[18] Among those developments that spurred the regime to action were reports of an 1883 *Los Angeles Times* article, entitled "Seductive Sonora," which claimed that Mexico would "see Sonora an American state within five years if the present influx of Americans continues." It was not the only article to play on Mexican fears that another embarrassing loss of territory might be imminent. Only days before the *Arizona*

Daily Star reported that a New York speculator had recently acquired then sold several Yaqui mines to an Englishman. Needless to say, the recent publicity surrounding Sonora deeply concerned the Porfirian government given its tenuous, and ever weakening, hold on the region.[19]

On March 31, 1885, then, Díaz launched a concerted military campaign designed to oust the Yaquis from the fertile river valley, and by early 1886, after less than a year of skirmishes of increasing intensity, federal forces finally overwhelmed the Indian "rebels." By this time, yellow fever and general malnutrition were taking their toll on the group, while the high morale that Cajeme had once inspired seemed to have vanished. In fact, the majority surrendered despite Cajeme's pleas that they continue fighting. As for the few who remained committed to Yaqui independence, Cajeme divided them into small bands and orchestrated a guerrilla campaign against federal troops, who, following the mass surrender, mistakenly thought themselves victorious. Tribal members sustained the guerrilla campaign, however, hiding out in Sonora's Bacatete Mountains between attacks, well into the twentieth century.[20] They would also remain subject to deportation well into the twentieth century. An official correspondence from 1904 estimated that 822 Yaquis had either already been deported or were awaiting deportation that year alone, while in 1908 that number reached 1,198. The program evidently peaked in 1908, and although exact figures are unknown, scholars are confident that several thousand of the estimated 30,000 Yaquis suffered through deportation. The tribe now appeared hopelessly fragmented, thinly spread across Mexico and the southwestern United States. As Edward Spicer observed, "Not even the Cherokees, whose deportation in 1835 from Georgia to Oklahoma had initiated a scattering over the United States, were so widely dispersed."[21]

The Mexican government launched another campaign to end the seemingly doomed Yaqui insurrection in early 1900, its goal being to wipe the Bacatete Mountains clean of rebel Indians. Tetabiate, Cajeme's successor, who had declared war against the Mexican government the previous year, managed to escape the onslaught, but several hundred Yaquis died in the conflict, with many simply jumping off cliffs to their deaths. Meanwhile, troops took approximately 1,000 women and children prisoner. One newspaper account reported that Mexican forces actually employed a gunboat in the campaign, while the Yaquis employed a Maxim gun. "Such a modern weapon in the hands of the aborigines of this continent is a circumstance well worthy of passing notice," the article editorialized. Passengers on a train bound for Hermosillo, another newspaper reported, were treated to a "ghastly sight" in 1905, when from the train they spotted the bodies of six Yaqui "chieftains" hanging from trees and telegraph poles. The Mexican military, the article claimed, often allowed executed Yaquis to remain strung up "for days and sometimes weeks as an example to others of their tribe."[22] The campaign had clearly taken a brutal turn.

Mexican officials, however, often bristled at the press coverage north of the border, frustrated that it too often assumed an anti-Mexican and pro-Indian tone. For example, one *Washington Post* article characterized the Yaquis as "exceedingly peaceful" unless provoked. In explaining why the Yaquis had gone "on the warpath" against the Mexican government, the article quoted one non-Indian American informant who claimed, "He may be a very bad Indian, and all his friends to whom he took rifles may be bad, but they are methodical in their hardness, and it does not seem entirely foolish to suppose they believe they have been badly dealt with by someone in their own country."[23] Another article from north of the border, written in response to the Mexican government's deportation campaign, characterized the Yaquis as "the most industrious, the most responsible, honorable, and virtuous of the working class in Sonora."[24] Mexican officials, meanwhile, claimed that the recent press coverage tended to exaggerate the size of the "rebel forces," often tried to justify the Yaqui rebellion, and, most seriously, often "belittled government forces" and their efforts to suppress what *they* viewed as indiscriminate Yaqui violence.[25] In fact, there is evidence that the state departments in *both* nations were working to limit the amount of press coverage the Yaqui campaign received.[26]

Regardless, following this latest campaign, the Yaquis entered into one of the most difficult eras in their history, one marked by a sharp decline in their standard of living and a sharp increase in both official and unofficial harassment. When turn-of-the-century census data indicated that an estimated 15 percent of Sonora's population was of Yaqui ancestry, officials took more drastic measures in singling out, then harassing and intimidating, the remaining Yaquis in hopes of breaking the resolve of those who still harbored separatist pretensions. In 1902, for example, newly elected governor Rafael Izábal ordered that Yaqui Indians over the age of sixteen don "identification passports," as one scholar called them, at all times. Those who refused to register and identify themselves as Yaqui, the governor warned, would be subject to arrest and even deportation. In 1906, Izábal expanded the law, simply ordering the arrest of *all* Yaquis, whether they were abiding by the regulation or not. "Frankly," the governor claimed, "I don't see any other solution for these *indios*."[27] But as one scholar gleaned from survivors of this tumultuous period, one attitude appeared widespread, namely, that the Yaquis "might be refugees or displaced persons for years and years, but Yaqui culture and the Yaqui homeland would transcend these temporary events."[28]

Not only would the Yaquis transcend the Mexican nation's extermination campaign, they would also transcend the Mexican nation itself. Unmentioned in John Kenneth Turner's *Barbarous Mexico* are those Yaquis who escaped persecution by turning to the United States for sanctuary. In the 1930s, Yaquis in Arizona would bitterly recount these transborder escapes, often hastily arranged and executed under cover of night in anticipation of the increasingly frequent raids by rural police on the Sonoran haciendas. To many Yaquis the United States appeared to offer the only alternative to the threat of deportation and an uncertain fate on the Yucatán plantations or a life of transience and uncertainty in area mountain ranges. It was an option that was not on the table for long, however. Because of a recession in the United States early in the twentieth century, officials stepped up their efforts to close the border to further immigration. While their efforts did not completely halt Yaqui migration north, they certainly managed to slow it. Other Yaquis steadfastly refused to leave the tribe's homeland. For example, when his family suggested they relocate to Arizona, Manuel Alvarez replied, "No. I have to die here." The following day he did just that. Mexican soldiers located Alvarez and hanged him from a mesquite tree for allegedly aiding Yaqui insurgents in the Sierra. Other Yaquis remained in Sonora, but either masked or completely abandoned their Yaqui identity, taking agricultural jobs, or working as artisans or laborers in any one of a number of Sonora's cities. It apparently was not uncommon for a portion of their wages to end up in the hands of Yaqui guerrillas.[29]

Despite the upending of their way of life in Sonora, those Yaquis who remained ultimately found their proximity to the border fortuitous for reasons other than convenient access to their Arizona safe haven. While conducting their military campaign against the Mexican regime, the Yaquis learned that they could cross the border into Arizona and easily earn wages to purchase much-needed supplies, supplies that could aid in their long struggle against the Mexican government. Mining enterprises in Bisbee in particular appear to have been popular destinations for Yaqui migrants. Arizona, then, became more than just a safe haven for Yaqui refugees. It also became a kind of arsenal.[30] Although ever more carefully monitored in the early twentieth century, the border was certainly not hermetically sealed. If queried by U.S. officials, these Yaquis sometimes claimed to be Mayos. The

Mayos, in the words of one Yaqui, were "favored by the Mexican authorities" because of their devout Catholicism, and thus often left alone. Some also claimed to be Opatas, which was another far less maligned tribe. And still others simply claimed the nationality of the nearest neighboring tribe.[31]

The United States, however, soon came under fire by Mexican officials as it became increasingly clear that Arizona was serving as an informal base of operations for Yaqui campaigns against Mexico and, more specifically, the Díaz regime. In fact, in 1904 the Mexican government demanded that the United States not only bar the sale of arms and ammunition to Yaqui Indians, but also more carefully monitor their movements throughout the state. At one point the city of Tucson even hired (with Mexican funds) a private detective, an American named Oscar Carrillo, to look into rumors of arms sales to Yaquis and to track suspicious tribal members. In the end, however, he had nothing incriminating to report. The Mexican consul in Phoenix accused the Tohono O'odham of helping the Yaquis acquire arms and ammunition, going so far as to request a thorough search of *all* area Indian reservations for evidence of complicity in the Yaquis' rebellion. Some Tucson merchants protested the ongoing crackdown on arms sales to Indians, such as José Ronstadt from the famous Ronstadt family, who balked at being denied the right to profit from the Yaqui rebellion, especially since, he claimed, dealers on the other side of the border in Cananea, Sonora, were happily outfitting Yaquis.[32] In short, a crackdown on arms sales to Yaquis was a problematic request. Those selling arms to the Yaquis were not doing so, in the words of one U.S. attorney, "with any design to provide the means for a military expedition or enterprise to be carried on against the government of Mexico," but were only trying to make a buck. U.S. officials needed evidence of "intentional equipping" of rebel Yaquis, in other words, in order to take action. U.S. officials did, however, agree to step up their efforts to enforce a provision of Arizona's criminal code that prohibited arms sales to Indians, and ultimately instructed a U.S. marshal in Arizona to take action in "breaking up the practice complained of."[33] It was a tall order. As one scholar put it, "The U.S. reservation system, the extensive social and economic networks of the Yaqui, the Yaquis' ability to pass as Mexican, and the easy availability of arms on the border facilitated Yaquis' participation in transnational circuits of power."[34]

Arizonan officials initially granted refugee Yaquis safe haven secure in the knowledge that mining and railroad companies would happily absorb them as laborers. That arrangement changed between 1906 and 1907, however, when an economic downturn tightened southern Arizona's labor market. Thereafter, American officials, acting on orders from the U.S. State Department, saw to it that recent Yaqui migrants were deported, even knowing full well that these migrants likely faced, at best, deportation to the henequen plantations and, at worse, extermination. Indeed, the Mexican government's coordinated campaign was still wreaking havoc on Sonora's Yaquis in the early years of the twentieth century. In 1885, the Mexican government estimated that the Yaqui population stood at around 20,000 (which was likely a conservative estimate). In 1900, a government expedition into the Yaqui River valley counted just over 7,000. In 1907, the first census conducted by the Porfiriato counted only 2,723. Another early twentieth-century survey found that only 1,680 were engaged in agricultural pursuits, which led authorities to conclude that the Yaquis had adopted urbanization as a survival strategy. It was a development that, in the words of one scholar, "signaled a dwindling connection to a Yaqui rural space of autonomy." The trend would not continue, however. With the Mexican Revolution of 1910 and the toppling of the Díaz regime, the deportation campaign immediately became a thing of the past, and the Yaquis came out of the figurative woodwork.[35]

Not surprisingly, in the wake of Díaz's ouster in May 1911, the Yaquis chose to side with Mexican revolutionaries. And their very visible participation in the Mexican Revolution, again not surprisingly, was rooted more in a determination to advance their claims to sovereignty than in an altruistic concern for the fate of the Mexican nation. Put simply, the objectives of the revolution, which included first and foremost a more equitable policy of land distribution, meshed well with Yaqui convictions and gave them some hope of reclaiming lost lands. They fought particularly hard on behalf of famed general Alvaro Obregón, presumably because rumor held he had some Yaqui blood. While the rumor was not accurate, Obregón had, in fact, been raised near a Mayo Indian pueblo and was just as fluent in Mayo as he was in Spanish.[36] Just prior to assuming office as the new Mexican president in 1911, Francisco Madero promised a delegation of Yaquis that, because of their service, he would not only restore their lands, but pay them a wage of one peso a day to serve as a sort of military reserve; invest in school, farm, and church development around the Yaqui River; and decree a thirty-year Yaqui tax exemption in return for their support. While the Yaquis' gamble appeared to be paying off, Madero's assassination eighteen months later ensured that the well-intentioned agreement never saw the light of day, and Yaqui resistance to Mexican authority continued.[37]

In 1916, Mexican officials negotiated an official armistice with the Yaquis. The terms of the armistice were simple: the Yaquis would agree to inhabit a series of villages selected by the government in the river valley, and the government, in return, would see to it that the Yaquis were well fed. The agreement also allowed the Yaquis to keep their firearms—a great selling point from the Indians' perspective, but one that the Mexican government likely regretted, since the armistice was short-lived. The following year, between 1,000 and 1,500 Yaquis, evidently feeling stifled, concluded that the villages were little more than Yaqui concentration camps and fled the area. They definitely did not go quietly, however, leaving what one scholar described as a "trail of destruction" in their wake. The federal government then declared war on the Yaquis anew in the wake of this incident, and sporadic violence once again became the norm.[38] "The Indian trouble is now considered more serious than in years," one observer concluded, adding, "The effect of a campaign of many months has thus been lost." Thereafter, however, the Yaquis began slowly filtering back into the Yaqui River valley, and the Mexican government, in a perennial budget crunch, was unable to respond in a meaningful way.[39]

Then around 1919, the Yaquis once again began lashing out at their non-Indian neighbors. That year, Yaquis attacked a group of Mexican travelers en route to Hermosillo, killing two. They then fled to the mountains west of Guaymas. Shortly thereafter, a local found two Mexican woodchoppers nearby who had been tortured and killed. The Yaquis also tortured and murdered a Mexican man and his five-year-old son. One official noted that "practically all the ranches had been abandoned" in those areas where the Yaquis were most active. In one instance, an estimated 200 Yaquis surrounded the town of Potam, just south of Guaymas, and attacked. Once a Yaqui stronghold (and one of the original eight pueblos), Potam was increasingly overrun with non-Indians. These inhabitants tried to defend themselves but finally fled the Yaqui onslaught. The Indians then proceeded to loot the town. Sensing that an attack on the immediate area's largest city might be next, the American consul in Guaymas warned the U.S. secretary of state, "Guaymas is absolutely without military protection, there being little to prevent a disastrous raid upon the city if the Yaquis choose to make it."[40]

The Yaquis again drew the ire of U.S. officials when, in 1919, they attacked and looted an American-owned mine named El Progresso, prompting U.S. officials to demand that Mexico step up its efforts to protect American lives and property. The Mexican military launched a counteroffensive a little over a month later to ferret out those Yaquis responsible for the assault on the mine, taking three Yaqui lives and recovering much of what the Yaquis had stolen.[41] The underlying cause of the latest surge in violence is not difficult to understand. The Yaquis had simply grown impatient waiting for the Mexican government to deliver on the promise made to them at the outset of the revolution, and thus began venting their frustration. As an American ambassador to Mexico explained in 1911, "The reasons given for the attitude of these Indians is that certain lands which were to have been returned to them at the close of the recent revolution have not been returned."[42]

Indeed, by the 1920s, thousands of Yaqui exiles had returned to southwest Sonora only to find the more fertile areas of the Yaqui River valley occupied by non-Indians. Still, they returned determined to reclaim their autonomy, even if it meant initially settling on the north bank of the river and submitting to life as landless agricultural workers. In 1925, Yaqui chief Francisco Pluma Blanca petitioned the Mexican government, as the historian John Dwyer explains, "under the constitutional provision that provided for the restitution of usurped property to indigenous communities." More specifically, the chief called for the return of lands that included Bacum, one of the original Yaqui towns established by the Jesuits. The administration of Plutarco Elías Calles denied the request. Compounding tensions in the mid-1920s was a surge in non-Indian migration to the region. Suddenly alarming amounts of water were being diverted from the Yaqui River for what turned out to be mostly American agricultural interests. In September 1926 the Yaquis took up arms once again, brazenly, though briefly, taking former president Obregón and some 150 federal troops hostage at the Vicam train station. Though freed without incident, Obregón vowed revenge. Soon thereafter, the federal government sent some 20,000 troops to attack Yaqui settlements. Hundreds of Yaquis died; many more fled into the Bacatete Mountains. Some were captured and conscripted into the Mexican army, and some were deported into the nation's interior. The fighting became even more ferocious when the Mexican government ordered the bombing of the nearby mountains by military aircraft. By the mid-1930s, Dwyer writes, "repression pervaded the Yaqui country, which resembled a military camp with thousands of federal troops stationed in Yaqui villages."[43]

Meanwhile, although many Arizona Yaquis returned to Sonora after the fall of the Díaz regime, still others remained in the United States with the intention of establishing what Edward Spicer called a "new branch of Yaqui society," bearing a "variant stream of Yaqui tradition."[44] The convoluted story of Lucas Chávez, relayed to Spicer in the 1930s, exemplifies the experiences of many Yaquis during this period. As a child, Chávez made regular trips with his father from the Yaqui River valley to Guaymas to buy in-demand products, such as needles or handkerchiefs, then would return to the Río Yaqui to peddle and barter. Guaymas was evidently not the most inviting place for a young Yaqui, and ridicule directed at Yaquis by Mexicans was common. "They would say 'chinga, chinga' all the time," he recalled. "Yaquis eat horses" was another popular taunt. He also recalled instances of Mexicans entering the Río Yaqui valley, violating young women, and generally doing "unjust things." In short, he understood the impulse, so prevalent among Yaquis, to fight the Mexicans. In fact, the elders of the tribe used to tell him, "Better for our lands to go into the hands of any other nation than to go into the hands of the Mexicans." After the death of his father, Chávez worked as a field hand in various locales until drifting into the United States in the 1890s to work on the railroad. He ultimately settled near Tucson, in Pascua, because of the growing Yaqui population there. Along with Pascua, Phoenix was a popular haven for Yaquis, since those willing to pick cotton could earn respectable wages there. After the season ended, however, many of these workers returned to Pascua. Chávez recalled a string of decent, fair Anglo "mayordomos," or bosses, one of whom married a Yaqui. "She spoke Yaqui all the time," he remembered. "And her daughters . . . they spoke Yaqui too." In the 1930s, he retired from manual labor, opted to stay in Pascua, and reportedly handled the mail for the village. Interestingly, when asked whether or not the Pascua Yaquis had a chief, he replied that it was unnecessary since "here political affairs are taken care of by the state government and Yaquis therefore don't need a Yaqui chief." "After all," he added, "are we not foreigners here?"[45]

Networks of migrating Yaquis like Chávez, many of whom had already worked in the United States, played a vital role in informing those who remained in Sonora of opportunities north of the border. In his autobiography, the Yaqui poet Refugio Savala recounts his family's experience after fleeing the "heartless killers" in Mexico. Savala's father had already been living in Arizona when the Mexican government launched its deportation campaign. After saving enough money, he returned to Sonora not only to retrieve his family, including his newborn son (appropriately named Refugio, or "refugee"), but also to spread word of good wages across the border. Many followed his example and undertook the trek to the United States. Savala's family moved their belongings to Arizona on the backs of four pack mules, and quickly found shelter, work, and food courtesy of the

Southern Pacific Railroad Company. The railroads apparently welcomed the Yaquis, and evidently treated them with a great deal of civility.[46]

Even though their unclear citizenship status and inability to speak English limited their opportunities, at least some Yaquis later characterized their first years in Arizona as carefree, affluent, and stable, standing in stark contrast to their people's troubled history. Yaqui migration to the United States slowed to a trickle after 1918 or so, however. The reasons for this were myriad. As mentioned above, a tighter labor market in southern Arizona meant that early twentieth-century Yaqui refugees were no longer welcomed with open arms. On top of that, World War I introduced into American popular culture a more general fear of "foreignness," or of the potential for non-native "undesirables" to, in the words of the historian Alexandra Minna Stern, "contaminate the body politic." Not coincidentally, then, the advent of the U.S. Border Patrol in 1924, which signaled the beginning of the border's militarization, roughly coincided with the end of the war, as did ever more rigorous immigration restrictions and new immigration procedures that required transborder migrants to possess passports and visas.[47] Although the Yaquis, in the early twentieth century, had established only a precarious transnational presence, the rest of the century would find them both cementing new ties and at least attempting to renew old ones, all against remarkable odds. Still, the existence of the border, at least in the wake of their dispersal from the Yaqui River, proved crucial for the survival of the tribe. "It seems fairly clear," concluded Edward Spicer, "that but for the U.S.-Mexico border there could well have been total extinction of the Yaqui people. The border allowed an alternative."[48] The border would continue to serve a crucial function well into the twentieth century, aiding and abetting the growth of the Yaqui nation. In this regard, the Yaquis had much in common with the Kickapoos.

The Kickapoo Retreat

Although eventually settling in the northern portion of the present-day state of Coahuila, Mexico, and Eagle Pass, Texas, the Kickapoos originated from a surprisingly far-flung locale. European records from around 1600 place them between Lake Michigan and Lake Erie, thousands of miles from what they today consider their spiritual homeland. By 1654 they had already fled the Great Lakes region in the face of increasing hostility from the Iroquois, taking refuge, along with the Sauk, Fox, and Potawatomies, in Wisconsin among the Menominee and Winnebago tribes. The arrival of the

French shook up power dynamics in the region, to the Kickapoos' ultimate detriment. Much later a tribal spiritual leader would drolly recount, "The first white people we met were French. We traded them deer hides and they said, 'Ah, these are very good hides.' Then they asked us for a small place to sleep." Unlike most Algonquian groups, the Kickapoos shunned European-produced goods, including alcohol, and exhibited a conspicuous and consistent hostility toward French Jesuits and their doctrine of forced acculturation. The Kickapoos soon allied themselves with neighboring groups, including the Mascoutens and the Fox, and eventually formed a confederacy. With their power solidified and European numbers increasing, open war was inevitable. The year 1712 marked the first open conflict between the Kickapoos and the French, when tribal members took a French messenger prisoner. The Hurons and Ottawas, allies of the French, retaliated by capturing a canoe filled with Kickapoos and slaying, among others, their principal chief. A formidable military campaign by the French soon followed, forcing the Kickapoos to make peace with the French. It was an uneasy peace, however. Loyalties continued to shift, with the Kickapoos sometimes at odds and sometimes allied with the French, until essentially reduced to pawns in the French and Indian War.[49]

Imperial struggles between the French and the British enveloped the Kickapoos during this period, and they decided to side with the French. Interestingly, in their ultimately successful attempt to gain the loyalty of the Kickapoos during the French and Indian War, the French presented the tribe with a Louis XV medal, which to this day remains one of their most coveted possessions, residing with the tribe in Nacimiento, Mexico, and serving, from their perspective, as one of many symbols of Kickapoo nationhood. However, the 1763 Treaty of Paris expelled the French from the Great Lakes region, and thereafter hostilities between the Algonquians and the British reached fever pitch. The Kickapoos were among many notable participants in Pontiac's Rebellion, which culminated in the Ottawa leader Pontiac's attempt to capture Fort Detroit. When British attempts at reconciliation failed to inspire the Kickapoos, one band fled the region altogether in 1765, taking advantage of an invitation from Antonio de Ulloa, governor of Spanish Louisiana, to settle near Saint Louis.[50] Some Kickapoos even worked as mercenaries for the Spanish as a kind of arm of Spanish Indian policy, roaming across Louisiana, Missouri, and Arkansas, taking Osage Indian scalps, prisoners, and plunder. In exchange, they received all the powder and shot they needed, along with tobacco and *aguardiente*, or brandy.[51] From here, the Kickapoos' history could be characterized as a near-constant retreat. As

Kickapoo Adolfo Anico explained in 1981, "The white man came and pretty soon they were all around us, so we moved south to what is now known as Kansas. Again, once more, the white man came and surrounded us. Again, once more, we moved south to what is now known as Oklahoma. Once again, we moved south into Texas, what is now known as Texas. There we live, and again we moved finally to Eagle Pass, into another area."[52]

Their journey to Eagle Pass was far more eventful than Anico's account implies, however. Following the American Revolution, the Kickapoos quickly identified land-hungry Americans as the new enemy, and allied themselves with the British. They fought American forces at the Battle of Fallen Timbers in 1794, meeting defeat at the hands of General Anthony Wayne. The Treaty of Greenville, which concluded the conflict, included a provision allocating a $500 annuity for the Kickapoos. Conflict continued, however, and tribal stability remained elusive. The group apparently had nothing but contempt for the Americans. They negotiated with the new nation only halfheartedly, usually engaging U.S. officials only when attempting to have some grievance addressed. In fact, an exasperated William Henry Harrison, realizing relations with the group had become a one-way street, once asked, "My Children, Why does it happen that I am so often obliged to address you in the language of complaint?" Tensions between the Indians of the region and Harrison soon boiled over into violence. The Kickapoos fought alongside Chief Tecumseh's brother, the Shawnee Prophet, at the 1811 Battle of Tippecanoe, and joined British forces during the War of 1812. During the latter conflict, 150 Kickapoo families joined Tecumseh and the Prophet in Ontario at a newly established intertribal village for Indian refugees. In the wake of this series of setbacks, the Kickapoos, during the presidency of James Monroe, ceded more than thirteen million acres of their land between the Illinois and Wabash Rivers in exchange for a tract of land in southeastern Missouri. It was a desperate attempt on the part of the tribe to, as one journalist put it, "avoid the swallowing giant called America." Roughly 2,000 Kickapoos relocated there, while two bands, each containing roughly 250 tribal members, mostly warriors, stubbornly remained in Illinois.[53]

By the 1830s, then, the Kickapoos appeared hopelessly fragmented. Numbering about 3,000, the tribe had now split into several bands and lived in small pockets from Lake Michigan all the way down to Mexican Territory. A group of roughly 350 held on in eastern Illinois; another group settled on the Osage River in Missouri; several bands, totaling around 900, roamed the Southern Plains; and about 800 settled on the Sabine River in the province of Texas at the invitation of the Mexican government in order to assist its Cherokee allies with frontier defense. They were part of a broader trend in which thousands of "immigrant Indians," as one scholar called them, entered Texas after being essentially pushed there by American settlers during the 1810s and 1820s. These Indians, who also included the Chickasaws, Choctaws, Creeks, Seminoles, and Shawnees, sometimes fought with and sometimes allied themselves with their non-Indian neighbors against Plains Indian raiders. Some had acculturated to the point that they kept domesticated livestock. The Texas Kickapoos initially prospered under the newly established Mexican government. In fact, in return for their loyalty, the Mexican government promised the Kickapoos the title to the lands they were then occupying. Relations between the Mexican government and the Texas Kickapoos deteriorated rapidly, however. The Mexican government instituted a generous land policy that quickly attracted Anglo settlers, the same settlers who, in 1836, rebelled and established the Republic of Texas.[54] The first group of Kickapoos to enter Mexico after the Texas Revolution did so in 1838. Numbering about eighty, they crossed the border to escape the Texas army, eventually settling near Morelos, and began serving as scouts and couriers within the Mexican military. According to one historian, these Kickapoo "mercenaries" were "highly esteemed by the Mexican government." However, they stayed for only about a year before pulling up stakes and relocating to Indian Territory.[55]

Texas president Mirabeau B. Lamar's 1839 Indian removal policy was at least partially responsible for the Kickapoos' relocation en masse to Mexico. Writing to Cherokee migrants that year, Lamar explained, "The people of Texas have acquired their sovereignty by many rightful and glorious achievements, and they will exercise it without any division or community with any other People." He wrote of his refusal to recognize an "alien political power" within Texas's borders and concluded with the insistence that the tribe had "no legitimate rights of soil in this country" and as such would "never be permitted to exercise a conflicting authority." Shortly thereafter, he addressed the Kickapoos specifically, ordering their "immediate removal out of the country . . . without delay." Although many left after concluding that accommodation with the Texans would be fruitless, others were evidently recruited by "Mexican Emissaries," according to one official, to help "wage a war of extermination against Northern Texas." The official predicted "more serious border warfare, than any we have ever yet experienced." By the eve of the republic's annexation by the United States in 1845, however, Texas officials had entered into a treaty with the Kickapoos, among other

Indian groups. It was a decision that at least some Texans considered ill advised. Writing in 1847, for example, one Texan argued that the treaty represented "great folly and indiscretion" on the part of the Texas government, since the Indians would inevitably interpret it as a "sanction to their intrusion and a right to settlement." Had Texas not been annexed by the United States in 1845, he continued, Indian numbers would have "alarmingly increased by immigration from the northern tribes of the United States." "Annexation," he concluded, "has arrested this evil."[56]

Just prior to the outbreak of the U.S.-Mexican War, Indian Commissioner George W. Bonnell put the number of Kickapoos residing within state boundaries at about 1,200. In the wake of the war, the Mexican government began shoring up its "new" frontier with military installations, partly in an attempt to protect settlers from Indian raiders. The government distributed some 200,000 pesos it had received via the terms of the 1848 peace treaty to frontier governors and ordered the establishment of eighteen military colonies along the border. It also granted lands to the Seminoles, Creeks, and Kickapoos in exchange for their vow to participate in frontier defense. Soon thereafter at least some Kickapoos relocated to Morelos, Coahuila, just south of Eagle Pass; then, in July 1850, they were joined by a contingent of roughly 500 Missouri Kickapoos, 100 Seminoles, and 100 Mascogos, or African Americans, at the behest of the Mexican government. The small settlement gradually evolved into a full-scale military colony. Local officials assigned these migrants sixteen *sitios de ganado mayor*, amounting to approximately 70,000 acres, on a temporary basis at the headwaters of the Río San Rodrigo and the Río San Antonio near present-day Ciudad Acuña. Federal officials threw their full support behind the colonization project, with one describing the migrants as "industrious," "hard working," and of good character and habits. The expectation was that they would form a "terrible obstacle for barbarous tribes" along the new border. The agreement between the migrants and Mexican president Benito Juárez further required that they maintain peaceful relations with citizens of both the United States and Mexico and respect the authority of the Mexican Republic. For a variety of reasons, the Mexican government, in 1852, relocated the Kickapoos and their Indian and African American neighbors to Hacienda El Nacimiento, twenty-three miles northwest of what is today the town of Múzquiz. The Seminoles and Mascogos gradually vacated the Mexican tract, many ultimately deciding to relocate to Indian country in Oklahoma, and by 1861 only Kickapoos remained on the tract. Then in 1864 their ranks swelled again when a contingent of Oklahoma Kickapoos migrated to Mexico rather than choose sides in the Civil War. Their trek was an eventful one. While en route, the 600 or so Kickapoo migrants were attacked by Confederate soldiers near the present-day town of Knickerbocker, Texas, along Dove Creek. The outnumbered and disorganized Confederates were routed by the Kickapoos, with some twenty left dead and nineteen left wounded. In the longer term the incident aggravated Kickapoo hostility toward Texans and further hastened their retreat across the Rio Grande.[57]

Those Kickapoos who chose not to migrate to northern Mexico typically did so because of several concerns. Some questioned the quality of the lands that had been offered by the Mexican government. As one group of Kickapoos later put it, "There was no grass and the land was no good, and the weather was too hot."[58] Some expressed concerns about the cost of moving, while others doubted that securing a claim to lands in Mexico was even possible given their migratory tendencies. Those who did choose to migrate, meanwhile, recognized the fact that, as one historian observed, "the terrain might have been forbidding, but that meant a thinner population." The "wildness" of northern Mexico, in other words, made it all the more likely that they could "live their lives without so much meddling" from agents of the United States government.[59] By roughly 1865, then, the majority of what are now referred to as the Southern Kickapoos had made their way south of the U.S.-Mexico border and put down roots. They apparently greatly appreciated the sympathetic reception they received from the Mexican government, and further admired Mexico's hands-off approach to Indian policy matters.[60]

Their agreement with the Mexican government, coupled with their location near the border, presented opportunities for the Kickapoos upon which they could not resist capitalizing. One U.S. consul observed that "so long as the Kickapoos have the protection of the Mexican Government and cross into Texas to loot, rob, and plunder, and as long as these acts are countenanced by the citizens of Mexico, and as long as the Kickapoo can find a ready market for their booty they will never willingly quit."[61] In fact, so profitable was raiding into Texas that Kickapoo warriors found they no longer needed to rely as heavily on agriculture to support their families. They sought and obtained the cooperation of local "political chiefs," as one historian described them, who would grant the Kickapoos both passports and titles to stolen livestock. Mexican customs officials at Piedras Negras and Nuevo Laredo rounded out the Coahuila "ring," helping to collect herds of horses and cattle transported by Kickapoo raiders across the Rio Grande in a canyon near Nacimiento. From there, a network of locals would assist in the disposal of Kickapoo "booty" in nearby Saltillo. Because of the extent of local collusion, these transactions were nice and legal, at least for all practical purposes. Texans did try to use Mexico's courts to reclaim their lost property, but typically to no avail. As one rancher put it, "It is evident to anyone who tries to receive stolen property from these Indians that they are protected by the Mexican authorities and the citizens of [Coahuila], as well as the merchants there, who . . . conduct an illicit trade with the Indians, encouraging them to raid into Texas." This phenomenon tends to be typical in border regions up to the present day. As the historian George Díaz put it, "Whereas the Mexican and U.S. governments considered smugglers as criminals and threats, border people regarded many of these same individuals as simple consumers, merchants, or folk heroes." And lest the Kickapoo case leave the impression that this was strictly a Mexican phenomenon, the historian Peter Andreas argued that the illicit flow of both goods and people, as well as the long string of campaigns to staunch that flow, did no less than help define and shape the American nation, while also serving as a "powerful motor in the development and expansion of the federal government." Regardless, the U.S. military was so determined to end these transborder depredations that in 1873 General Phil Sheridan authorized an attack on the Kickapoos on Mexican soil. Sheridan of course did not consult the Mexican government before launching this particular campaign. His orders were reportedly as follows: "Let it be a campaign of annihilation, obliteration, and complete destruction." The military arrived to find that most Kickapoo men were out hunting, so the campaign did not culminate in violence. Those Kickapoo whom they did manage to take captive, however, were subsequently forcibly relocated to Oklahoma.[62]

Failing to dislodge them through military means, the U.S. government attempted to *legislate* the removal of the Kickapoos from El Nacimiento and relocate them to the home of their Kansas counterpart. The reasons were myriad. U.S. officials were evidently upset that so many Kickapoos had taken advantage of what one described as the "partial paralysis of the authority of the United States" during the Civil War and slipped out of its borders, and now sought to return these Indians "to their condition before the war." U.S. officials were also evidently under the impression that Mexico was either unable or unwilling to provide for the welfare of the Indians, and that transborder raids would remain a fact of life so long as this remained the case. "There is but little doubt," two Texans wrote to President Andrew

Johnson in late 1865, "but with the proper inducement held out by the U.S. Government they could be induced to return to their Reserve, which would be the most economical and humane way of disposing of them." Another argued that the sole reason a portion of the tribe remained in Mexico was in order to provide "a place of safety for [their] stolen property," including horses, cattle, and even captives. Those responsible for the raiding in Texas only had to "cross the River to their kindred who remain in Mexico" whenever "pushed hard" by authorities north of the border. The resultant legislation, passed in 1874, called for "the removal of the Kickapoo and other Indians from the borders of Texas and Mexico," while also promising support for the relocated Indians. The U.S. Congress evidently sensed problems more serious than Indian depredations on the horizon. "The importance of restoring peaceful relations within the border infested by these roaming and predatory Indians," the act reads, "cannot be too highly estimated; and their removal to the Indian territory will, it is believed, relieve the authorities of Mexico and the United States from a condition of things which jeopardizes the continuance of friendly relations between the two governments." Congress predicted that the Kickapoos would, "if encouraged and assisted by the government," willingly join the "three hundred already removed to the Indian Territory." "It is difficult to see," wrote one U.S. official, "what substantial advantage Mexico can expect from retaining these Indians. So long as they remain where they are now, they are tempted to plunder and commit other acts of violence, not only upon Mexicans but upon the American side of the Rio Grande." In the United States, he claimed, "the Indians are kept from harming others and have a chance of materially benefiting their condition." When it came time to remove the Indians, however, the Mexican government was not cooperative, the citizens of nearby Santa Rosa were not cooperative, and the Kickapoos, most of all, were not cooperative.[63]

One problem with removal was that the Kickapoos doubted that the Texans would let them pass through the state peacefully. When asked what would alleviate their fears of passage through Texas up to Indian Territory, one Kickapoo communicated his wish that "a delegation from the reservations in the United States [would] come to them . . . and lead them back" in order to ensure their safety. They were assisted in their recalcitrance by Mexican officials and citizens who had their own reasons for obstructing U.S. efforts to "repatriate" the Kickapoos. After arriving in Mexico, the U.S. legation sent to coordinate removal ran into a host of problems. Local officials, first of all, demanded that the United States pay for the Kickapoos' houses, which, they claimed, the Indians were "wrongly in possession of," according to one member of the legation. Local law enforcement also demanded the U.S. legation pay for horses that the Kickapoos had allegedly stolen. Local citizens, meanwhile, according to the same source, "combined to put up prices on beef, flour, coffee, corn, and sugar to such outrageous prices that I had to send off to surrounding towns for such as the Indians required." "I have absolutely refused to make any more purchases here," the head of the legation declared. Once the legation managed to acquire flour, the Indians who consumed it immediately sickened. "The flour was undoubtedly poisoned," he complained, "with the expectation that the Indians would attribute the act to me." The Mexican government, meanwhile, claimed that they simply lacked the authority to assist the U.S. legation in their efforts to relocate the Indians, since their laws made no racial distinctions among their citizenry and, thus, *all* Mexican citizens enjoyed the same constitutional protections. Although the legation attempted to appeal to what one official vaguely described as a "spirit of internationalism and comity," cooperation was not forthcoming on any level, and the U.S. ultimately made little progress in returning the Kickapoos to their old lands. The fundamental problem was that Mexican officials gave the Kickapoos the option of which nation they preferred to call home. Most Kickapoos were apparently happy where they were.[64]

In one case, however, a group of fifty-five Kickapoos, with "jefe" José Galindo as their mouthpiece, notified Mexican authorities that they desired to leave Mexico and return to the United States. It was evidently not a common request. Although a Chihuahua-based Mexican official notified the U.S. War Department of the Kickapoos' wishes, Mexico's cooperation apparently ended there. Writing in 1878, John W. Foster, a member of a subsequent legation put in charge of repatriating the allegedly wayward Kickapoos, expressed surprise and frustration over the fact that "upon learning of the desire of Galindo and his band to return to their reservations in the United States," Mexican officials did not "indicate a willingness to follow the course adopted by the past administration of Mexico and extend facilities for their return."[65] It would not be the last time U.S. officials would encounter that lack of willingness when dealing with Mexico.

Meanwhile, the 1887 Dawes Act divided the Kickapoo reservation in Oklahoma into eighty-acre allotments, the idea being to hasten assimilation by replacing tribal with private land ownership. Allotment as a policy was generally despised by the Kickapoos. As one Oklahoma resident and acquaintance of the tribe put it in the late nineteenth century:

> The Kickapoo Indians had been, as we called it, "forcibly allotted," and the "kicking" Kickapoos were very persistent in resisting any effort the government might make to reconcile them to accept their land or to accept their money, $211. They would have nothing to do with it. They were so prejudiced against the allotment that they even would not drive on a wagon road over the land that had been allotted to them. If they had been starving to death, they would not have signed for provisions for fear they might be signing something that would be an acceptance. They at that time were wild and suspicious Indians . . . they kicked against the treaty; they kicked against the allotment. They were opposed to anything that the government wanted them to do.

Ultimately, the Kickapoos were among many Indian groups for whom the act proved devastating. In fact, roughly 90 percent of Kickapoo lands ultimately fell into non-Indian hands because of the new policy. However not all of those who had allotments succumbed to the temptation to make a quick buck off of them, however, and a small number maintain allotments to this day. Still, this latest assault on their autonomy led many frustrated Oklahoma Kickapoos to relocate to Mexico on a more or less permanent basis, further swelling the ranks of Kickapoos living south of the border year-round.[66]

As an Oklahoma-based attorney with a long history as a tribal advocate revealed, "From the first I knew of them, and always, their life's dream has been to return to Mexico to be reunited with their children. The first Kickapoo I ever talked with said to me—an old decrepit man—'If they take my allotment, do you think it may in some way lead to my getting away from here?'"[67] Relocating from Oklahoma to Mexico could also mean escaping more mundane annoyances involving non-Indian neighbors. As another Oklahoman familiar with the tribe explained, "If an Indian's horse got into a white man's pasture it was $3. If a white man's horse got into the Indian's fields and ate up his crops and the Indians took it up, the white man came to the corral and tore it up and said, 'To the devil with you. This is not Indian country.' The Kickapoos can not live in a country like Oklahoma."[68]

Even though south of the border, the Kickapoos were not beyond the reach of non-Indians in Oklahoma who were determined to divest them of what little land remained theirs. In 1905, U.S. Acting Commissioner of Indian Affairs C. F. Larrabee complained to the secretary of the interior that white Oklahomans were conspiring to fraudulently acquire titles to Kickapoo lands in Oklahoma by sending negotiators to Mexican Kickapoo settlements. The U.S. district attorney for Oklahoma had evidently warned Larrabee that this latest development was "one step in robbing the Kickapoo Indians of all the lands they have and inducing them to remain in Mexico until the robbery is complete." Larrabee went on to express sympathy for the group, claiming that they were "less intelligent than the average full blood Indian," were inhabiting a "tract of worthless land" in Mexico, and were generally in a "very bad way in that country." Thus, he proposed a two-pronged investigation south of the border, one to explore the matter of the land deeds, the other to more generally assess the Kickapoos' living conditions. In so doing, Larrabee hoped to avoid a scenario whereby the U.S. government would be forced to "expend considerable money in removing the Kickapoos from Mexico." Larrabee was aware of the implications of conducting an investigation in a "Foreign State," and promised to acquire Mexico's consent. Evidently, the Mexican federal government agreed to grant U.S. authorities passage, but only reluctantly. And even then, authorities in Múzquiz remained defiant when the investigation commenced, apparently refusing to "recognize certain duly appointed persons by the Interior Department of the United States," according to the American embassy in Mexico.[69]

Investigators traveled from Shawnee, Oklahoma, to Coahuila in June 1906, led by Frank Thackery, U.S. superintendent of Indian schools. Upon arrival on Kickapoo lands, Thackery reportedly "found the Indians mostly all dancing." Soon thereafter local police asked the Americans to leave the Kickapoo village, thereby signaling that local cooperation would not be forthcoming. Upon their arrival in Múzquiz, however, the party immediately located eight men who were paid representatives of "many other men in Oklahoma who have sent the cash here to pay the Indians for their lands." Sensing that his hands were legally tied while on foreign soil, Thackery recommended hiring a Mexican attorney to begin prosecuting those involved in the allegedly fraudulent activity. A Mexican attorney, Thackery also hoped, would help ensure that the Kickapoos' rights under both Mexican and U.S. law were protected. Should the Kickapoos lose everything they own in the United States, Thackery feared, it was very likely that they would ultimately end up "paupers," and it would then not be long before Mexico called upon the United States to remove the group. Thackery also recommended clearing up confusion over the exact nature of Kickapoo land ownership south of the border. "The United States," he concluded, "should have an equal interest in their getting a proper title to lands in Mexico in order that [the Kickapoos] may not drift back upon us penniless."[70]

What Thackery did not bother to learn, however, was that the Kickapoos had plans of their own for the Oklahoma allotments. According to Oklahoman E. W. Sweeney, whom the Kickapoos, in Sweeney's words, "frequently solicited to attend councils . . . where I did the writing for them," at least some Kickapoos "seemed to have very little regard for their land in Oklahoma." Sweeney continued, "They wanted to return to Mexico and on every available occasion, at their homes and in council, or anywhere that I might meet a group of them, their foremost thought seemed to be to get away and return to Mexico." Not only that, but at least some of them "had agreed amongst themselves . . . that they would sell their land in Oklahoma and put it all in a pot together and buy a reservation in Mexico." Clearly, officials were giving the Kickapoos too little credit. The Indians understood that the allotment policy, although almost universally despised, could be used to their ultimate advantage.[71]

Few corners of Mexico remained untouched by the Mexican Revolution, and Nacimiento was no different. With the outbreak of revolution, the Mexican Kickapoos fought for Francisco Madero and then, after his assassination, for Victoriano Huerta. Huerta's overthrow by Venustiano Carranza proved disastrous for the Kickapoos. Carranza's soldiers took one contingent of Kickapoo soldiers prisoner in retaliation for their loyalty to Huerta, while another group of Carranza's men forced the Kickapoos to flee their village. The Kickapoos evidently spent the balance of the revolution hiding out, fearing another visit from the troops. In the 1920s, they returned to their tranquil, somewhat isolated existence. However, a seven-year-long drought that began in 1944, coupled with the loss of groundwater due to excessive pumping by the nearby American Smelting and Refining Company (or ASARCO), forced many Kickapoos out of their village yet again, this time in order to seek employment. As one writer put it, "At Nacimiento they had no water except for barely trickling springs. Their wheat crops failed, their cattle starved, and the mountains nearby were largely hunted out. Though Mexico had been generous with loyalty and land, it offered neither jobs nor government assistance." As they had during crisis after crisis in previous decades, the Kickapoos looked to the border for a solution. It was during these years that they began entering the migrant labor stream north of the border, adopting Eagle Pass, Texas, as their transborder way station, then pouring back into Nacimiento during the winter months.[72] It was a strategy that would serve them well, effectively sustaining the small group throughout the twentieth century. Still, it presented almost as many problems as it solved, problems that only worsened as the twentieth century progressed and transborder traffic came under ever-increasing scrutiny. But even had the Mexican government been more forthcoming with offers of jobs or other forms of aid, it is not likely the Kickapoos would have accepted. Like many of Mexico's indigenous peoples, they were determined to stay indigenous. In other words, embracing federal assistance might mean inviting federal intrusion and potential overreach. The Kickapoos would make it clear again and again that any entrée into the modern economy would occur in a limited fashion, on their own terms, and in such a way as to not compromise their political and cultural autonomy.[73]

The Tohono O'odham Divided

Unlike in the cases of the Yaquis and Kickapoos, the Tohono O'odham's division by the U.S.-Mexico border was not the result of forced migration, but of the imposition of an international boundary by outsiders. The 1853 Gadsden Purchase cut the Tohono O'odham in two, leaving half on the U.S. side and half on the Mexican side. At one time their lands stretched from present-day Phoenix, Arizona, south to Hermosillo, Sonora, and west to the Gulf of California.[74] The Tohono O'odham were one of a handful of Sonoran tribes who managed to remain aloof from Spanish and, later, Mexican authority and who were only indirectly affected by missionization efforts. In fact, the historian Jack Forbes suggested that the whole of Sonora was unique in that "all or almost all of the aboriginal groups had survived after some 288 years of warfare and contact, and 211 years of Christian missionary activity."[75] As with the Yaquis, part of their success in maintaining that aloofness was due to their efforts to forge a cooperative relationship with the Spanish early on. For example, they were immediate allies in Spain's long war against the Apaches, whom the O'odham simply referred to as "Enemy." Yet because of a variety of cultural and political changes wrought by colonialism, they increasingly found themselves viewing the Spanish, as one scholar put it, "across a chasm of distrust and misunderstanding," which would strain that relationship and, consequently, strengthen their determination to maintain their independence.[76]

The Tohono O'odham evidently first beheld Europeans in 1540, when the Coronado expedition clipped the eastern edge of their lands. The sight of hundreds of armed men on horses no doubt impressed them. The Spanish explored their lands further in ensuing years, but after finding no marketable commodities they left the O'odham, whom they eventually dubbed the Papagos, alone for more than a century. In the seventeenth century, mining activity in Sonora increased, and Spanish settlement grew in tandem. Further, missionary efforts gradually reached farther and farther north into Sonora throughout the first half of the century, culminating in the arrival of Father Eusebio Francisco Kino in the far northwestern edge of New Spain, a region the Spanish called the Pimería Alta. Spanish missionaries eventually encountered a variety of linguistic relatives of the Tohono O'odham. For example, the Hia C'ed O'odham lived northeast of the Gulf of California, while the Akimel O'odham, whom the Spanish called Pimas, lived along the banks of various rivers, such as the Gila. Apparently none of these groups had a sense of themselves as a "tribe" or any other kind of political entity. Rather, their villages and rancherías were politically semiautonomous, though it was not uncommon for these groups to forge temporary alliances in times of trouble. In 1697, Kino entered the Santa Cruz valley, in the heart of O'odham territory, to launch a ranching enterprise. What was initially a business venture evolved by the late 1700s into the massive San Xavier del Bac mission, which would later become the seat of the O'odham reservation. Under Kino's supervision, the O'odham built a string of missions in present-day Sonora along the Magdalena and Altar Rivers and the Santa Cruz River in present-day Arizona. Kino remained there, teaching, preaching, and exploring, until the end of his life. He also often acted as a moderator when problems arose between the Spanish and the O'odham.[77]

Despite some initial success in administering to their Indian charges, the missionaries gradually fell out of favor with the O'odham. They monopolized the most fertile lands in the Pimería Alta, and as mining activity increased Spanish settlers began hemming in the O'odham. While some O'odham stayed near the mission or continued laboring on Spanish farms, many who had lost complete use of their land came to depend more heavily on seasonal migration in the pursuit of game and water sources. Their movements, however, were not always economically motivated. Since the missionaries could only administer to so many O'odham, a significant number of Indians got into the habit of traveling to the missions in the winter months so that their children could be baptized with Spanish names and educated in Christian doctrine. This practice gradually evolved into a popular annual religious pilgrimage that continued well into the twentieth century. The O'odham eventually selected the town of Magdalena, just south of Nogales, for its final destination. After Kino's death in 1711, missionary activity waned, and non-Indian settlers, realizing their vulnerability to Apache and Seri depredations, began filing out of the Papaguería.[78]

Up until Mexican independence, the O'odham adhered, technically speaking, to the Spanish colonial system of government, in that they elected a village representative who was then confirmed by the provincial governor. Yet they had comparatively little contact with Spaniards. In fact, any aspects of Spanish culture adopted by the O'odham likely came from their regular visits deeper into New Spain rather than from their contact with Spaniards on their own lands.[79] Because of their isolation, the Tohono O'odham remained, by and large, at peace with the Spanish and then the Mexican government. Although the Mexican government colonized O'odham lands west of Hermosillo in order to help control the increasingly troublesome Seri Indians, the O'odham lived fairly independently until 1853. With the Gadsden Treaty, however, the U.S. military rounded up any O'odham they managed to locate south of the new boundary, ultimately numbering about 1,000, and relocated them north to two small reservations, San Xavier and Gila Bend, both near Tucson.[80] Even so, many O'odham evidently remained unaware that a change of government had occurred. As the historian Winston Erickson explains, "Where other Mexican citizens were located within O'odham lands, information about the change of government was available, but some O'odham still maintained allegiance to Mexico decades later because no one had told them about the new international boundary."[81]

Although perhaps unaware of the boundary's precise location, at least some O'odham were aware of parties of boundary surveyors moving through their lands during the 1850s. Surveyors moved through the lands of not just the O'odham, but also the Apache, Pima, Maricopa, Yuma, Cocopah, and Diegueño Indians. Some of these Indians served as guides, sources of food and information, and even ethnographic subjects. When the Americans arrived on the lands of the O'odham, they found a people who were mostly living in splendid isolation, with one notable exception. "For generations," one scholar explained, "a group of distinct bands known collectively as Apaches had raided Pima, Maricopa, Tohono O'odham and Mexican settlements in a cycle of retributive violence." The American surveyors, then, would have observed a "border landscape littered with abandoned settlements and barricaded towns" and border peoples who nursed a deep hatred of the Apaches (a hatred that was mutual, by the way) that lingered into the early twentieth century. These border peoples, including the O'odham, would go on to cooperate with civil and military officials in protecting the region from incursions not just by the Apaches, but also by American filibusters who were intent on violating Mexico's territorial sovereignty either for personal gain or to add additional territory to the United States. The Tohono O'odham were actually instrumental in thwarting the efforts of one of the most notorious of these filibusters, Henry A. Crabb, who entered northern Sonora in 1857 with a small army of co-conspirators. Within days of their arrival, the O'odham and a collection of soldiers and volunteers managed to locate and surround the American invaders. The O'odham then reportedly shot flaming arrows at the hay-roofed houses into which the Americans had retreated, thereby forcing their surrender and prompting the execution of every member of the filibuster expedition save a sixteen-year-old boy. It was only through the collective effort of Mexican settlers, indigenous communities, and civil and military leaders that, in the words of one scholar, "the boundary line stayed in place and a sense of Mexican national identity continued to develop along the border.[82]

The O'odham, meanwhile, remained insistent on preserving their independence despite this burgeoning, mutually beneficial relationship with non-Indians. While they happily accepted gifts from the Americans, including tobacco, beads, cotton cloth, various tools, and American flags, they also made it clear that they intended to protect the integrity of their culture, their political structures, and, especially, their territorial holdings. As one O'odham explained to a group of non-Indians in 1856 or 1857, "Every stick and stone on this land belongs to us. Everything that grows on it is our food . . . The water is ours, the mountains . . . These mountains, I say, are mine and the Whites shall not disturb them."[83]

Perhaps not surprisingly, officials in the United States had a difficult time containing the O'odham north of the border, particularly during hard times. Between 1871 and 1872, Indian agent R. A. Wilbur, in a series of letters to an official within the Bureau of Indian Affairs, warned of worsening conditions around San Xavier brought on by drought and famine. Writing in October 1871, Wilbur described daily visits by O'odham in an "almost a destitute condition" with requests that he provide "the necessaries of life." "I have explained to them my inability to extend to them any immediate relief," he wrote, "but promised to represent their case to you." While some O'odham remained on their designated lands, the looming threat of starvation forced many to seek employment in Tucson, while "by far the greater portion" crossed the border into Sonora "in search of food to keep from starving." The solution to the O'odham's increasing woes, Wilbur suggested, was the establishment of a larger reservation. "The settlers are fast crowding them around San Xavier del Bac," he explained, "and taking up the best portions of the land." Wilbur's letters take on a tone of urgency in ensuing months, culminating in a stern warning in December 1872: "I cannot urge too strongly the importance of securing a Reservation for these Indians." Apparently his advice went unheeded. The following year, the O'odham were still on the migratory trail and, in Wilbur's words, "in the habit of crossing the line to aid farmers in Sonora owing to the fact that there was not sufficient work to employ them all here."[84]

Indeed, they willingly participated in the cash economy when necessary, laboring on both Mexican and American ranches, plantations, and mines even at the expense of more long-standing subsistence patterns. Some even worked transporting and selling salt to area miners from a salt lake near the California coast. The so-called salt pilgrimage was, in fact, a long-standing tradition in O'odham culture, a practice that now supplied the O'odham with a marketable commodity. Increasing mining activity in Sonora during the nineteenth century brought many O'odham south of the border to work in the expanding agricultural sector. The downside, however, was that increased demand for land in Arizona meant that, once "abandoned," their lands often fell into non-Indian hands. Meanwhile, the same pattern of gradual land loss played itself out on the lands of southern O'odham. Opportunities south of the border waxed and waned throughout the second half of the nineteenth century until, by the turn of the twentieth, very few O'odham chose to live in Mexico. The end result was that the O'odham quickly slid into a pattern of dependency on both sides of the border, and regular migration in search of employment became a fact of life. And although typically characterized as a peaceful people, the O'odham were evidently not above raiding and violence. In the late 1880s, for example, Mexican officials complained that O'odham raiders were stealing Mexican cattle from settlements at Sonoita and El Plomo and then retreating across the border into the United States. Then in 1889 the O'odham launched a transborder raid targeting the Mexican village of El Plomo. The plan was to free a group of relatives that Mexican officials had imprisoned, recover lost O'odham cattle and horses, and then return to the other side of the border. It did not exactly go off without a hitch, however, and five O'odham lost their lives in a shootout with Mexicans before being forced to retreat. One scholar observed that "their self-conscious use of the border," as during the El Plomo raid, "reflected the growing importance of the boundary in their lives." And it would only grow in importance over the course of the next century.[85]

Compounding their economic woes, the O'odham were suffering through significant territorial losses during the second half of the nineteenth century.

At roughly the same time, both the United States and Mexico initiated nationwide programs to transfer public lands into private hands with the expectation that this would help spur economic development. The United States passed the 1862 Homestead Act and the 1877 Desert Land Act to achieve these ends, while the Mexican government contracted a series of surveyors to oversee the transference of so-called *terrenos baldíos* (or vacant lands) to private individuals. In turn, these surveyors received vast tracts of land for their efforts. "These policies privatized huge amounts of land," one scholar explained, "but were also characterized by inaccuracy, inconsistency, and inequity, leading to the appropriation of millions of acres that were inhabited, used, or claimed by Indians and other borderland people." The Tohono O'odham in particular lost an untold amount of territory in these efforts at privatization on both sides of the border. It did not take long for Mexican and American ranching enterprises to expand to the point that they directly intruded on lands actively being used by the O'odham, which led to regular conflict over access to the scarcest of resources along the western Arizona-Sonora border: water and grazing land. Many Sonoran O'odham responded to the specter of continued, and potentially worsening, conflict by crossing into the United States, where at least some of them followed the lead of many Arizona O'odham and took low-paying jobs with area ranching outfits. All the while, O'odham dispossession from tribal lands continued.[86]

These developments, taken collectively, prompted U.S. officials to finally discuss placing the O'odham under the auspices of the Bureau of Indian Affairs and, especially, creating a larger reservation. After all, the harsh, unforgiving environment in which the O'odham lived required plenty of room to roam.[87] Very few O'odham actually lived on either the San Xavier or Gila Bend reservations, likely because neither reservation contained a government agency to administer to the tribe. Nearby agencies, meanwhile, had their hands full with the Gila River Pimas and the Salt River Maricopas. Further, without proper surveillance of O'odham lands by government authorities, squatting by non-Indians was a constant problem. The O'odham's difficulties accelerated when U.S. officials applied the 1887 Dawes Act, which had already divided up Kickapoo lands in Oklahoma, to the O'odham's lands. In the early 1890s, officials allotted San Xavier's lands, then totaling roughly 69,000 acres. The 363 O'odham at San Xavier each received between seventy and one hundred acres (the U.S. government considered the excess acreage worthless). Only if the tribe's agent deemed them competent in managing their own affairs, the order stipulated, would individual

O'odham receive the legal title to their allotment. However, the O'odham had little experience with the concept of private ownership of land, and just as on Indian reservations throughout the United States, problems soon arose. For instance, officials granted an O'odham named Pedro Eusebio a fee-simple title to his plot in 1909, and Eusebio, in turn, quickly sold a significant portion of his land to non-Indian outsiders, apparently unaware that he was signing away the rights to his allotment. Eusebio died soon thereafter, and his son fought to regain the lost acreage, testifying before the Indian Commission that his father had made an ill-informed decision. His son, however, was unsuccessful, so for many years non-Indians owned land right in the heart of O'odham country. These kinds of misunderstandings perhaps explain why officials never implemented an 1894 executive order calling for the allotment of lands on the Gila Bend reservation. Not surprisingly, then, as the turn of the century loomed, the O'odham found themselves just barely surviving. They were less able to sustain their former way of life and increasingly dependent on the cash economy, working as cowboys, railroad laborers, construction workers, and even domestics.[88]

The obvious difficulties facing the tribe prompted one Tucson newspaper to query, "What shall we do with our Indians?" The article, published in 1895, assured locals that there were, in fact, "some good Indians who are not dead Indians," and that it was the government's responsibility to tend to their welfare "in return for the good done to our people, by them in the dark days of Indian warfare and border strife." Regarding their meager economic resources in the wake of a "change of circumstances," the article asked, "What is there for the Indian to do but steal or die?" The community of Tucson evidently held the O'odham in high regard. "It is common for the white man to characterize the Indian as thriftless and good for nothing," the article continued, "but so far as it applies to the Papagos, it is not true as those familiar with them can bear abundant testimony." The article described young O'odham women being thrust into prostitution and young men faring little better, since perpetual unemployment often reduced them to "loafers and bummers on the streets." "Give the Papagos farms and they will work," the article concluded, adding, "Beyond a little labor it will cost our people nothing."[89]

The O'odham's proximity to the border was also proving problematic. O'odham cattlemen complained to Indian agents repeatedly that tensions across the border, including transborder raiding and the U.S.'s military incursions into Mexico in pursuit of Pancho Villa, had made it too dangerous to round up cattle, particularly those that strayed across the then unfenced international boundary. O'odham leaders also requested (and actually received) arms and ammunition, which they claimed would help them defend their property from "pro-German" attacks from south of the border. It was an unlikely scenario, but one that nonetheless attracted sympathetic attention from U.S. officials. They ultimately surmised that a protected land base with formally delineated boundaries was the best defense for the precariously located tribe.[90]

In 1915, the O'odham received a visit from Indian Commissioner Cato Sells. While there, Sells stressed the importance of education and agricultural training for Arizona's 40,000 indigenous peoples, not only for their own well-being but also so that, in Sells's words, "it will be possible to cut down the appropriations of the government for the Indians." Sells went on to compliment the O'odham directly, lauding their "genius of necessity" and highlighting the fact that they "fought a winning fight" out in the desert, utilizing "everything in order to live, every bit of water and even the cactus." Sells ultimately visited every reservation in the United States to get a firsthand idea of general reservation conditions—a first in the history of the office of the Indian Commissioner. Although he met with numerous local officials while in the Tucson area, Sells insisted, according to one newspaper account, that he had "nothing of local interest to announce, as his was . . . entirely an inspection trip."[91]

In January 1916, however, a telegram arrived in an O'odham village from Sells announcing that President Woodrow Wilson had, by executive order, established a permanent reservation for the O'odham. It was a stunning about-face by a government that still enforced the Dawes Act. Officials expressed the hope that the reservation, encompassing a staggering 3.1 million acres, would provide the 5,500 tribal members ample space to farm and keep cattle in their desert environment. In other words, while the old lands at San Xavier and Gila Bend were, according to one newspaper, a "reservation to all intents and purposes," the lands selected for the new reservation had been "formally recognized by the government as Indian territory."[92] Further, while the former reservations, in terms of allotted acreage, had proved insufficient again and again, the new reservation was, and remains, among the largest Indian reservations in the United States. It encompasses roughly the same area as the state of Connecticut or the country of Belgium. "The advantages to the Indians," one article concluded, "are so evident that they scarcely need to be enumerated."[93] Although it comprises only a portion of the Papaguería, which extended into Sonora, the reservation is indeed fairly extensive. It includes lands between the Baboquivari Mountains to the west and the Ajo Mountains to the east down to the border and up just south of Interstate 10. There are also small parcels of O'odham-controlled lands at Gila Bend, San Xavier, and Florence, Arizona. The reservation boasts roughly seventy villages, but only one proper town: Sells, which is the capital of the Tohono O'odham Nation. Visible from nearly every corner of the reservation is perhaps the most significant landmark in O'odham culture, Baboquivari Peak, which one scholar described as "the Garden of Eden and the Promised Land, rolled into one." It is also regarded as "the center of the Tohono O'odham universe," since the O'odham believe it to be the home of their creator, I'itoi. I'itoi is said to live in a cave beneath the mountain, and tribal members still visit the site and leave offerings such as key chains, rosary beads, cigarettes, and chewing gum. The peak is difficult to miss. A contemporary of Father Kino's nicknamed it "Noah's Ark," and more recently it has become a popular point of reference for undocumented migrants crossing on foot and heading toward jobs in central Arizona (they call it el Tambor, or the drum).[94]

While one newspaper welcomed the reservation grant, suggesting that the O'odham finally had an "adequate" reservation, another lambasted local officials, accusing them of "napping" while Cato Sells seized "500 acres of land for each Papago buck, squaw, and papoose." Aside from pointing out that the land grant comprised over one-half of Pima County, some of it likely containing the most fertile agricultural lands Arizona had to offer, the article was also careful to note that many of the O'odham were "nomadic Indians from the Mexican side."[95] Those who claimed that the O'odham were American Indians, another article argued, simply had not done their research. "The home of the tribe," it argued, "is at Poso [sic] Verde, Sonora, from whence they send their children 'across the line' when they want them educated, and from which they come to the Papago country in the beneficient [sic] land of Cato Sells to plant their annual temporals [sic], always returning, with few exceptions, to their Poso Verde home."[96] Policy makers evidently heard the uproar, and responded in February 1917 by reducing the size of the reservation through an executive order that returned about 475,000 acres to the public domain. These lands came to be known as "the strip" since they ran more or less through the middle of the reservation. Although the government eventually returned the strip to the tribe, as Winston Erickson noted, "that they were removed shows the displeasure and power of those who did not want the lands in Indian hands."[97]

Although generous by reservation standards, today the reservation encompasses only about a quarter of O'odham lands recognized in Father

Kino's time. Further, it does not include any O'odham lands in Mexico, leaving southern O'odham to fight their own battles with a different—and often less sympathetic—government.[98] In the end, the creation of a reservation within U.S. borders and U.S. borders alone only further inhibited the tribe's transborder mobility. Even more than the U.S.-Mexico border, it clearly delineated where the O'odham could live and, by extension, where they could not, at least in the eyes of U.S. officials. Thus, although O'odham migration continued in subsequent years, it nevertheless became increasingly difficult. Born in Pozo Verde, Sonora, in the early twentieth century, Rita Bustamante recalled how normal it was to work on both sides of the border. "I remember when there was no boundary," she stated. "We O'odham just came and went as we pleased."[99] But with the outbreak of World War I, suddenly crossing the border became problematic. It had been common for both O'odham and Mexicans to round up cattle along the border every six months or so. In 1916, however, Mexican soldiers prohibited the O'odham from entering Mexico for the first time. Soon thereafter, the O'odham began receiving word that Mexicans were killing and eating O'odham cattle, while also driving the tribe's horses farther south, making their retrieval by their O'odham owners unlikely. The O'odham spent three years going through diplomatic channels in an effort to reclaim their cattle, but by that time their herds were largely depleted. "They must have longed for the days," Erickson contends, "when, faced with a similar problem, they armed themselves and retrieved their cattle by force." Then in the years following the war, the O'odham increasingly began appealing to U.S. officials for help regulating traffic though their reservation, traffic that was resulting in stolen livestock and the smuggling of arms and ammunition into Mexico.[100] The O'odham found the latter trend particularly troubling, in part because the Mexican government, on more than one occasion, had accused them of assisting the Yaquis in their aforementioned struggles over land and autonomy by serving as a conduit for arms and ammunition. Although U.S. investigators found no evidence of O'odham complicity, the Bureau of Indian Affairs decided that it was high time the border running through O'odham land was fenced. "In theory," Erickson explains, "they continued to have unrestricted access across the border, but as times changed, that access would become less free."[101] The fence, though not exactly an insurmountable obstacle to transborder migration, was nonetheless a powerful portent of things to come.

The Yaquis and Kickapoos assumed a transnational orientation out of necessity, as a strategy for survival, effectively adapting long-standing migratory patterns to new and ever-changing circumstances. While the

O'odham found their transnational orientation imposed without their consent and, in some cases, their knowledge, they responded in much the same way as the Yaquis and Kickapoos. All three groups turned to the U.S.-Mexico border to find solutions to persistent problems in their homelands, adopted or otherwise. And they were remarkably successful in maintaining tribal cohesion, cultural continuity, and a persistent vision of nationhood even while straddling the borders of the United States and Mexico. Yet increasing contact with these two powerful, looming nation-states often interfered with their hard-won freedom to traverse the border when convenient, expedient, or necessary. In just the first three decades of the twentieth century, the border would evolve from a minor obstacle (at best) to a formidable barrier. U.S. immigration officials especially would step up their efforts to control transborder traffic through inspections and literacy tests, and, as one scholar explained, "Native people who had long identified themselves on the basis of their ties to places and kinship groups [would struggle] to assert their rights in a new national context in which citizenship was an important source of power and privilege."[102] Thus, their often uncertain citizenship and/or legal statuses, products of their unusual orientation and migratory habits, meant that non-Indians more frequently challenged their sovereign status as Indians, along with their religious customs, cultural practices, and, especially, patterns of economic subsistence that required transborder mobility. Legislative and policy trends on both sides of the border further complicated efforts at maintaining hard-won transnational networks that enabled tribal cohesion and cultural continuity. In sum, all three groups found themselves facing obstacles that were far more formidable than any border fence. These Indians' responses to these myriad twentieth-century challenges, however, displayed a level of ingenuity, resourcefulness, and determination that, while remarkable, would not surprise those familiar with their long, troubled histories. In a sense, their early histories had primed them for what lay ahead. The Kickapoos alone had contended with, as one historian observed, "different native nations, the Spanish and the British empires, Mexico, the Lone Star Republic, the Confederacy, various states in the US and Mexican federal systems, and local officials in places like Coahuila and Eagle Pass" over the course of the nineteenth century. The relative stability of "boundaries and spheres of influence" during the twentieth must have come as a relief for peoples so used to shifting political sands underfoot.[103]

2 The Indigenous Race Is Abandoned

Indian Policies

· ·

In his 1979 essay "Mexico and the United States," the Mexican poet Octavio Paz attempted to account for the profound social, economic, and psychic differences that have plagued relations between Mexico and the United States since the middle of the eighteenth century, when, he asserted, Mexicans, then under Spain, first became aware an emergent national identity. He briefly focuses his attention on the question of the Indian presence in both countries and its function in their national narratives, concluding:

> Mesoamerican civilization died a violent death, but Mexico is Mexico thanks to the Indian presence. Though the language and religion, the political institutions and the culture of the country are Western, there is one aspect of Mexico that faces in another direction—the Indian direction. Mexico is a nation between two civilizations and two pasts. In the United States, the Indian element does not appear. This, in my opinion, is the major difference between our two countries. The Indians who were not exterminated were corralled into "reservations." The Christian horror of "fallen nature" extended to the natives of America: the United States was founded on a land without a past. The historical memory of Americans is European, not American.[1]

Paz went on to examine the influence of Hispanic Catholicism and English Protestantism on each country's fundamental assumptions about the role indigenous populations would later play in political, economic, and cultural spheres. With Hispanic Catholicism, he argued, "the notions of conquest and domination are bound up with ideas of conversion and assimilation," whereas in the English Protestant tradition, "conquest and domination imply not the conversion of the conquered but their segregation."[2] In his essay "The Emancipation of America," the Mexican historian Jaime E. Rodríguez O. took this distinction one step further, writing, "Whereas educated members of both communities emphasized the unique characteristics of their land and peoples, the Spanish Americans incorporated their Indian heritage into their interpretation of American identity, while the British Americans did not."[3] While both Paz and Rodríguez O. have a point about New Spain's determination to carve out a place for indigenous peoples within colonial society, neither Spain nor its successor government were above at least de facto segregation.

In fact, although Paz and subsequent observers have emphasized differences in how both the United States and Mexico viewed Indian populations and conducted Indian affairs, one can locate remarkable parallels in even a superficial examination of broader policy currents and patterns of thought regarding the Indian presence in both countries. First of all, both the United States and Mexico ultimately opted for Indian policy agendas that included the forced acculturation and assimilation of Indian peoples, or the stamping out of their essential "Indianness." This required that each nation at least attempt to dismantle Indian peoples' cultural, religious, and political institutions, leaving only those of non-Indians in their stead. Both nations then developed massive, and expensive, bureaucratic machinery through which they hoped to accomplish this objective. And finally, both nations reached a point where they grudgingly admitted that they had failed in their efforts and would have to acknowledge and even respect the determination on the part of indigenous communities to maintain at least a semiautonomous political and cultural existence. But above all, both nations have historically exhibited a sustained preoccupation with the Indians residing within their borders. As the historian Francis Paul Prucha put it, Indians have been "consistently in the consciousness of officials" on both sides of the international boundary, and for good reason.[4] They had survived seemingly against all odds, and it seemed that no matter how aggressive officials were in attacking their land base, undermining their subsistence strategies, and promoting their acculturation and assimilation, indigenous peoples found a way to persist in some form or other as separate cultural, and often political, entities.

Yet the question remains why parallel "problems" within both nation-states failed to produce parallel solutions. In other words, why did Mexico not develop the kinds of "blanket" Indian policies that characterized late nineteenth- and early twentieth-century Indian policy in the United States? And even more fundamentally, why did the Mexican government not opt for the reservation system as an arena in which to enforce acculturation, as did the United States, despite a similarly strong desire to stamp out more overtly "Indian" practices within its borders? Although the historian Claudia Haake argued that "at a most basic level the similarities [between U.S.

and Mexican federal Indian policies] outweigh(ed) the dissimilarities," a closer look reveals some notable impediments to the formulation and implementation of a coherent, consistent "Indian policy" in Mexico, impediments that often owed their origin to a dogged determination to forge a single nation from what seemed like a dizzying array of extant and competing nations, coupled with a pragmatic realization that any "blanket" policies would inevitably prove insufficient and even counterproductive in accomplishing this task.[5]

This chapter examines these similarities and dissimilarities in order to, above all, contextualize the experiences of the Yaqui, Kickapoo, and Tohono O'odham Indians during the late nineteenth century and through the twentieth century. Scholarship on U.S. Indian policy is abundant, whereas scholarship on Mexican Indian policy is considerably less so. This is partly due to Mexico's aforementioned lack of any blanket policies, which makes policy currents difficult to identify and less subject to generalization. But much like the U.S. government, the Mexican government frequently changed direction with regard to those legislative measures designed to catalyze change within indigenous communities in the pursuit of some kind of broad policy objective. Depending on the presidential administration, the ideological climate, and, especially, the availability of funding, Indians were sometimes celebrated and subsidized, sometimes maligned and marginalized, and sometimes ignored altogether. Yet non-Indians in Mexico consistently viewed Indians as social, cultural, and economic impediments to national progress, and often treated them as such. Although policy climates on both sides of the border did not always directly impact the Yaquis, Kickapoos, and Tohono O'odham, they do often explain the mobility of these groups, or at least their resolve to maintain control over their respective destinies in the face of policy currents seemingly designed to undermine that control. Their resolve, in turn, frequently led them beyond their own borders and across international ones, where they knew they could escape national prerogatives that too often proved detrimental to Indian peoples, their sense of community and peoplehood, and their nationalizing agendas. Yet federal Indian policies could also serve as tools for Indian peoples, or as a means of pursuing an immediate or long-term tribal agenda. Appealing to policymakers and/or submitting to prevailing policy currents, in other words, could also prove vital to the maintenance of at least a semiautonomous existence for at least portions of these indigenous nations. However, as will be shown, cooperation and compromise came with consequences. For a whole host of complicated reasons, some of these Indians were, in the end, forced to choose the lesser of the two evils when it came to U.S. and Mexican Indian policies, which often meant finally severing the ties that bind at the increasingly formidable U.S.-Mexico border.

From virtually the United States' inception, it recognized the legal legitimacy of three types of government: federal, state, and tribal. The Americans, like the British before them, relied on the treaty system, a system built upon a mutual recognition of national sovereignty, to govern relations between federal, state, and/or tribal governments. As the Commerce Clause (article 1, section 8) of the Constitution puts it, "The Congress shall have Power . . . to regulate Commerce with foreign Nations, and among the several States, and with the Indian Tribes." Although the U.S. government did not permit tribal nations to raise armies or issue currency, tribal sovereignty otherwise remained intact. Native nations had the authority to define citizenship, devise law enforcement and justice systems, regulate and tax property, and otherwise govern the domestic affairs of its citizens.[6]

The late nineteenth century would witness an escalation of unprecedented proportions in federal involvement in Indian affairs in the United States, and throughout the twentieth century that involvement would only deepen. Prior to that, however, early U.S policymakers favored a simple policy of physical removal and segregation of Indian peoples, particularly after the acquisition of the Louisiana Territory in 1803 made this strategy more viable. The failure of Indian peoples to acculturate and assimilate, from the perspective of U.S. policymakers, necessitated such drastic measures. Although the Indians' physical removal was far from voluntary from the very beginning, it was not until the administration of Andrew Jackson (1829–37) that removal became an official government program. Well-intentioned reformers promoted the policy as the only means of preventing the Indians' destruction, giving them what reformers believed to be much-needed time and space to prepare for acculturation and eventual assimilation into white America. The federal government, meanwhile, enthusiastically adopted the rhetoric of Indian reformers, but tended to harbor less noble motivations for implementing removal. Simply put, Indian removal had the added benefit of pushing Indians beyond the perimeters of white settlement, thereby opening up their lands for the nation's expansion. The advent of the Bureau of Indian Affairs (BIA) in 1824 slightly predated the implementation of removal. Initially situated within the War Department, the BIA moved to the Department of the Interior in 1849.

Charged with the management of Indian lands and the implementation of Indian policies, the BIA would henceforth become a constant, almost domineering presence in the lives of Indian peoples. With the BIA at the helm, removal as a policy proceeded with a remarkable rapidity. By 1840, in fact, lands east of the Mississippi River had been largely cleared of Indian tribes, though some tribal members opted to remain as individuals and obtain U.S. citizenship. The government sometimes relied on diplomacy to persuade Indians to relocate, though military action was an option that negotiators rarely took off the table and sometimes implemented without hesitation.[7]

Removal and relocation as a policy, however, quickly fell out of favor. With the nation's dramatic territorial acquisition in the wake of the U.S.-Mexican War, coupled with the discovery of gold in California, Indian lands once again came under siege by non-Indians who were either passing through or slowly expanding in ever-increasing numbers onto lands set aside by the federal government. Government policy, then, responded to this turn of events with the reservation system, which policymakers sometimes referred to as the policy of concentration. Pretty soon even the so-called Great American Desert, or the Great Plains, once thought fit only for Indian inhabitants, was suddenly reimagined as the nation's "heartland," or a land of boundless agricultural potential. Concentrating Indians on even further reduced landholdings, then, had the dual benefit of making Indians easier to supervise, acculturate, and ultimately assimilate while also opening up surplus acreage in this "heartland" for white settlement.[8]

Gradually it became obvious that the strategy of either isolating native populations on reservations or moving them westward was no longer viable given the expense of administering the Indian reservations and the nation's rapid growth. The U.S. government then began implementing a long series of measures designed to force the integration of Indians into the dominant social and economic order, thus relieving itself of the responsibility for their well-being. The aforementioned Dawes Act represented perhaps the most ambitious federally sanctioned attempt to detribalize and "Americanize" Indians. Under this act, Congress essentially legislated many reservations out of existence. It forced select Indian tribes to accept individual allotments in lieu of collectively held lands, the goal being, in the words of one reformer, to "awaken in him wants," or to encourage private enterprise and competition among Indians by undermining communal landholding patterns. Massachusetts senator Henry Laurens Dawes, for whom the law was named, along with the majority of his self-styled Indian reformer contemporaries, viewed this as the most logical and expedient way to break the communal, and thus cultural, bonds between Indians and to force their integration into surrounding communities. However, it ultimately resulted in the loss of two-thirds of the Indian land base. As the Kickapoo case demonstrated, allotments regularly fell into non-Indian hands, as Indians were either swindled by speculators or surrounding landowners or sold their allotments for quick money.[9]

With their focus remaining squarely on a policy of forced assimilation, policymakers concurrently experimented with Indian education as a means of supplementing the aims of the Dawes Act. Reformers during this period (roughly 1875–1928) viewed education as the preferred method for introducing and instilling Christian values in Indian youths, since the majority of reformers shared the sentiment that older generations were, so to speak, lost causes. Sure, older Indians could be forced to accept allotments, build houses, and submit to Anglo-American laws and customs, the argument went, but in their hearts they would always remain Indian, forever bound to tribal traditions. Thus, removing Indian children from the reservation and placing them in boarding schools would, reformers hoped, preclude the possibility of a tribal identity taking root.[10] The fact that the U.S. government could legislate its will over the American Indian population as a whole both without their consent and in a blatant spirit of paternalism illustrated the fact that Indians' collective fate was now at the mercy of ever-shifting currents in popular political thought. The BIA, meanwhile, gradually emerged as a bureaucratic powerhouse, exercising what one scholar called "a nearly unfathomable degree of authority." This late nineteenth-century emphasis on forced assimilation, however, ultimately fell out of favor with policymakers, owing partly to its uneven results, but also to a shift in attitudes among reformers and policymakers that was in part inspired by the spirit of the Depression-era New Deal.[11]

The 1934 Indian Reorganization Act (IRA), the legislative arm of the so-called Indian New Deal, embodied this shift in attitudes. Under the direction of Commissioner of Indian Affairs John Collier, who served from 1933 to 1945, the BIA launched a massive campaign to preserve, protect, and foster the growth of what remained of Indian land and culture. Essentially, federal Indian policy under Collier concerned itself with the reversal of previous policy measures that favored forced assimilation, such as the Dawes Act. Through the IRA, Collier hoped to promote notions of cultural pluralism and tribal sovereignty, while reinforcing the concept that reservations should be viewed as permanent homelands.[12] Although the law did not fulfill all of Collier's desired aims, it did result in adequate economic success and, perhaps more importantly, had a profound psychological impact, leaving many tribes more secure in their identities and more hopeful for their futures. It also ended the allotment of Indian lands and helped reconstitute tribal governments, which left Indians feeling more confident that their reservations and reservation-based institutions had acquired enough legal legitimacy to withstand future attacks.[13] As for the issue of indigenous nationhood in the United States, one study characterized the IRA as a "two-edged sword," explaining:

> On the one hand, they gave form and status to tribal governmental institutions, ending an era in which many tribes were either effectively powerless and run as wards of the federal government or largely neglected but unable to assert authority that federal and other authorities would recognize. On the other hand, they commonly proved to be ineffective systems of government for tribes. For many, many tribes, governments organized under the IRA entailed a fatal flaw: they were boilerplate systems that ignored the wide variety of legitimate governing forms tribes had used to rule themselves for innumerable years. Perhaps like trying to impose a monarchy on the United States today, foreign systems in Indian Country have generally lacked legitimacy and support—and therefore effectiveness.[14]

It would be yet another challenge nascent indigenous nations like the ones discussed herein would face in reclaiming and/or protecting tribal sovereignty. Although policymakers never viewed the IRA as a complete failure, the act was nevertheless allowed to languish during the war years. Congress began the 1950s with yet another legislative about-face in the form of a new policy current ominously referred to as "termination." Essentially, termination comprised twelve measures aimed at severing trust relationships between the federal government and all tribes located in Florida, New York, Texas, and California, and individual tribes such as the Menominee, Klamath, Flathead, Chippewa, and Potawatomi. The new legislation relegated governmental responsibilities in the areas of social welfare, education, law enforcement, and economic assistance to the individual states, thereby effectively terminating tribal ties with the federal government and abolishing some reservations.[15]

Termination resembled the Dawes Act not only in its ultimate objectives, which included complete cultural and economic mainstreaming and the revocation of tribal sovereignty, but also in its ideological origins. The Dawes

Act reflected prevailing national sentiment in the post–Civil War years, as the country united in an attempt to redefine "nationhood" by calling for some semblance of national unity in the face of continued cultural diversity. In this environment, the conspicuous presence of political and cultural "islands" was particularly distressing.[16] Similarly, in the post–World War II era, with McCarthyism in full swing, reservations came under attack, with pundits claiming that they represented socialist institutions sanctioned by and situated within the confines of the self-proclaimed "greatest democracy in the world." The emphasis placed on American Indian tribalism and cultural regeneration and preservation during the Collier era of Indian affairs would find an ideological complement in the Indian rights movement of the 1960s and 1970s. Put simply, termination, much like the Dawes Act, failed to bear fruit, instead only deepening the Indians' dependence on the federal government while doing little to alienate them from their tribal identities. The second half of the twentieth century witnessed the formation of AIM, or the American Indian Movement, which maintained a presence, in sometimes aggressive fashion, in the national political arena on behalf of Indian peoples across the country. It also witnessed the passage of the 1975 Indian Self-Determination and Education Assistance Act, which represented a further attempt at placing more political power in the hands of the Indians themselves.[17] In the 1960s, as in the 1930s, the United States found itself swept up in a spirit of reform that touched many aspects of federal policy, leading many to renew their commitment to the "Indian cause." From here Indians would experience a surge in cultural pride, a renewed commitment to protecting hunting and fishing rights, an erosion of the authority of the BIA and of non-Indian religious institutions, and the strengthening of tribal governments and courts. "It is the great irony of nineteenth-century Indian policy," the legal scholar Charles Wilkinson points out, "that the sharply reduced tribal landholdings, which Native peoples bitterly protested, later became cherished homelands and the foundation for the modern sovereignty movement."[18]

Pinning down such currents in Mexican thought and federal action is a much more difficult task, since pinning down what it means to be an Indian in Mexico is more complicated. Being "Indian" in Mexico, generally speaking, has tended to have more to do with economic status than ethnic or cultural makeup. Mexicans have often equated "Indianness" with "ruralness," the idea being that isolated populations are more likely to cling to "tradition." Mexicans have also commonly employed the term *indio* as an insult, understood as not quite a racial or cultural category, but more as a suggestion of "otherness." Or, on another level, it can simply imply a "lack of cool."[19] At one time, these attitudes even pervaded the scholarly community. For example, Albert Bushnell Hart, a professor of political science at Harvard University, wrote in 1914, "The fundamental trouble in Latin America, and particularly in Mexico, seems to be that the population is substantially of native American origin," and as a consequence the region had "not acquired the coolness and political reasonableness which are the basis of modern civilized government."[20] Over time Mexican thinkers revised and refined definitions of Indianness. Writing in 1942, the Mexican scholar Ramón G. Bonfil argued that the most "valid" marker of Indianness is the existence of a "different mentality," one "which makes [Indians] live beyond our laws, creating special patterns of social organization, different forms of labor than we have, and a cultural tempo distinct from that in which we live." He also added that perhaps as a consequence these individuals tend to be situated at the bottom of the "pyramid of Mexican society," which has historically left them vulnerable to exploitation.[21] Another longtime marker of Indianness in Mexico has been one's language. As the anthropologist Miguel León-Portilla explained, millions of Mexicans "retain such pre-Hispanic survivals as a diet based on corn, and the use of 'huaraches' instead of shoes," so officials had to ignore these and similar cultural traits and instead look toward language in order to "most easily" identify Indians.[22] Yet, as one historian noted, "Still, more than five hundred years after Columbus 'discovered' Indians, there is confusion today over what exactly constitutes an Indian in Mexico."[23] At least in a legal, constitutional sense, Mexican Indians ceased to be "Indian" in the wake of the Mexican Revolution. Thus, any special status as "indigenous" was supposed to become a thing of the past. Compounding the difficulties in separating Mexican Indians from non-Indians is the fact that racial mixing evidently occurred in Mexico to a much greater extent than in the United States. And as one scholar succinctly explained, "Where there are no Indians there can be no Indian policy."[24]

This was not always the case in Mexico, however. In fact, under Spain, Mexico had a fairly well-defined Indian policy, particularly since Spanish colonial officials viewed Indians as childlike and therefore in need of guidance and oversight. The crown considered it a moral obligation to expose infidel Indians to Catholicism and Hispanic civilization. This did not mean, however, that Indians were unfit to labor on the Spaniards' behalf. Colonial Indian policy thus established various mechanisms, including the *encomienda* and mission system, to extract labor from Indians while, ostensibly, saving them from both themselves and an afterlife of torment.[25] Lofty goals notwithstanding, in the end the Spanish were far more successful in integrating Indians economically than culturally, gradually coming to believe that the former goal was realistic and worthwhile and the latter was not.[26] The fundamental problem was that the Spanish never stopped viewing Indians as children. Although Indian acculturation consistently remained the goal of Spanish policymakers until the end of the colonial period, few Spaniards made an honest effort to meaningfully integrate Indians into Hispanic communities, instead opting to keep them concentrated in missions or self-contained Indian communities. Indians, then, had to take it upon themselves to challenge their segregation and marginalization, and they did so most often by entering the market economy. As the historian David Weber explains, "In many places, it seems that exposure to the market economy and the workaday world of Hispanic frontier society did more than missions to alter Indian society and culture." Indians learned the Spanish language, learned Spanish trade protocol, and even learned to "drink, swear, and gamble in the Spanish way." Many Indians, however, let their "acculturation" go only so far. Some continued to use stone tools, for example, despite the general availability of metal tools. And while some significantly altered their religious beliefs to accommodate Catholic doctrine, the pull of more traditional forms of worship and systems of belief typically remained powerful. After all, religions are often born out of the process of assigning meaning to the spaces in which peoples live and work. Catholicism could rarely compete with such so-called emplaced religions. While the Spanish could alter behaviors and even some beliefs, divesting these spaces of meaning was another matter altogether.[27]

The 1821 Plan de Iguala, which established Mexican independence, attempted to further undermine the distinction between Indians and non-Indians so firmly established during the Spanish colonial period. It declared all Mexican nationals, regardless of their ethnic and cultural backgrounds, equal citizens of the newly independent republic. Although this was a largely symbolic gesture, the declaration demonstrated that, unlike the United States and Canada, Mexico was determined to break with Indian policies that it now viewed as irrelevant and even counterproductive relics of its colonial past and thus at odds with the nationalizing project it now had to undertake.[28] The break, however, often had grave consequences for the nation's indigenous peoples, since it placed them in an even more vulnerable position. For example, in 1863, President Benito Juárez announced a federal initiative in which *terrenos baldíos* would be divided up and sold in order to fight French efforts to colonize Mexico. The new laws resulted in the loss of 4.5 million acres of land over the course of four years, the vast bulk of which belonged to indigenous peoples who were unable to provide proof of ownership. Although Juárez's initiative predated the Dawes Act by a couple of decades, it had an eerily similar impact on Indian peoples. While intended to provide small farms to members of Indian communities, federal and state initiatives aimed at land distribution more often than not led to their displacement. Indians, in turn, often ended up laboring on large haciendas, the owners of which had the influence and financial means to simply purchase those lands intended for redistribution. Another fundamental problem was that land alone did not always deliver on the promise of productivity or economic security. Local environments, especially desert environments, were not always suitable for agriculture, and local indigenous peoples were not always eager to be molded into mestizo farmers by the Mexican state. Mexico often appeared to be among those states that have been, as the political scientist and anthropologist James Scott put it, "driven by utopian plans and an authoritarian disregard for the values, desires, and objections of their subjects." In Mexico's attempt to foster "huge, utopian changes in people's work habits, living patterns, moral conduct, and worldview," it either failed to note or chose to ignore a whole host of realities on the ground, many environmental in nature, that would inevitably complicate these efforts.[29]

As in the United States, one can easily detect patterns of anti-Indian thinking in nineteenth-century Mexico, at least among Mexican officials. They excluded native languages from legal and administrative discourse, and liberals as well as conservatives came to conclude that Indians must either be transformed and assimilated or exterminated altogether. It was a process one scholar characterized as an attempt to "whiten the nation" through institutional means.[30] Near the end of the century, however, Mexican intellectuals took the lead in defending indigenous populations from these assaults or in encouraging their integration into the Mexican nation through a deeper understanding of their cultures and histories. Their efforts, though laudable, would amount to very little during the Porfiriato (1876–1911), when the Mexican government, with the dictator Porfirio Díaz at the helm, was far more likely to promote an image of Indians as impediments to national progress. In fact, in confronting those impediments, Díaz attacked their land base first, opening up supposedly vacant lands to foreign immigration and cultivation, a strategy that, again, had much in common with that of Dawes-era reformers north of the border. He also permitted individuals operating under the auspices of his "colonization programs" to ignore Indian *ejidos*, or lands held in common by Indian groups. In the end, about two million acres of communal lands fell into non-Indian, and often non-Mexican, hands.[31] This is one policy development that *did* profoundly impact the Indian subjects of this book, as will be shown. One contemporary noted that Díaz's reforms made Indians feel like "a son whose father denied him food while at the same time inviting strangers to dine." Although Díaz took a few halting steps in developing a system of Indian education, as reformers in the United States were then doing, he did so halfheartedly and with few successes. Most of the Indian schools established during the Porfiriato floundered due to the lack of a sustained financial commitment. The Indians, too, had something to do with these early failures. For example, in 1909 the Kickapoos burned down their new school before it had even opened, which, as will be shown, would not be the last time they would go to such extremes in resisting non-Indian education.[32]

In a nation whose history is peppered with noteworthy indigenous figures, anti-Indian sentiment in Mexico proved problematic. How could one reconcile the Indians' alleged inferiority given so much historical evidence to the contrary? As one historian put it, "Mexico's historical experience demonstrated the absurdity of the racist position. The lives of Juárez, Altamirano, Ramírez, and many others proved that Indians had the same capabilities as white men."[33] Francisco Belmar, a member of Mexico's Supreme Court, acted on this increasingly pervasive sentiment in 1910 by founding the Indianist Society of Mexico. He hoped his organization would encourage the study of Mexican Indians in order to ultimately "redeem" them, or in a sense rescue them from poverty and supposed misery. His ideas caught on in a big way in subsequent years. In fact, in a brave display of defiance, a member of the organization, speaking in the presence of Díaz himself, stated bluntly, "I come, gentlemen, to confirm that the indigenous race is abandoned, and that this is not just."[34]

An unprecedented *official* push for Indian assimilation into the Mexican nation began in 1910 with the Mexican Revolution, which precipitated Díaz's downfall. In yet another parallel to the Dawes Act north of the border, Plutarco Elías Calles's government attempted to incorporate Indians into the national fold by depriving them of their lands. With the 1916 Decree No. 33, the Calles government addressed the Indians of Sonora specifically in the form of a thinly veiled threat, warning, "The nomadic tribes and those of the Yaqui and Mayo River will not enjoy the right of Sonoran citizenship as long as their farms and villages maintain their anomalous organization."

In return for joining the national fold, the decree promised that those indigenous peoples who instead lived in "the organized communities of the state" would enjoy the "privilege of citizenship."[35] The obvious problem was one of incentive. The lure of citizenship simply was not powerful enough for the nation's semiautonomous indigenous groups to vacate their lands, forfeit their autonomy, and relocate to "organized communities." It was a problem that had plagued non-Indians in North America for centuries: How does one go about controlling those Indians who, in the words of David Weber, "successfully maintained their political and spiritual independence" and "continued to assert their claims, often with gun and powder"?[36] In some regions of North America, this "problem" persists to the present day.

Still, as in the post–Civil War years in the United States, internal conflict in Mexico in the early twentieth century encouraged an aggressive pursuit of national unity that very often targeted Indian populations. Mexican leaders placed a similar emphasis on conformity, declaring that Indians who fought in the revolution needed to be reminded that they were Mexicans first and foremost. For example, in 1925 Mexico's Education Ministry founded the Casa del Estudiante Indígena in Mexico City, which attempted to "civilize" Mexico's indigenous peoples through an education in and exposure to Mexican culture. In the 1930s Mexican officials began opening similar schools in various Mexican states, each designed to stamp out tribal cultures, teach indigenous peoples the Spanish language, and replace their allegiance to the tribal unit with Mexican patriotism. The program specifically targeted indigenous boys, calling for their removal from indigenous communities and their total immersion in modern Mexican society. It was an Indian policy initiative that suggested a familiarity with the boarding school experiment in the United States.[37]

These efforts were an early expression of a broader trend in twentieth-century Mexican history that Mexican intellectuals termed *indigenismo*. While postrevolutionary Mexico demanded Indian integration into Mexican society and the body politic (though, of course, only after acculturating), it also often voiced pride in its Indian heritage. In fact, Mexico's postrevolutionary political and intellectual elite came to view indigenous peoples as central to the nation's identity. The historian Rick López explains:

> These urban elites interpreted Mexico as falling horribly short of
> new ideas about what it meant to be a modern nation. They felt
> that to be modern a nation had to be a culturally, economically,
> and politically distinct and unified people with deep historical

roots . . . Indianness, they argued, was the thread that would unite the diverse populations living within the territory of the Mexican Republic and distinguish Mexico among a global family of other nation-states. To be truly Mexican one was expected to be part Indian or to demonstrate a concern for the valorization and redemption of the Mexican Indian as part of the nation. Those who rejected the country's Indianness were publicly chastised for their foreignness and lack of nationalist zeal.[38]

Thus, *indigenismo* was, as another historian succinctly put it, an attempt to challenge "the exclusive association of modernity with whiteness." Yet while reformers used indigenous peoples as a rallying point in jump-starting their nationalizing project, they were also keenly aware that their message was not likely to resonate with the very peoples they were celebrating. So beyond playing up their centrality to Mexican national identity, reformers promised to provide at least those Indians who fought in the revolution with a variety of opportunities to participate in the local and national economy. Inviting them into the economic fold, the reformers reasoned, might help foster the nationalistic impulse that they felt lacking among Mexico's indigenous population, which, in turn, might lessen the sociocultural gap between themselves and the nation's Indian peoples.[39] "We do not accept the thesis," stated one official, perfectly summing up Indigenista ideology, "that the Indian's backwardness is due to innate deficiencies which he has neither will nor ambition to overcome. On the contrary, we believe that his backwardness is the fault of those who have made him an object for exploitation."[40] Another Mexican official stated his case more forcefully, arguing, "That builder, that creator, that patriot is, as we all know, the humble, naked, poor, despised Mexican Indian. The destiny of the nation lies today, as it did yesterday and as it always will, in the hands of this powerful titan." Before the nations of the Americas could progress, he concluded, the Indian must be allowed to "descend from the cross of misery and ignorance where the wicked ones mercilessly tied him."[41] The image of Indians as having been callously exploited and marginalized by their selfish, greedy, non-Indian countrymen was evidently a powerful one.

It was also an accurate one. As the historian Alexander Dawson points out, Mexican Indians in the first half of the twentieth century "lived in misery, and were broadly perceived as a crippling burden to the nation." Near midcentury some Mexican officials began expressing concerns that *indigenismo* had stagnated and that more aggressive steps needed to be taken to

spur Indian acculturation.[42] This more urgent emphasis on Indian acculturation coincided with an increasing faith in scientific investigation to address such perceived social ills. Following the lead of Indian enthusiasts
such as Belmar, government officials came to the conclusion that they must
first *understand* Indians if they were to improve their standard of living
and, ultimately, incorporate them into the Mexican nation. The Mexican
government had taken the first steps in this mission back in 1917, when it
created the Department of Anthropology, and the mission gained momentum under the direction of the influential anthropologist Dr. Manuel Gamio
in the years that followed. Scientific studies were one thing; however, reformers soon identified the need to *apply* these studies. In the 1930s, the
government created the National Institute of Anthropology and History
and the Autonomous Department of Indian Affairs in order to bridge the
gap between scientific study and practical application. In 1947, the Mexican government placed the Autonomous Department of Indian Affairs under
the Ministry of Education, renaming it the Department of Indian Affairs.
The following year, the government created the National Indian Institute
and charged it with working in conjunction with the Inter-American Indian
Institute toward the establishment of multiple "coordinating centers" throughout Latin America to administer participating governments' acculturation
programs. The base of operations for these various organizations remained,
for decades, Mexico City. A host of journals, including the bimonthly *Boletín Indigenista* and the quarterly *América Indígena*, supplemented their
efforts, serving as what one publication called 'information organs." These
too were based in Mexico City.[43] As in the United States, the bureaucratic
machinery that aimed to govern the lives of Indian peoples was seemingly
growing more complex with each passing decade.

Still, Mexico worked diligently to foster the impression that its program
was hemispheric in scope, even devoting financial resources to international
outreach. For example, in 1941 the Mexican government invited Pueblo
Indians from the United States to meet with various Indian communities
across Mexico. A performance at Mexico City's Palace of Fine Arts, during
which the Pueblos presented songs and dances, capped off the visit.[44] And
beginning in 1940, the Department of Indian Affairs inaugurated an annual
Day of the Indian. Held every April at the Fine Arts Plaza in Mexico City,
the affair celebrated Indian contributions to broader American history while
providing the opportunity to reflect on ongoing problems facing the hemisphere's indigenous peoples. At one such Day of the Indian, in fact, Sonoran
Yaquis and Kickapoos from Coahuila treated attendees to tribal dances.[45]

At the 1953 gathering, Dr. Alfonso Caso, director of the National Indian Institute of Mexico, explained the purpose of the Day of the Indian:

> The ceremony we hold every year on this day is more a symbol than an act of remembrance. We are not here to commemorate the past glories of the Teotihuacán, Toltec, Aztec, Maya, Zapotec, Mixtec, Tarrascan, Chibcha, Inca and many other great civilizations that used to flourish on the continent . . . Today's celebration is not only for the purpose of recalling the greatness of our Indian ancestors; it serves to indicate the firm will of the governments and people of America to destroy an often secular injustice that reduced this Indian race, at one time lords of the Continent[,] to the state of material and cultural impoverishment in which it now finds itself. That is why I say that today's ceremony is a symbol; it means that the people of America have definitely decided to solve the problem of the great Indian masses of America and bring them what they lack: communications, schools, health services, land and water, protection of their forests, and protection against non-Indian groups that have exploited them for centuries.[46]

In this mission, Latin America also looked to the United States for an example. Ecuador's ambassador to Mexico, Dr. Jorge Villagómez Yépez, singled out the New Dealer John Collier, whom he referred to as the "wise president" of the Institute of Ethnic Affairs, in praising the United States' activism. Collier, he asserted, "has proclaimed the need for an 'orderly withdrawal' and for the reintegration of the North American Indian into the general life of the country. The magnificent idea behind this is cultural pluralism which favors protecting the distinctive characteristics of underdeveloped ethnic groups and aiding in their special development."[47] Although he seems to have misinterpreted Collier's broader mission of revitalizing Indian cultures through a strengthening of reservation communities and tribal governments, his remarks do demonstrate that Indigenistas went to great lengths to promote a mission that they believed had attained an air of universality, or at least one that was on the cutting edge of Indian policy currents. As Dawson explains, Indigenistas "took the radical view that the nation was made up of a plurality of cultures, and called for self-empowerment, the inclusion of locals in decision making, and ultimately even recognized the right of indigenous peoples to self-determination."[48] Generally speaking, however, Mexican policymakers frowned on the reservation system employed by the United States. One Mexican official summed it up nicely, stating, "To imprison [the Indian] theoretically or practically on 'reservations' is to condemn him to a sterile life, and ultimately extinction."[49]

Thus, Indigenistas took great pains to learn from what they perceived to be the United States' Indian policy failures. In the mid-1920s, for example, a Mexican official toured Indian schools and reservations in the United States, and was troubled by what he witnessed. First of all, despite the long push for Indian assimilation in the United States via the Dawes Act and the Indian education experiment, Indian peoples, in his words, "continued to form a separate social group," completely cut off from "the rest of the components of the American union." Second, Indians obviously resented the fact that while pushing for their assimilation, the U.S. government appeared simultaneously determined to "not make them an integral part, neither as citizens nor as social subjects, of the great national family." One must take this official's observations with a grain of salt, however. As the historian Stephen Lewis aptly observed, "In a predominately mestizo nation, the idea of 'social separation' was a disturbing one, even if it existed in practice."[50] And at least in the case of the Tohono O'odham, Mexican officials put forth little effort in dissuading the O'odham from relocating en masse to the Arizona reservation. As has been shown, there was in fact a concerted push in late nineteenth-century Mexico to, as the historians Andrae Marak and Laura Tuennerman put it, "eliminate corporate identities and communities—especially those of the Catholic Church, peasant pueblos, and indigenous groups—and replace them with wage laborers and capitalist yeoman farmers who, it was hoped, would view themselves as Mexican citizens." The O'odham watched as Mexican settlers entered their lands in search of precious metals or a piece of the expanding cattle industry. They also had to contend with a railroad, which had been constructed to connect Guaymas, Sonora, and Nogales, Arizona, that now ran through the heart of their ancestral lands. It is little wonder, then, that so many opted for life on a reservation in the United States, however distasteful and counterproductive Mexican reformers found the reservation concept to be.[51]

In the end, the process of acculturation failed to progress to the satisfaction of reformers, despite unprecedented efforts on the federal government's behalf. And when elected in 1934, President Lázaro Cárdenas helped many of the nation's Indian peoples maintain a buffer zone between themselves and their non-Indian neighbors through a series of land reform measures. As Claudia Haake observed, "Cárdenas saw the *ejido* as more than a transitional device and rather as a model to capitalistic agriculture." In a very real way, then, the *ejido* designation, as interpreted by Cárdenas, had much in common with reservations in the United States, which, at least during the Collier era, came to be viewed as permanent homelands for Indian peoples. Also among Cárdenas's initiatives was the redistribution of roughly eighteen million hectares of land to an estimated 800,000 recipients, many of them members of indigenous communities. The number of landless in Mexico fell from 2.5 million to 1.9 million.[52] As will be shown, the Yaquis in particular were beneficiaries of this new trend in the history of Mexican "Indian policy."

Still, not all Indians embraced Cárdenas's efforts at reform. In fact, in the 1930s Mexican educators conducted a survey of Indian communities and encountered staunch opposition to integration into Mexican national culture and the Mexican economy. Thus, as the twentieth century progressed it tended to be the Mexican government and non-Indian mestizos who felt "abandoned" by indigenous peoples, *not* the other way around. Put simply, they were surprised and dismayed to receive so little in the way of cooperation from indigenous communities. Indians were, in the words of one scholar, "refusing to fall in line with postrevolutionary visions of a modern Mexican state," a situation non-Indians found disappointing and, ultimately, troubling. For example, non-Indians continued to regard the southern O'odham as at best "proto-citizens" who desperately needed state tutelage and at worst, at least according to one historian's assessment, "lazy, drunken . . . thieves," a "wandering people," and an ongoing "problem" the nation had still not managed to solve despite its best efforts. And the clearest sign that the O'odham had "abandoned" the Mexican nation was that fact that by the second half of the twentieth century so many had permanently left their lands in Mexico, choosing instead to reside on the Sells reservation in Arizona.[53]

Thus, while the national government had invested heavily in a twofold strategy that, again much like that of the United States fifty years before, during the Dawes era, focused on economic integration and education as key to assimilation, Indian populations remained resistant to their efforts. And it was through that resistance to federal programs that Mexico's indigenous peoples made their voices heard, and, at least temporarily, forced the federal government to reimagine Mexico as more a plurality of nations than a single nation. Simply put, Indigenistas were perhaps overly ambitious from the outset in that they attempted to, as Dawson explains, "create a new state and extend its authority across a national territory that remained largely outside the scope of federal control." Unlike the indigenous peoples they were working hard to reform, early Indigenistas believed that modernity and nationhood were one and the same. Creating a nation, they maintained, required the undermining of Mexico's many pockets of indigenous autonomy.[54]

Mexico's Indians were not as malleable or compliant as the Indigenistas had anticipated, however, and the goal of assimilating Indians into the Mexican mainstream ultimately proved unrealistic. Simply put, the Indians refused to forfeit their own cultural convictions, and were growing more and more adept at limiting the reformers' access to their communities.[55] Another barrier to their nationalizing efforts involved, again, persistent difficulties in identifying who was Indian. Dawson explains, "*Indigenistas* used a variety of racial and cultural data, along with their own imaginations, [to identify] both the Indian and the mestizo," ultimately concluding that Indians comprised between 30 and 50 percent of Mexico's population—figures that must have led to a reevaluation of their nationalizing mission. In other words, since the Indian population appeared to be growing in tandem with the rest of the population, Indians no longer appeared to be a shrinking, doomed minority despite decades of efforts aimed at their acculturation.[56]

In the end, the problems encountered by Indigenistas forced them to abandon many of their initial goals and move to a surprising new line of thought. Continued diversity within Mexico's borders, they were beginning to conclude, was in fact a source of strength. Dawson explains, "Mexico, they decided, was not one nation but many, each with a right to self-determination based upon their distinct histories, geographies, and cultures." They found no reason to eliminate local systems of government, such as councils of elders (an institution the Kickapoos once maintained), and instead portrayed such systems as a way for indigenous peoples to exist in modern Mexico with dignity. It was a revolutionary new intellectual direction, and one that would have staying power. One intellectual went so far as to suggest that more "advanced" Indian tribes should be recognized as separate nationalities within Mexico's borders, and, as such, should be allowed to conduct their own affairs in their own language and according to their own local needs.[57]

Whether or not federal policies affected any real change in indigenous areas within Mexico is difficult to ascertain due to the absence of any "blanket" Indian policies, such as the Dawes Act, the Indian Reorganization Act, or the termination measures, coupled with persistent difficulties in actually identifying Indians. In their efforts to incorporate Indian peoples into the social, economic, and political orbit of the Mexican nation, officials consistently downplayed the Indians' separateness, or the socioeconomic gulf that stood between them and their non-Indian neighbors. Unlike the United States, which differentiated between "recognized" and "unrecognized" Indian groups (with the former enjoying a host of legal privileges and exceptions), Mexico made no such distinction. Generally speaking, post-revolutionary governments in Mexico have largely confined their efforts, where indigenous peoples are concerned, to land distribution. Furthermore, their efforts targeted not just landless indigenous peoples, but *all* of Mexico's landless poor (even though the government has been well aware that the vast majority of Mexicans comprising the "landless poor" are of indigenous ancestry). In explaining the government's continued lack of activity in the arena of Indian affairs, at least when compared to the United States, Claudia Haake contended, "It may be that the state was not strong enough for a coherent policy towards the members of the indigenous members of the nation, or, more likely, that it was unwilling to face the consequences this would have brought." Furthermore, it has historically been in the best interest of the Mexican nation to ignore the "Indian problem" by simply pretending that, at least in an official capacity, Indians did not exist. Policies more generally aimed at "peasants," then, could maintain the fiction of national unity while relieving the government of additional responsibilities. As Haake astutely observed, since the Mexican Revolution, Indians have been a "people disowned," struggling against a "policy disguised." Policies emanating from the Mexican government, in other words, rarely treated Indian peoples and mestizos the same. The most expeditious way to confront the "Indian problem," it turned out, was to acknowledge their Indianness, or their political and cultural uniqueness, and then strategize accordingly.[58]

Luckily for these reformers, the bulk of the twentieth century witnessed far less dramatic forms of indigenous resistance than the previous century on both sides of the U.S-Mexico border. At least in the case of the Yaquis, Kickapoos, and Tohono O'odham, new patterns of resistance would emerge in courts, before congressional committees, in communications with immigration or other federal authorities, and in letters to connected politicians, scholars, or even these Indians' transborder counterparts. In other words, at a certain point the various Yaqui, Kickapoo, and Tohono O'odham communities more or less stabilized. Patterns of transnational mobility that had so often led to violence, instability, and uncertainty during the previous century gave way to a new (and, it turned out, more viable) survival strategy: working *through* the system rather than continuing to operate beyond its purview or in open defiance of its prerogatives. Oftentimes these groups adopted this new strategy by choice, engaging one or the other nation-state in order to meet an immediate or long-term agenda, while other times government bureaucrats attempted, with varying degrees of success, to impose their will on these determined but increasingly divided indigenous nations. In the end, transnational networks that had once flourished would, almost across the board, constrict to the point that little transborder human traffic flowed unfettered. What had once been a symbol of opportunity and possibility had become an obstacle that seemed less and less worth the effort to confront. Still, indigenous peoples on both sides of the increasingly formidable border would keep their eyes fixed on the terminuses of these once flourishing transnational networks, always with a sense of themselves as part of something larger than a single nation could contain.

3 God Gave the Land to the Yaquis

The Beleaguered Yaqui Nation

· ·

In the earliest hours of the first day of Lent, 1934, Yaqui Indian Rosalio Moisés had what he described as a "very good dream." In it, a group of white men arrived in the Yaqui River valley to aid the beleaguered group in their seemingly endless struggles with their non-Indian neighbors. In fact, Moisés was not the first Yaqui to be visited by this dream. Years prior, José María Nóteme often told Yaqui audiences, including a young Moisés, of a recurring dream of his own in which the Mexican military began waging war on the Yaquis anew, this time threatening to "finish off the Yaquis" for good. Then, just when all seemed lost, the white strangers arrived from the north and, as Moisés later recounted, "ask[ed] the Yaquis about all that had happened to them and little by little help[ed] them to make a happy living." Only days after Moisés's dream, a group of white men did, in fact, arrive in the valley. "When I heard this," Moisés remembered, "I thought, 'These are the white men I saw in my dream, and my dreams never lie to me.'"[1]

The "white men" were actually members of a nine-man expeditionary party headed by the anthropologist William Curry Holden and sponsored by Texas Technological College in Lubbock. They set out to study, in the words of a Lubbock-based publication, "the physical, social, religious, governmental, and economic aspects of . . . the last unconquered primitive people of the North American Continent." The travelers arrived during a precarious peace between the Yaquis and the Mexican military, and on the heels of one of the largest indigenous revolts in North American history, a revolt that, late in the previous century, nearly resulted in the tribe's complete removal from the Yaqui River valley. Meanwhile, in addition to the "half-subdued groups in the garrisoned villages," the expeditionary party heard tell of Yaqui "holdouts" still populating area mountain ranges, continuing the tribe's tradition of resistance to non-Yaqui authority. In fact, one member of the party casually recorded in his diary during the expedition's early days, "A Yaqui was killed today by some soldiers in the mountains."[2] The Yaqui River valley in mid-1934, then, was still a volatile place.

In the interest of keeping the peace, the Mexican government evidently had the Yaquis on the military payroll, though the Indians possessed no uniforms, nor did they ever report for duty. The government was, according to one account, simply "paying the Yaqui to be good." This was, in fact, the government's strategy. Allowing the tribe to maintain at least some sense of military pride, as well as a semblance of independence, they reasoned, would make the Yaquis easier to control. In entering Yaqui country, the party from Texas had to acquire the consent of both the Mexican military and Yaqui leaders. The outsiders reportedly received the cold shoulder from the Yaquis initially, since they had requested Mexican cooperation *before* consulting the tribe. It was a minor affront, however, upon which the tribe did not dwell. In fact, the Yaquis quickly overcame their initial suspicion and befriended the Texans after realizing that they had once shared a common enemy: the Mexican government, whom the Texans, the Yaquis recalled with delight, had soundly defeated in their *own* bid for independence.[3]

If the party had entered Yaqui country twenty years earlier, they might not have survived that initial encounter. The anthropologist Ralph Beals recalled traveling to the Yaqui River with his brother Carleton and two other American companions in 1917 despite warnings by residents of nearby Guaymas that they steer clear of the region altogether. They soon came upon what appeared to be a Yaqui war party destroying a railroad bridge. For reasons that were unclear to Beals and his brother, their two American companions decided to approach the Yaquis. Suddenly the situation turned violent, and Beals and his brother watched in horror as the Yaquis beat the two men to death with clubs. He and his brother quickly retreated to Guaymas, shaken but otherwise unharmed. The encounter made a lasting impression on Beals, however, and in time he would come to regard the Yaquis as, in the historian Ruben Flores's words, "a powerful symbol of resistance to the power of the state." While their fierce determination to "preserve their community by maintaining clear boundaries to the outside" was put on full display that day in 1917, it was their "rabid sense of nationalism" that most impressed Beals.[4]

Holden and crew apparently shared that sentiment. They would later claim to have witnessed firsthand the inner workings of what one account characterized as "the only 'state within a state' to be found in the western hemisphere." Although the Yaquis lived within Mexican borders and "under the muzzle of Mexican army guns," they had maintained their right to "administer their own justice, obey their own laws, have their own military organizations and—above all—pack their own guns." One party member characterized the Yaqui military as "like a foreign legion." "This couldn't happen in our country" was the general consensus.[5] It should be added, however, that this was not strictly a "Yaqui problem" the Mexican government had on its hands. Flores further argued that in early twentieth-century Mexico "neither the state nor industry had yet accelerated to the point of destroying the panoply of cultural communities that defined the country."[6] These "cultural communities" only needed to remain steadfast in the face of the state's efforts to undermine their uniqueness and even their sovereignty, as the Yaquis had been doing so effectively.

The concerns of those Yaquis who remained in Mexico, then, diverged dramatically from those of their Arizona-based counterpart. Taking shape in Sonora was a more militant Yaqui nationalism, one characterized by a marked indifference to and suspicion of outsiders. Their primary preoccupation was the maintenance of the group's political and cultural autonomy, which required the maintenance of their land base, which just happened to contain some of the richest farmland in North America. Yaquis in Arizona, meanwhile, mostly inhabited Pascua Village on the outskirts of Tucson, though a lesser number inhabited nearby Barrio Belén. Older Yaquis in the region, the anthropologist Edward Spicer observed, lived in "an atmosphere of the recent past." They gathered often to share stories of Cajeme, of violence, of flight, and of escape. A favorite was the story of Francisco Valencia, who went so far as to join a circus troupe in order to cross into the United States. "They are all refugees, and they do not forget it," Spicer wrote. Pascua formally came into being in 1921 with the assistance of local businessmen. It was the first step in their effort to forge, in Spicer's words, a "Yaqui Nation in Arizona." But although they were gradually cementing their presence in Tucson, they kept a keen eye on developments among their southern counterpart, always eager to reenter at least the cultural orbit of their relatives.[7]

Thus, the Yaquis faced a new set of challenges as they entered a new phase in their collective history. While the previous phase was characterized by near-constant rebellion, from this point forward violence was, with rare exceptions, a thing of the past. Instead, the process of reconciling the Yaquis' presence in both the United States and Mexico with their persistent claims to nationhood would occur in legislative and legal circles rather than military ones. Yet, as one reporter observed in the 1970s, "Now that overt persecution has ended, tribal culture and unity face more subtle, change-producing pressure." Much of that pressure would come in the form of measures designed to restrict Yaqui movements and blunt their claims to sovereignty. Officials on both sides of the border would begin employing new surveillance technologies such as the telephone and relying on emergent institutions such as the *rurales*, the Arizona Rangers, the Border Patrol, and consulates to limit the Yaquis' ability to subvert national authority.[8] Changes wrought by these efforts would, in the end, dramatically complicate the maintenance of the Yaqui nation.

This chapter, then, examines the new role the boundary between the United States and Mexico played in Yaqui life over the course of the twentieth century as the tribe gradually solidified its transnational presence. This process would entail not only continued resistance south of the boundary, but also the continued insistence that Yaqui settlements in the United States contained much more than dwindling contingents of temporary sojourners. However, while the border symbolized opportunity for some, whether in the pursuit of economic security or spiritual and/or cultural sustenance, for most it increasingly came to represent little more than a barrier, an obstacle that kept some Yaquis in, some Yaquis out, and, in the end, stymied the efforts of Yaquis on both sides to fully reclaim lost sovereignty. It also created cultural rifts between these two centers of Yaqui life, often steering patterns of life and labor down two separate, and sometimes incompatible, evolutionary paths. Thus, while the tribe initially began rebuilding on two separate foundations, one in Arizona and the other along the Yaqui River, the new priority, at least for most of the twentieth century, became bridging the gap between these two centers, or forging a reconstituted, autonomous Yaqui nation that transcended international borders. First, however, they would have to contend with what the historian Oscar Martínez called the "troublesome border," which was *also* entering a new phase in its history. Keeping transborder lines of communication and physical movement open would prove easier said than done.

In his autobiography, written in the late 1960s, Yaqui Rosalio Moisés recounted in further detail his people's initial meeting with Holden and his nine-man crew during that 1934 Lenten season, a crew that included a physician, an ethnobotanist, an ornithologist, an archaeologist, and a historian. The party approached the village of Torim and explained to a group of Yaqui officials that, in Moisés's words, they "wanted to learn what had happened to the Yaquis in their own land, and they wanted to put everything in a book for people to read. This, they said, would help the Yaquis make a better life in the Rio Yaqui." The introduction reportedly put the Yaqui chiefs at ease, and they allowed Holden and crew to visit Pluma Blanca, or the group's primary chief. Pluma Blanca, however, responded to the newcomers' book proposal somewhat angrily, exclaiming, "Are we not like other human beings? We [all] have five fingers on each hand and five toes on each foot."⁹

Eventually the Yaquis allowed Holden and his crew to begin their field-work, though one cannot help but imagine the consternation the Yaquis must have felt watching their men submit to an invasive series of anthropological measurements using, variously, a spreading caliper, a sliding caliper, and a steel measuring tape. The party measured the Indians' height, weight, arm span, torso length, shoulders, hips, and, finally, heads, then had each of their subjects pose for a headshot in order to draw conclusions about Yaqui facial characteristics later. They also managed to secure, according to Holden, 144 "museum specimens," a small collection of botanical specimens, roughly 600 photographs, 1,200 feet of movie film, and countless sketches before leaving the valley.[10] One member of the 1934 expedition, in fact, described a typical day during the first expedition, observing, "Again Ethnology is being pursued lustily."[11]

The party also demonstrated the practical benefits of allowing the new-comers to have access to their communities. Dr. Charles Wagner, for example, ultimately performed operations on more than a few Yaquis. "Their confidence and gratitude were delightful," he later wrote. One particularly memorable experience involved the removal of a cancerous tumor from the back of a fourteen-year-old Yaqui boy. Had it been left untreated, he likely would have died. Wagner also removed a bullet from Yaqui Juan Serrena, one of several Serrena acquired after a "little misunderstanding" with Mexican soldiers, and that had been lodged in his back for nineteen years. Wagner no doubt felt out of his element, performing the surgery in front of a large crowd, while his assistants had to contend with insects, dust, and "emaciated, omnipresent dogs." The operation was a success, however, and won the expeditionary party additional goodwill.[12]

Holden and crew returned later that year to resume their fieldwork, and ultimately gathered a great deal of information on Yaqui history and culture while also making off with a large number of tribal artifacts. They also, evidently, spent time in discussions with Yaqui leaders in an effort to better understand their relationship with the Mexican government. Shortly after this second expedition, in fact, Holden wrote to Moisés with encouraging news: he had personally been to Mexico City to discuss the Yaquis with government officials, and had found a receptive audience. "I guess he explained things very well," Moisés later recalled, "because soon some Mexican officials came to the Yaqui villages." They listened while the Yaquis aired their grievances, and then shortly thereafter assigned a new Mexican general to police the so-called Yaqui Zone, a general who was ultimately far more effective in maintaining calm in the region. Then, in February 1935, a boxcar arrived at the village of Vicam that contained pants, jackets, huaraches, blankets, and agricultural tools, all courtesy of the Mexican government. Unfortunately for Moisés, however, the shipment had already been picked over by local Mexican soldiers, and Yaqui chiefs and government officials hoarded the rest for themselves and their families. "All day I stood there watching," Moisés remembered. "I did not get a single blanket." Still, Moisés could not help but laud Holden's efforts on the Yaquis' behalf, and in fact gave Holden full credit for the Mexican government's sudden interest in their well-being. "Dr. Holden had got the government officials in Mexico City to listen about the plight of the poor Yaquis," Moisés concluded. "But the *torocoyoris* [Yaqui traitors] and Mexican soldiers stole everything, and nothing was changed for the poor Yaquis."[13]

In a series of correspondences with Yaqui Ramón Torry, who served as an interpreter for Holden and crew, we can best see Holden's sustained, though sometimes reluctant, efforts to defuse the volatile atmosphere along the Yaqui River. For example, writing in the wake of the first expedition, Torry complained to Holden about worsening conflicts with their Mexican neighbors, conflicts that usually involved access to Yaqui lands. "I remember you," Torry wrote in somewhat broken English, "because when you ride around here with me, you were speaking a lovely voice with my peoples and that we got a little hope from you." He asked Holden to take the Yaquis' complaints straight to "the American governor of U.S.A."[14] Holden replied to Torry the following month. "Your letter makes us very sad," Holden wrote, adding, "I am afraid that I am not much good at giving advice to your people." In what was likely an attempt to put Torry's mind at ease, however, Holden continued, "I was in Mexico City last Christmas and talked with a number of the high officials about the Yaquis. They all seemed to want to do the right thing by the Yaqui people. They have plans to help all the Indians of Mexico." He concluded with the somewhat vague assurance that "everything will turn out alright."[15]

Torry wrote Holden again the following year with word that the Yaquis' relationship with their Mexican neighbors was not improving. This time, Torry asked Holden to return to the Río Yaqui to personally assist the tribe before things turned violent.[16] Holden responded soon thereafter, urging the Yaquis to avoid resorting to violence, instead encouraging them to appeal directly to Mexico's president. "[Lázaro] Cárdenas seems to be a good man," he wrote, "and if the grievances of the Yaquis were put up to him squarely he would perhaps see that they received justice."[17] Only days after urging Torry to take matters into his own hands, however, Holden forwarded Torry's complaint to Ramón Beteta, the head of Mexico's Statistics Agency of the Secretariat of Industry and Commerce. "From [Torry's] letter," Holden wrote to Beteta, "it seems that trouble is brewing in the Yaqui country . . . I am in a delicate situation as an outsider and a foreigner taking note of matters which are strictly internal problems of the Mexican government. My purpose is to let you know the nature of the friction which may, if allowed to go on, terminate in trouble both for the government and the Yaquis." Yet after presenting himself as an unwitting participant in this ongoing drama between the Yaquis and the Mexican military, Holden politely but firmly asked Beteta to do whatever he could to clear up the "misunderstanding" between the Yaquis and the Mexican government.[18] Although this would not be the last exchange between Holden and Beteta, it would take nearly four years for Beteta to relay encouraging news. "As you know," he wrote to Holden in 1938, "the Government finally decided to take a firm stand in the Yaqui question once and for all. They have already received their lands which will insure permanent peace in the Yaqui Valley."[19]

Beteta was referring to a series of presidential decrees, courtesy of President Cárdenas, that, taken collectively, sanctioned the return of those "mountain holdouts" to the river valley and officially designated the Yaquis' lands a Zona Indígena. Thus, Cárdenas was instrumental in reformalizing the Yaqui presence in Sonora, guaranteeing their right to inhabit the valley through the establishment of agricultural cooperatives, and even affirming, with some conditions, their right to govern themselves by designating the tribe an "indigenous community."[20] The extent to which Holden influenced this decision, whether or not his advocacy forced the Mexican government's hand, is difficult to ascertain. But, as already indicated, at least some Yaquis gave Holden and his crew credit for their dramatically changing fortunes. Holden remained involved in the lives of some Yaquis on a personal level as well. It was not unusual for him to provide assistance in acquiring immigration papers or arranging work in the United States, for example. In fact, Holden hired Moisés to help with the construction of his new home and, later, with the construction of a Yaqui-style ramada for Texas Tech's museum. And when the Yaqui River valley suffered a devastating flood in 1949, Holden and several other members of the university community donated a few dollars each to help Moisés and his family recover. It was also not unheard of for Moisés to request small loans during other tough times. One particularly lean summer, for example, he sent Holden a request for twenty dollars, and later remembered, "[Dr. Holden] must have mailed the money as soon as he received my letter, because a letter containing two ten-dollar bills came right away."[21] The friendship between the Yaquis and Holden and his crew did not end in 1934. In fact, subsequent expeditions, also sponsored by Texas Tech, took place in 1938, 1940, both spring and winter of 1953, and 1955, all culminating in a "commemorative" expedition in 1984.[22]

While these expeditions came and went freely, Yaquis who wished to migrate on a transnational scale were not always as unfettered, and became even less so as the century progressed. The Yaquis, like the other indigenous groups discussed herein, would have to struggle with immigration authorities and policies that, over the course of the twentieth century, became increasingly inflexible. Put simply, the early decades of the twentieth century marked the arrival of a new phase in the history of the U.S.-Mexico border, one in which officials on both sides focused their efforts as never before on managing transborder migration. Yet the border, at least temporarily, remained what one scholar characterized as a "social fiction." Although border inspection stations lorded over formal crossing points by the late 1920s, having now become permanent, ever more imposing features on the new border landscape, migrants had little trouble skirting these crossing points and identifying alternate routes to and from their transborder destinations. As the historian Patrick Ettinger explains, "Rural, remote, and mostly uninhabited, the southwest border invited subversion of the national border." Individual migrants only needed to expend a bit of "creative energy" in order to ensure that the border remained permeable. Officials did go to great lengths to fortify the border during the early decades of the twentieth century, but, as Ettinger concludes, the border "could only be as strong as its weakest point, and it still largely consisted of weak points."[23]

One new trend was that officials (particularly north of the border) would periodically crack down on transborder migration, especially during periods of economic turmoil and/or when the supply of labor exceeded demand. The economic depression of the 1930s, for example, spurred a massive "repatriation" of Mexican workers, while Operation Wetback during the 1950s encouraged a similar trend under the guise of ferreting out potential political subversives. Yet another crackdown occurred during the recession of 1974–75, a crackdown characterized by what Oscar Martínez called "Gestapo methods" at U.S. border inspection stations.[24] All of these changes in political and legal dynamics sent shock waves throughout the region's indigenous communities, which had come to depend on, and in fact expect, unfettered transborder movement. Although this trend is less obvious in the Kickapoo case, the Indians discussed herein would find their interests diverge considerably depending on which side of the border they happened to reside. This forced these nascent nations to acknowledge that the border drawn by the United States and Mexico could ultimately prove insurmountable in the face of their efforts to forge some semblance of national unity.

Thus, although Yaqui migration between the new place and the old place never stopped altogether, it had slowed to a trickle by the early twentieth century, and remained so thereafter. How many Yaquis ultimately migrated to Arizona during the late nineteenth century and the first two decades of the twentieth century is difficult to ascertain, but Edward Spicer, the leading expert on Arizona's Yaquis at midcentury, speculated that it was possibly as many as 5,000, while only about 2,000–3,000 Yaquis remained scattered throughout Sonora. The rest, amounting to an estimated 8,000, evidently submitted to forced relocation, ultimately assimilating into the broader Mexican social milieu. Others simply disappeared. The Yaquis were not entirely unused to family members seemingly falling off the map, and the disappearance of loved ones was particularly common early in the century when the tribe's presence in Mexico had not entirely stabilized. In the 1930s, Juana de Amarillas reflected on these years. She recalled losing her husband shortly after arriving in Sonora, adding, "The soldiers took him away. We didn't know anything about what happened to him . . . I don't know where he got killed or whether they sent him to Yucatán or what happened." She also lost her son under similarly mysterious circumstances. "He was taken [to La Paz] by the soldiers," she claimed. "He died and they sent me a paper saying he was dead. That was all I ever knew about it. That was a sad time. That's the way it is in Sonora."[25]

Further, the move from the old place to the new, and vice versa, was not always a permanent one, as the somewhat atypical story of "General" Guadalupe Flores illustrates. Flores was the self-proclaimed "jefe" of Barrio Pascua during the early twentieth century, and served as a key link between Sonoran and Arizona Yaquis. He left Sonora in 1928 with a small band of Yaquis who were fleeing yet another period of violent conflict with the Mexican government, only to face detainment by Border Patrol agents shortly after entering Arizona. The Border Patrol, after several days, allowed Flores and his band to remain in Arizona as refugees, and officials in Washington eventually granted the band refugee status, alongside their Yaqui brethren already in Arizona. They initially labored on small farms in the Santa Cruz valley before settling in Pascua, which by then contained a stable, and even burgeoning, Yaqui population. According to one report, they were able to lead "the same life they were accustomed to below the border, except for the absence of their farms." Instead, they found employment on others' farms. Flores was different from his fellow Yaquis, however, in that he purportedly never "stooped to the menial labor engaged in by his followers." Oddly, rumor held that his subsistence depended on the generosity of a mysterious benefactor. "At regular intervals when nights are dark," one local paper reported, "an automobile is said to stop at the general's door, leave several large sacks of food, and depart. No one has shown a willingness to investigate this mysterious source of food."[26]

Flores served an important function in Arizona. He frequently sent runners into Sonora to maintain open channels of communication with the tribe's southern counterpart, who, still fearing deportation, kept to "the highest ridges in their travels" and who often went without food and water, instead eking out an existence "from the meager offerings of the desert," according to one newspaper account. Flores actually attained prominence in Arizona after befriending a local Border Patrol agent named Ivan Williams and, at Williams's request, producing what became known as the "shirt-tail" history of the Yaquis. Flores reportedly sent his runners to Sonora through trails between the Bacatete Mountains and the border, and shortly thereafter they would return with portions of the tribe's history written on their shirts, often, oddly enough, in blood. When Border Patrol agents apprehended one of Flores's "historians" in the desert, then noticed the writing, the "shirt-tail" nickname was born.[27]

Evidently, however, Flores did not wish to remain in Arizona, nor did at least some of his fellow migrants. In 1931, in fact, the city editor of the *Arizona Daily Star* appealed to the Mexican consul in El Paso on behalf of these migrants, writing, "According to their chiefs, headed by Guadalupe Flores, the Yaquis wish to return to their own country along the Yaqui River. However, due to their status in part as political refugees, they wish first the assurance of protection and guarantees of the Mexican government that they will not be molested if they return to their own country." "At the present time," the letter continues, "the status of these people might be termed as a parole from the military authorities of the United States, to whom they surrendered their arms when they entered the United States." He assured the consul that the small group of Yaquis had been living a "peaceable quiet life" and promised to "remain at peace if permitted to return to their own valley."[28]

In July 1936, after ten years of exile, Flores got his wish. By this time the Mexican government had actually begun appealing to expatriates and encouraging their return in an effort to shore up the economy and implement a broader "nationalizing" campaign among its indigenous peoples. The request also, perhaps fortuitously, corresponded with the aforementioned Depression-era repatriation campaign in the United States, in which authorities subjected Mexican (and even some Mexican American) workers to forced deportation in hopes of alleviating the nation's economic crisis. As incentive, the pro-Indian administration of Lázaro Cárdenas promised that returning Yaquis could participate in government-sponsored agricultural projects. Small farms, their thinking went, just might produce self-sufficient Yaquis while also stoking the regional economy. Flores, for one, appears to have welcomed the opportunity to return. While he evidently had no farm of his own in Sonora, he maintained that several friends in the Yaqui pueblo of Torim would provide assistance. Flores's "lieutenant," Luciano Alvarez, and his housekeeper, Guayvi de Olivas Epifania, ultimately accompanied him on the trip home, as did his dog Lobo. "He is muy malo," Flores said with giddy excitement, "and will make those Torim dogs run like hell."[29] However, even though the Mexican political climate turned in the Yaquis' favor during the 1930s, it appears that few Arizona Yaquis followed Flores's lead. The younger generation of Yaquis, especially, had little desire to return to the Yaqui River. As Yaqui Cayetano Lopez remembered during the 1930s, "there wasn't anything to do in Sonora. This is the only country we know." Further, as he had heard tell from more recent Sonoran Yaqui immigrants, "the Yaquis down there is [sic] all just the same as here," so he did not feel as if he was missing much.[30]

In Sonora, Yaquis were filtering back into the Yaqui River valley in increasing numbers following the aforementioned Cárdenas reforms of the 1930s. Cárdenas had emerged as a major champion of the Indian cause. While traveling the country during his 1934 presidential campaign, he could not help but notice the dire poverty in which indigenous peoples lived. He actually passed through Yaqui country that year and called for land restitution, the establishment of agricultural zones, and the shoring up of irrigation infrastructure, all in an effort to, as he put it, "resolve definitively the eternal Yaqui problem." He considered them "a strong and pure race that should fully expect vindication for the despoliation of their lands by past governments."[31] Cárdenas used his presidency to launch a concerted effort to improve social and economic conditions in the nation's indigenous communities more generally, ultimately calling for the formation of a federal department devoted to harnessing the expertise of Mexico's intellectual community to address these perennial problems.[32] It should be pointed out, however, that Cárdenas had little interest in preserving Mexico's many indigenous cultures, and instead envisioned their acculturation and assimilation into the Mexican nation. But the Yaquis were different. Dwyer argues that it was the Yaquis' "resilience, militancy, and tendency to side with any political faction that endorsed the return of their homelands," coupled with Cárdenas's "political weakness in Sonora," that resulted in the tribe receiving "more material largess and political autonomy" from the administration than other indigenous groups. Further differentiating the Yaquis from many other Indian peoples in Mexico was the fact that, again in Dwyer's words, "the Yaquis had a written literary tradition and preserved their institutions outside of the religious cargo system, which made their cultural restoration more acceptable to Cárdenas and other revolutionary leaders."[33] Although his incorporationist notions slowly fell out of favor among Indigenistas, Cárdenas still felt that the methods favored by his administration were far superior to those of the U.S. government, which treated Indians as separate from the mainstream.[34]

Cárdenas's broader plan called for the initiation of a "vigorous development project" along the Yaqui River under the departments of agriculture, economy, and defense. It promised federal funding for potable water and irrigation, road construction, the construction of power and light plants, credit for agricultural workers, the clearing of timber, the planting of coconut, orange, and lime trees, and the distribution of 10,000 hectares of "high-grade" land on the right bank of the Yaqui River to tribal members, among other goals. Ultimately, the Yaquis received livestock, farm machinery, trucks, tools such as shovels, machetes, and hatchets, barbed-wire fencing, and, finally, seeds and fertilizer. The decrees also promised credit and guaranteed that the price of wheat would remain steady and high. The objective of this "generous experiment," according to one decree, was to bring "work and prosperity to a sizable nucleus of the Yaqui population" while also incorporating "a zone, until now ignored, into the nation's production."[35]

The government no doubt had less altruistic motives as well. As one scholar explained, "The greatest fear of any government was that the Yaqui tribe, with an estimated population of 8,400 to 9,600 in 1937, would join a regional rebellion to defend their ancestral lands and culture, as they had done on many occasions, as recently as 1927."[36] The 1927 rebellion had required a yearlong effort on the part of the Mexican military to suppress, with the army even employing bomber planes in an effort to ferret Yaqui rebels out of the Sierra de Bacatete. The 1927 campaign also, incidentally, produced another temporary surge in Yaqui migration to Arizona. Meanwhile, centuries of conflict with the Yaquis had left their non-Indian neighbors with an irrational fear of the Indians that bordered on the absurd. The Indians, for example, were thought to possess mysterious powers, such as immunity to rabies, and were also believed to have an inhumanly long life span.[37] It was in this context that the Mexican government instituted what one Yaqui referred to as a "bi-weekly money gift," mentioned above, that they hoped would help keep the peace in the region. It turned out to be an effective strategy. One Yaqui told Edward Spicer that the Yaquis "would all be back in the hills in a few weeks" if the payments ceased, since "they are far from conquered."[38] Still, by the mid-1930s the Yaquis were so closely allied with the Mexican government that the federal army employed a Yaqui battalion in a campaign against Mayo Indian rebels as well as, surprisingly enough, against Yaqui cattle rustlers in the Sierra de Bacatete. It was an unusual arrangement, but one that seemed to be working.[39]

Cooperative Yaquis also benefited from an economic boom of sorts in Sonora during the Cárdenas years. By the mid-1930s, Sonora had become Mexico's breadbasket, so to speak, producing about 11 percent of the nation's wheat. Assisting this growth was a series of government-sponsored reclamation projects that gradually brought thousands of hectares of land into production. In fact, the Yaqui River valley had only 10,000 hectares of arable land in 1911. By 1943, that number reached 70,000—a startling figure considering that as late as 1890 the region was, as one scholar put it, "a largely uninhabited wasteland," with the exception of small strips along the river.[40] Part of Cárdenas's strategy became incorporating the Yaquis into the regional economy as industrious and virtuous farmers, and in this he initially appeared to be succeeding. Yet he also realized that the group would remain peaceful only as long as they were able to maintain some elements of Yaqui culture. Another component of his strategy, then, involved establishing boarding schools throughout Yaqui country staffed by teachers who spoke the Indians' language. Yaqui students learned about tribal history and the spiritual significance of their land base, all while surrounded by murals celebrating tribal culture. Cárdenas also instituted a ban on alcohol, overconsumption of which had long plagued the Yaquis, in the Zona. His efforts were warmly received. As one scholar put it, "If there is any Mestizo whom the Yaqui regard as a tribal hero, it is Lázaro Cárdenas."[41]

The Yaquis themselves acknowledged that, as one told Spicer, "after Cárdenas came in things were better and the Indians were allowed to work." They were also finally able to begin openly reconstituting Yaqui culture along the Yaqui River without fear of persecution, and evidently did so with a great zeal. In a 1947 newspaper article, Spicer insisted that Yaqui culture, at least in Mexico, was "as distinctive and vigorous as it was in the 19th century." The article continues, "The old ways of life . . . throughout Yaqui land are strong enough to influence the tribe's members who are coming back to the 'reservation,' and the culture is being revitalized." Yaqui religious groups also began cultivating relationships with the Catholic Church, a notable development considering the tribe had more or less shunned the Church since the end of the Jesuit period. The Yaquis' government also appeared more vital than ever at midcentury, though authority tended to flow up from the village level rather than down from some centralized authority. Spicer described village organization as a blending of "unmistakably Medieval European" traditions with preconquest Yaqui traditions. For example, the Yaquis recognized two different sets of authority figures: village governors and village elders. Spicer observed that the two groups "always meet, and transact business together, but generally their members perform different functions." The governors were responsible for chairing meetings and administering decisions, while the elders were responsible for advising the governors and serving as spokesmen for the villagers. He also noted that the titles for official positions, positions that were analogous to, for example, governor, sheriff, captain, and sergeant, often sounded like "Yaqui modifications of Spanish words." Finally, he could not help but notice that the Yaquis regarded their government as "quite independent of the state-municipality organization of Sonora," and that it appeared to function as such.[42]

Shortly after Mexican independence, the new government had ordered the Yaquis (among other indigenous groups) to create municipal governments staffed by democratically elected local officials and to adopt their policy of individual land ownership. The Yaquis had already organized town governments under the Spanish, however, and by the nineteenth century had established a pattern of political autonomy and what Spicer called "vigorous Yaqui separation" that proved too powerful for the Mexican government to overcome. Spicer continues: "The two features on which the Mexicans focused as necessary for bringing the Indians into the nation—individual land holding and political hierarchy—flew in the face of the previous two centuries of development. Political equality with Mexicans was meaningless in the limited context of the Yaqui River communities." Thus, through a sustained interest in a "Yaqui nation," effective patterns of resistance, and what Spicer referred to as "an unusual combination of circumstances," the Yaquis managed to avoid true political and economic incorporation into the Mexican nation up to the era of the Cárdenas reforms.[43]

However, even with this sudden surge of interest in their well-being, the group was far from confident that hard times were behind them. Yaqui Paulino Valenzuela revealed to Spicer in 1942 that "there may be another revolution shortly," since some Yaquis were demanding "a U.S. protectorate, like Cuba, where the U.S. helped everybody get more freedom."[44] Although the Yaquis believed they were moving closer to what a Sonora-based military official described as "a Yaqui Indian Reservation as in the United States," in the end the Cárdenas administration, like so many administrations before it, proved unresponsive to those concerns that most preoccupied the Yaquis. For one, Mexicans continued streaming into the Yaqui River country despite official government property protections. One Yaqui explained to Spicer, "Fifteen years ago there were no Mexicans . . . now there are hundreds," ultimately forcing them to contend with a "gradual encroachment on their lands." Further, the Cárdenas administration did not return all of the tribe's old territory. Although the decrees returned about 1.2 million acres of land to the Yaquis, two of the original eight pueblos had been permanently lost to Mexican settlers during the very tumultuous previous decades, namely, Cócorit and Bacum. The decree also left the physical boundaries of the Zona hopelessly vague, though most likely by design. Still, six of the eight original eight pueblos, including Vicam, the political center of the pueblos, remained intact, with Potam emerging as the most populous. Further, the Yaquis had managed to retain or reclaim those lands with the most spiritual significance. The left bank of the river, the side that contained the most fertile agricultural lands, simply did not hold as much spiritual import. Interestingly, communities of Yaquis also managed to establish permanent villages in the Sierra Bacatete, once a popular haven for Yaqui rebels and refugees, and began openly producing beef, cheese, and liquor for the regional economy.[45]

Despite some progress, in the end many of the programs promised by the decree either failed to materialize or did not last. In the 1940s, one Yaqui asked Cárdenas, "Tata Lázaro, do you remember the hospitals, the schools, and the lands that you gave us? The hospitals are now cantinas, the schools are occupied by soldiers, the lands belong to the newly rich." Another asked

Spicer if he would mind presenting their case to the *U.S.* government. They were disappointed when he refused.[46] By the end of the 1930s, then, it was clear that Cárdenas's plans to develop the Zona had stalled. Roads and canals were not being maintained and had thus fallen into disrepair. All the boarding schools had closed save one, and the majority of its students were non-Indians. Alcohol still flowed into the valley unabated, cattle rustling remained a fact of life, and state-sponsored governments had ceased to function. A 1939 government-sponsored report concluded, "Complete anarchy reigns in the administration of the Yaqui Colonies."[47] Although Mexican bureaucrats were evidently failing in their mission to civilize and integrate the Yaquis, their efforts did usher in a long period of peace and relative stability in the region, as well as modest economic growth. The Yaquis, meanwhile, were able to enjoy near-total autonomy within a more or less secure Yaqui enclave, imperfect though it may have been.[48]

The Mexican government did not give up on the tribe, though, and came back with a similar, though considerably more ambitious, development plan in 1951. The Inter-Ministerial Commission for the Yaqui River Valley Region had a budget of over fourteen million pesos to implement a broad program aimed at shoring up the economy of the valley and, in turn, improving the tribe's standard of living. Like the earlier development plan, the 1951 initiative also promised potable water and credit for agricultural projects, while including provisions for a series of "welfare units," schools, and even sports fields. "We cannot yet say," one official reported, "that the Yaqui problem is solved, for many of the projects and plans for economic reconstruction are at present in the process of being carried out, but we can say that all the important and necessary steps have been taken for the felicitous and rational incorporation of these tribes, which used to be rebellious and are now dedicated to their own progress and that of Mexico."[49] Reporting on the progress of the initiative in 1962, however, one Mexican official stated, somewhat vaguely, "In practice, for various reasons, the action of these bodies has been limited."[50]

The status of their "incorporation" into the Mexican nation remained somewhat unclear thereafter, and Yaqui control of the valley, once relatively secure, seemed increasingly tenuous. One observer described political life within the Zona as "complex," explaining that while the Yaquis were "theoretically" entitled to govern themselves, the army considered the Zona merely a "sub-zone" of the military district headquartered at nearby Esperanza, a district that included all of the Yaqui River valley. As such, they claimed that martial law trumped Yaqui law within the Zona. The state of

Sonora also claimed governorship of the Yaquis, and thus repeatedly tried to extend its authority over the Zona. However, although the state collected taxes on both motor vehicles and wagons, kept a handful of "functionaries" in the main pueblo, and occasionally sent road scrapers to maintain major thoroughfares within the Zona, the task of governing the Yaquis continued to be performed by Yaqui governors within each pueblo. In other words, despite claims of authority emanating from both the local military apparatus and the state, Yaqui governing institutions remained intact. The Yaquis, meanwhile, largely stayed out of Mexican politics. Even though they enjoyed the right to vote in state or national elections, they expressed "little or no interest in national or international politics," as one observer claimed.[51]

Although not much changed politically that would have sounded alarms throughout Yaqui country, the economic and demographic situation was much different. In 1952 a federal highway officially opened that bisected the Yaquis' land. Men, machinery, crops, and livestock were now easier to transport to and from the Zona. Mexican middlemen began arriving in Yaqui country to purchase firewood, charcoal, cattle, and horses. Similarly, non-Indian storekeepers, blacksmiths, bakers, mechanics, carpenters, saloon keepers, and the like began filtering into the Zona to cater to Yaqui businesses and communities, while the federal bureaucratic machinery in the Zona necessitated the presence of even more non-Indians. In fact, one scholar estimated the Mexican population of the Zona to have reached between 6,000 and 7,000 by the end of the 1950s, a number nearly matching the number of Yaquis, which the 1959 census estimated to be just below 8,000 (though scholars believe this estimate to be quite conservative). It was a development that the Yaquis found troubling. However, the new highway also made possible the development of Yaqui agricultural societies, and the resultant (admittedly modest) economic progress meant that Yaquis could often afford trucks. This convenient mode of transportation facilitated the movement of Yaquis to fiestas, such as the Fiesta of Saint Francis at Magdalena or the Fiesta of the Virgin near Bataconsica, as well as to urban centers in the region, such as Guaymas and Ciudad Obregón, where they often sold cheese, goats, and garden vegetables. This development provided a renewed opportunity for tribal members to either forge or strengthen transborder tribal ties through interactions with their Arizona counterpart.[52]

Like the new highway, the completion of the Alvaro Obregón Dam in 1952 also produced mixed results for the tribe. In years past, the Yaquis engaged in subsistence farming and cultivated their fields manually. Irrigation came via biannual flooding courtesy of the Yaqui River or shallow, temporary channels that delivered the river's waters to Yaqui agricultural sites. This meant a predictable and plentiful source of irrigation for Yaqui subsistence farmers and thousands of acres of Yaqui land, but with a couple of caveats. First of all, non-Indians often diverted the bulk of the water well south of Yaqui territory, while the narrow canals constructed to deliver water to the Yaquis lacked adequate capacity. Even so, Yaqui elders would later remember, in the words of one scholar, "idyllic country scenes in which children played alongside the river, of fields where watermelons, beans, sweet potatoes, bananas, and sugarcane grew in abundance." The situation post-1952, however, prompted one Yaqui to lament, "The Rio Yaqui is dead."[53] Second, and perhaps most significantly, Yaqui farmers now had to pay for the water from the river, which left many in dire financial straits. As one scholar explained: "The Yaquis now found themselves fully integrated into the cash economy. Beholden to the bank and overextended in their credit, they became extremely vulnerable to disruptions in the harvest. Loans were defaulted on at an alarming rate. Many Yaqui farmers, no longer able to obtain credit from the bank, found themselves forced to work as wage laborers on their own land, now rented out to non-Yaqui farmers who could afford the substantial capital input required for modern agriculture."[54]

But there was a much more fundamental reason why the Yaquis simply were not content with their arrangement with the Mexican government at midcentury. Put simply, their desire for their old lands trumped their interest in participating in the regional economy. They mobilized in the 1970s to reclaim their lands and towns on the other bank of the river, but were ultimately unsuccessful. The historian and anthropologist Thomas McGuire contends that their failure was due in part to their rather complex political situation. The tribe was, in his words, "constrained by its own autonomy." Their economic dependence on external, non-Indian financiers left the tribe vulnerable, internally divided between those who sought assistance from the state and those who feared this would bring about an acceleration of state control. Still, tribal members remained united in their determination to claim lost lands, partly out of habit and partly because, as McGuire concludes, "that demand does not implicate the more crucial and rupturing issue of finance."[55]

As for their Arizona counterpart, the bulk of these Yaqui migrants slowly but surely secured their presence in their adopted homeland. In 1909, in fact, they formally announced their intention to begin rebuilding Yaqui culture in Arizona by requesting, and ultimately receiving, a permit from the local sheriff that would allow the tribe to conduct their annual Lenten and

Easter Ceremony north of the border for the first time. Although Mexico would still figure prominently in the ceremonial lives of many Arizona Yaquis (for example, the annual fiesta de San Francisco, held every October in Magdalena, Sonora, continues to lure Yaquis from both sides of the border), the Lenten and Easter Ceremony would, in ensuing decades, increase in significance and, in the process, become a regular event on the Tucson community calendar as both a local and a tourist attraction.[56] The U.S. government, meanwhile, proved to be alarmingly proactive in identifying Yaqui aliens within its borders, a practice that was consistent with the aforementioned early twentieth-century trend toward tightening border traffic. Immigration officials twice launched regional "alien" registration drives, one in 1918 and the other in 1940. In the latter year, local newspapers ran an announcement by the local director of alien registration demanding that Chinese and Yaqui immigrants register with local officials. "Many of the latter," the announcement read, "have lived in this country for years after fleeing from Mexico, and are actually a people without a country, no longer being citizens of Mexico, and unable to become citizens of the United States."[57]

As the century progressed, then, this popular perception of the Yaquis as "men without a country" meant that immigration officials were especially wary of waving tribal members through border crossings, as they once had. They also evidently went one step further, regularly sending immigration agents to Yaqui communities throughout Arizona in order to identify any unregistered migrants from Sonora. Ironically, however, these agents often emerged as advocates on behalf of tribal members. As Spicer explained in the 1940s, "These officers frequently become trusted friends of Yaquis, if they can speak Spanish, and often help them in various ways in their relations with state and city agencies. It may be said in this connection that it is only the border patrolmen who fully understand the citizenship status of the Yaquis."[58]

The first clarification of these Yaqui migrants' status north of the border came in 1940, when the U.S. government instituted a series of regulations to address Mexican immigration more generally. The regulations declared that all persons who migrated from Mexico prior to 1924, regardless of whether they possessed papers demonstrating that their entrance had been legal, could not be deported unless they could be classified as "criminals." However, law-abiding immigrants were eligible for citizenship only if their date of immigration occurred before July 1, 1906, and they had not returned to Mexico and reentered the United States in the interim. The latter provision, then, meant that roughly 75 percent of Arizona's Yaquis could not obtain citizenship. And even those Yaquis who migrated prior to 1906 still faced obstacles in acquiring U.S. citizenship. For example, one Yaqui man applied for citizenship in 1937 after having resided in the United States since 1903. On his application, however, he noted that he was "a real Yaqui Indian." The immigration office rejected his application, since at this time only those classified as Caucasians or as individuals of African descent were eligible for citizenship. Oddly, if he had listed his nationality as "Mexican," the office explained, he would have been approved, since Mexicans qualified as Caucasians under U.S. immigration regulations.[59]

Meanwhile, mobility, though not always of the transborder variety, remained the norm among Yaquis in Arizona. While the Yaquis claimed to have "roamed the country even before the coming of the Spanish," Spicer argued that they were actually not all that exceptional in their migratory habits. Much like Spanish-speaking Mexican Americans and English-speaking Anglo-Americans in the borderlands region, the Yaquis had "shifted residence from town to town, moved from town to cotton ranch and back again, worked where work was available, gone on relief, and helped to build the railroad, the highways, and the irrigation centers." Spicer acknowledged a certain sense of distinctness among Yaquis that is apparent not only to tribal members but also to non-Indian neighbors, yet he also characterized them as "very much a part of the conglomerate, mobile society of the rapidly growing southwestern state in which they have lived for more than fifty years." Although one Mexican scholar claimed that constant warfare was to blame for forcing the Yaquis onto the migratory path, Spicer argued that they possessed a *variety* of motives, many shared by both Indians and non-Indians in the burgeoning American Southwest. Further, in the fifty years between the Yaquis' settlement in Arizona and the time of Spicer's study, the Yaquis remained relatively scattered, with some living with and even intermarrying with the Tohono O'odham both on and off the O'odham reservation, some residing on the nearby Pima reservation, and some intermarrying with African Americans and Anglos. In this dizzying variety of social, political, and cultural contexts, maintaining an emotional attachment to their Yaqui heritage proved challenging, but it did happen. For example, in his study of the Yaqui village of Potam, Spicer observed a vigorous pattern of correspondence between these far-flung settlements, noting that "knowledge on the part of the Potam people of living conditions and events in the non-river settlements is often very detailed as a result of the interchange of letters." Some Yaquis, he discovered, divided their time between Potam and Arizona, with some even expressing homesickness for Tucson or Phoenix, cities where some had spent their youth and/or buried their parents. He estimated that perhaps several hundred Potam residents had spent at least a few years in the Arizona communities. Sporadic, voluntary migration out of the community and across the border, thus, was not uncommon, and those Yaquis who did not regularly return to the Yaqui River evidently remained very much in the emotional orbit of their southern counterpart.[60]

In the realm of employment, from the outset Yaquis in Arizona generally gravitated toward a somewhat narrow range of occupations. Between the late 1800s and the early 1940s, Yaquis worked on railroad gangs, made adobe bricks, and worked on farms and ranches. The latter had become the occupation of choice by the World War II years, when cotton picking, as Spicer explained, became "a feature of the agricultural rhythm which affects almost all Yaquis." Most Yaqui families (90 percent according to a "conservative" estimate) resided in a string of cotton camps all across southern Arizona for three to four months at a time, resulting in the virtual depopulation of Yaqui settlements across the state.[61] The Bracero Program, implemented during World War II to both encourage and control the flow of migrant workers across the border, opened up additional employment opportunities for Indians in the United States. Employers began recruiting Indians for agricultural work in increasing numbers, since the new program restricted the number of Mexican workers allowed in the United States. This practice was particularly prevalent in Arizona, though the primary beneficiaries tended to be Navajo Indians.[62] Spicer noted, however, that the Yaquis largely shunned steady employment. "Habits of steady work," he explained, "are regarded as a handicap to anyone who aspires to village prestige, because they get in the way of activities necessary for the latter." Quitting a job, therefore, could earn a tribal member more respect than the wages one could earn through steady work.[63] As long as work remained relatively easy to come by, then, Yaquis avoided more than a tenuous commitment to any one job.

Yaquis in Arizona thus recognized two distinctly different forms of work: that for wage labor and that for ceremonial purposes. Steady employment for wage work would obviously translate into a more comfortable lifestyle, but it did not necessarily translate into a higher social status within the group, nor did the size of one's income or the extent of one's possessions. It was ceremonial participation that really counted within the tribe's prestige system. Although Yaqui laborers constantly struggled to balance their employment obligations with their ceremonial life, the latter most often won out in the end. Their employers, however, typically valued the Yaquis as laborers, and thus tolerated their seeming eccentricities. While they were periodically absent and, according to some employers, had occasional problems with alcohol, their honesty and commitment to quality work typically outweighed these minor problems.[64]

Unfortunately, for these Yaqui workers the post–World War II years witnessed a downturn in cotton production, which left growers with massive surpluses. Decreased demand for labor, coupled with the mechanization of the cotton industry by the mid-1950s, meant that Yaqui families no longer enjoyed this predictable source of income and instead had to transition into jobs outside of the agricultural sector. This sudden downturn in employment opportunities also forced many Yaquis to seek government assistance for the first time as they adopted new subsistence patterns.[65] Adding to these difficulties was the fact that, as Spicer put it, "the typical Yaqui is a squatter." Few owned immovable property, and few even paid rent. Instead, they typically lived in villages established by growers who valued their labor, or, after its establishment in 1910, in the village of Guadalupe. The federal government set aside the roughly forty-acre Guadalupe plot for Yaqui refugees with the understanding that they would eventually pay for their plots. Few ever paid, however, since few possessed the means to do so. "The conditions under which they may continue to live there are not clearly defined by law," Spicer observed. The city of Tucson or, more specifically, a real estate company, allowed Yaquis to occupy another village site, which became Pascua, on Tucson's immediate outskirts, but these plots were not tax-exempt, and thus initially not particularly desirable. As mentioned earlier, however, Pascua would evolve into a kind of population center for Yaquis in Arizona as the century progressed. Others squatted along the banks of the Santa Cruz River in South Tucson, and still others managed to purchase lots either south of Pascua, in the aforementioned Barrio Belén, or in Tucson proper.[66] At least for the time being, then, the Yaqui presence in Arizona was fairly diffuse, a fact of life that hindered the growth of the nationalistic impulse that was so strong south of the border.

While the movement to Arizona provided a wealth of new opportunities for Yaqui migrants, their southern counterpart regularly alleged that life in the United States was exacting an unacceptable cultural toll, an assertion that consequently complicated relations between the two groups. Even area ranchers, who enthusiastically employed Yaqui laborers, noticed a gradual change in behavior among those Yaquis who resided primarily north of the border. One rancher and frequent employer of Yaqui laborers observed, "The first ones that came in were first-class workers, better than any Mexicans . . . But now they aren't so good anymore. The young ones drink a lot. They're getting too Americanized."[67] The reality was more complex than the rancher suggested. Yaquis in Arizona found themselves occupying what one historian described as a "liminal cultural and political space between two nations and their status as Mexican and Indian." They often lived and worked alongside ethnic Mexicans, shared the uncertainties that came with their precarious legal status, and conversed in Spanish, which all suggested a retreat from tribal culture. Yet Anglo-Americans often viewed them as American Indian because of their connection to Arizona's broader indigenous community. As mentioned earlier, the Yaquis also lacked a formal governing body, which further suggested a kind of disconnect with tribal traditions. But as one tribal member explained, "We live under the law of the United States." For many Yaquis, a governing structure was simply unnecessary. Tensions emerged over time, with some Yaquis wishing to safeguard their presence north of the border by pushing for a legal status as American Indians, and others fearing that doing so would compromise both their culture and their autonomy. It was the latter group that was most likely to cultivate transborder cultural ties to challenge those lines of ethnicity and culture they saw being drawn in the United States, lines that did little to acknowledge the transnational nature of their Yaqui identity.[68]

Despite going to great lengths to adapt to life in the United States, many still lived with a well-founded fear of deportation. Local officials periodically (every three to four years, according to Spicer) revived plans to send the Yaquis back to, in the words of one senator, "their wild hill-life in Mexico." Such plans always fell by the wayside, but not before making Arizona's Yaquis understandably nervous.[69] Such deportation plans also emanated from south of the border. During the 1930s Pluma Blanca, who, as mentioned earlier, served as the liaison between the Yaquis and the Mexican government, proposed a complete repatriation of Yaquis living north of the border. One Yaqui who had spent time in Oregon, Arizona, and California, however, reported to Sonoran Yaquis that tribal members were actually better off in the United States, and thus argued against forced repatriation. Tribal elders in Sonora *also* argued against forced repatriation, but did so out of a fear of returning Yaquis' American influence. Put simply, they believed these returnees would swell the ranks of Yaqui "progressives" who, according to one account, sought to "introduce those ways into the stronghold of the fierce fighters of Mexico," and thus possibly corrupt them. Pascua especially seemed to stand in stark contrast to Yaqui villages in Mexico. There, at least according to one account, "the old ways have been disappearing as better houses, more stable family life, and better education have evolved." This was not the first time Yaqui elders expressed a fear of the potentially contaminating influence of outsiders. They had, for example, steadfastly resisted those efforts by President Cárdenas to, in his words, "fuse their high civilization with that of Mexicans," and at one point actually demanded that Cárdenas remove the Southern Pacific Railroad from the Yaquis' homeland, fearing that with the railroad came the potentially dangerous Mexican influence. But as Spicer put it, "Those extreme demands have not, naturally, been met."[70]

The assertion that they might somehow contaminate Yaqui culture tended to put Arizona's Yaquis on the defensive. A later history written in conjunction with the tribe and published in English, Spanish, and Yoeme singled out religion. It claimed that Yaqui spirituality actually *thrived* in the United States, since "the religious ceremonies, which the people refused to give up, were practiced more openly in the United States than in Sonora," while in Sonora these same ceremonies "had to go underground for survival." Further, they insisted that ties to the homeland remained strong. "Whether in the new place or the old place," they concluded, "the Yaquis have a place of their own."[71] Spicer agreed, arguing in the 1970s that the cultural foundation laid by Arizona's Yaqui population "[had] now persisted for three-quarters of a century and [seemed] more solid than at any time in their existence," despite its deviance from the cultural norm.[72]

Indeed, over time the fears experienced by new arrivals that they would somehow be "discovered to be Yaquis" abated, and distinctly Yaqui customs, including religious observances, reemerged. As mentioned above, tribal members reestablished the all-important Lenten and Easter Ceremony, which was a central Catholic-Yaqui event that the tribe had suppressed in earlier decades in an effort to conceal their Yaqui identity from Mexican officials. The revival of at least this aspect of the Yaqui faith in Arizona eventually inspired a similar revival in Mexico, signaling a growing trend toward bridging the cultural gap between the old and new Yaqui homelands. Put simply, the fact that the Yaqui faith now spanned two nation-states provided an impetus for the renewal of transborder tribal ties. Attesting to the growing influence of the Arizona settlement, this trend emanated from a far-flung locale that had once been little more than a haven for Yaqui refugees. Now Arizona's Yaquis were having a decisive impact on the tribe's ancestral home.[73] In ensuing years, the ceremony would prove important "not only to the Yaqui sense of self but also as an identifying symbol for outsiders," as one historian put it. In other words, it "demonstrated through public performance their 'Indianness,' thus serving to define them as something other than Mexicans." For Yaquis in Sonora, this was advantageous in that it served to remind non-Indians how little they understood of Yaqui society and culture and thus helped maintain and even reinforce boundaries between Yaquis and their Mexican neighbors. For Yaquis in Arizona, the ceremony similarly helped differentiate them from Mexicans, which proved fortuitous during, for example, the Depression-era repatriation campaign that targeted Mexican laborers for deportation. It also helped strengthen their case that they merited a special status as Indians. The Lenten and Easter Ceremony thus became, according to Thomas McGuire, "entertainment put to the service of efficacy" on both sides of the border.[74]

Though increasingly comfortable and secure in Arizona, many Arizona Yaquis evidently still nursed a desire to return to the tribe's homeland, and returning to the river, according to one scholar, remains a "positively valued practice" up to the present day. Arizona Yaquis would return to Sonora to witness more elaborate versions of the dances they perform, the ceremonies they observe, and the fiestas they attend in their smaller settlements. Others trek north to attend baptisms, first communions, weddings, and funerals. And Sonoran Yaquis evidently take a great deal of pride in seeing Yaquis return to "the cradle of Yaqui culture and society."[75] Even decades away from the Yaqui homeland, it turned out, did not extinguish the desire to return for some Yaquis. For example, just as soon as she could regularize her immigration status, Yaqui Antonia Valenzuela returned to the valley in 1960, after having been away since 1904. She enjoyed her time there so much that she extended her stay to three months, after having initially planned to stay only a few days. She got acquainted with new relatives and reacquainted with old, and attended two fiestas, which were reportedly "the only ones she ever enjoyed." Her husband, although somewhat upset with her for staying so long, made his own long-anticipated trip to Sonora three years later.[76]

Sadly, others remained alienated from *both* centers of Yaqui life. In the 1970s, Yaqui and longtime Hermosillo resident Chepa Moreno was debating the merits of remaining in Hermosillo versus returning to the Yaqui River valley. She was at an advanced age, and feared that remaining in Hermosillo would mean that upon her death she would be buried in a nameless pauper's grave. If she died among Yaquis, however, she knew she would be buried in front of a church and given a proper farewell. In the end,

Moreno decided to remain in Hermosillo, where a small income she still received from employers allowed her to indulge in her favorite luxury: a fresh pack of cigarettes each day. She also did not want to abandon her cat, a rarity in Hermosillo's lower-class barrios. Unfortunately, Chepa's worst fear ultimately came to fruition. Her death was, according to one anthropologist who was familiar with Chepa's life history, "devoid of any Yaqui ritual," and her beloved cat was senselessly and violently killed shortly after Chepa's passing.[77] Chepa seems to represent a small minority of Yaquis, however, since the vast majority appears to have gravitated toward either their older settlements along the Yaqui River or their new settlements in Arizona.

Although Yaquis in Arizona appeared to have been making progress in stabilizing their presence, those who remained in Sonora, despite their recognition by the Mexican government as an autonomous political entity, found their admittedly limited freedoms eroding in more recent decades. Though they had managed to remain more or less ethnically, culturally, and even politically distinct from surrounding Mexican communities, they were nonetheless increasingly bound up in the regional system of commercial agriculture, a system that did not always accommodate the Yaquis' complex and rigorous ceremonial schedule. Reconciling their unwavering commitment to a demanding religious calendar with their increasing domination by market forces has proved to be a tall order. As McGuire succinctly put it, "Yaquis are as politically autonomous as they are economically dependent."[78]

Their circumstances may have been less than ideal, but Yaquis south of the border were not exactly in dire straits. Fast-forward to April 1984, when Texas Tech University hosted a symposium, entitled "The Year of the Yaqui," to commemorate and reflect upon its fifty-year relationship with the Yaqui Indians. The university's intentions could not have been better. For the symposium, a group of anthropologists, historians, archaeologists, and Yaqui Indians from both sides of the border gathered to assess the tribe's political, economic, and cultural evolution, to investigate historical and contemporary challenges faced by Yaquis in both Sonora and Arizona, and to enjoy performances by Yaqui dancers and exhibitions by Yaqui artists.[79] Shortly thereafter, university faculty and other employees launched a final expedition to Sonora. The party included the historians John Wunder, Willard Rollings, and Dan Flores, the archaeologist Robert Campbell, and two members of the university's mass communications department. Their objective was, as Flores wrote in a diary of the expedition, "to observe cultural change [and] continuum since the first expeditions," an objective that he privately admitted was "not really clear-cut." More concretely, they hoped to film the group's annual Fiesta de Gloria, or Easter ceremony, as previous expeditions had done. Incidentally, they also brought with them cartons of cigarettes and groceries to assist in preparations for the fiesta, per the advance instructions of the Yaquis.[80]

But when the party arrived in the river valley, the Yaquis refused to allow the taping of their ceremony. As Flores wrote, "What we have discovered . . . is that Yaqui culture, in the 20 years or more since the last filming . . . has undergone many radical changes, and among them is a growing dislike for being the subject of camera lenses and curious gringo ethnographers." Somewhat ironically, however, hundreds of Yaquis attended the screening of a film from an earlier Fiesta de Gloria. Flores described delight and frequent laughter among the many Yaqui attendees as they watched their relatives in action. Still, the Yaquis remained firm in their refusal to allow further filming. Much had changed, then, since the last expedition. Yaqui homes by and large contained electrical power, which the Mexican government provided in the 1960s, although the Yaquis still refused indoor plumbing, which they considered "unnatural and unnecessary," according to Flores. He noted that the Yaquis in the 1980s were far more "corpulent" than the earlier, "wasp-waisted" generation observed by Holden.[81] He also noted the presence of schools, automobiles, tractors, and barbed-wire fences where there had once been only Carrizo fences, as well as the use of propane gas and the substitution of brick for adobe in construction. He even noted the presence of a crop-dusting plane. Flores mused, "I yet find it most incongruous to see a traditional Carrizo cane lodge with a John Deere tractor and a television antenna on the flat roof! Nonetheless, the sight is common." In sum, then, he considered cultural change among the Yaquis to be "considerable."[82] Regardless, the Yaquis appeared to have stabilized, with some perhaps even prospering.

In fact, by the turn of the twenty-first century, the Yaquis had acquired a reputation as, in the words of one scholar, "the richest tribe in Mexico." It was an assertion, she continues, "made to me by nonindigenous Mexicans in casual conversations and during interviews, on buses and at parties. It was something I heard repeatedly." The Yaquis possessed an enviable amount of land and at least theoretically exclusive rights to abutting ocean resources. Some non-Indians also could not help but "speculate aloud, imagining a wealth of mineral resources lying dormant, unexploited in the foothills of the reserve's Bacatete Mountains." The Yaquis acknowledged these economic advantages over Mexicans in the region, but often claimed, in the words of one Yaqui, "The reality is that the Yaquis are not rich. They have the land but not the means to work it."[83]

Indeed, a closer look betrays the fact that the Zona was an economically depressed area within a largely prosperous region. Underemployment and unemployment were endemic. Vast tracts of Yaqui lands were being rented out to non-Indians (as much as 90 percent, according to one estimate). "Anyone who has traveled International Highway 15, which passes directly through the Yaqui Zona," one scholar noted, "has witnessed the crumbling walls of wattle-and-daub houses, their trapper roofs held down with rocks and bottles and soil, the dirt roads that wind away from the main thorough-fare, the conglomeration of cramped, dusty stores, rusty bicycles, and limping cars." But even more seriously, economic conditions were catalyzing yet another pattern of out-migration, with many crossing the border into Arizona. As Yaqui Indian and Vicam resident Luz García put it: "The Yaqui youth are once again nomads. They are leaving their pueblos because they need work . . . Many, many modern young people . . . are leaving the country, to the tribe which we have over there, in Tucson . . . They are no longer working in [professions related to] what they have studied, mind you . . . Many of them studied to be agricultural engineers, architectural engineers, ecological engineers . . . [Now] they have come to know this work of waiters, restaurant workers, or they simply work picking lemons or oranges or vegetables there in the United States."[84]

As for transborder movement, although border crossings were never a simple affair for tribal members, they became more difficult as the century progressed. The roadblocks encountered by a party of Yaquis en route to a wake are illustrative. In December 1984 the Pascua Yaquis lost a young tribal member to leukemia. Following Yaqui religious tradition, the deceased's family scheduled a celebration and extended invitations to Yaqui relatives and dancers, some of whom happened to reside on the other side of the border. Tribal members considered such gatherings a religious imperative, having been decreed, in the words of one Yaqui, "not by Federal Recognition but . . . by our Creator [eons] before what the white man called Christianity." However, as relatives from the Río Yaqui attempted to cross the U.S.-Mexican border into Arizona, an immigration officer flatly denied their entry on the grounds that they were not immediate family, an action the tribe later characterized as not just insensitive, but "anti-culture, anti-Indian, and offensive to Indian religion." In a letter of complaint submitted to the United States Immigration and Naturalization Service just days later, the tribe stated, "Many of our people who have come to visit on religious and other occasions have had their passports confiscated for no reason at all." "If officers . . . who seem to have anti-Indian attitudes are left in charge of the temporary entry of Yaqui Indians into the United States," the complaint continues, "then our Yaqui Pueblos in Arizona are going to have a lot of problems this coming Lenten Season." To allay the evidently common fear that these Yaqui pilgrims might take up permanent residence in the United States, the letter assures officials that only about "one percent" of Mexico's 23,000 Yaquis had ever expressed a desire to live and work in the United States. Instead, the vast majority visited on a temporary basis, if at all. "Yaquis in Mexico are too attached to our land in Mexico after fighting and dying for [it] from 1533 to 1927," the letter concludes.[85]

A more in-depth account of the episode surfaced a few days later, one authored by its Yaqui participants, Andres and Rebecca Flores and Guadalupe Valenzuela. They had traveled from Tucson to Vicam, one of the eight pueblos on the Yaqui River, to notify relatives of the death in the family, and returned with Vicam Yaquis Leonardo and Francisca Buitimea to attend the wake. Unfortunately, Francisca had not completed the application process for entry in advance. "Rules are rules," the guard told the travelers, "and I'm not about to break any rules for anyone." When one of the officers allegedly assumed a "rude and angry tone of voice," the Yaquis asked to speak with a supervisor. "That won't do any good," was the officer's reply. When one of the Yaquis attempted to explain that as Native Americans the travelers had certain rights, the officer interrupted, exclaiming, "You guys aren't American Indians." He paused for a moment, then corrected himself, explaining, "I mean they aren't," motioning to the Yaquis from Vicam. Shortly thereafter, the officer's supervisor arrived, whereupon one of the tribal members attempted to explain that immigration officials normally let Yaquis pass for religious ceremonies. A quick call to the tribe's chairman in Arizona, David Ramírez, they assured the supervisor, would iron things out. "It wouldn't do any good," he reportedly replied, adding, "It's just a waste of time." When one of them asked for the supervising officer's name, he responded: "Intimidating us won't do any good. We people who work have to deal with people like you every day." Although the officers eventually spoke with Ramírez, they remained steadfast in denying the Indians' entry. Both Leonardo and Francisca Buitimea took a bus back to Vicam that same day. "I and the others signed below," the complaint concludes, "would like to submit this affidavit as to the type of torment Our People have to go through in order to practice Our Religious Rights as Yaquis."[86]

The frustration these Yaquis felt at the port of entry could also cut the other way. Yaqui Rosalio Moisés described one such encounter that occurred while he was traveling from Arizona to the Río Yaqui. When Moisés reached the port of entry, a Mexican official asked for his passport. "I really do not know what you mean by a passport," he replied in all seriousness. The official then asked a series of questions concerning his place of birth, his destination in Sonora, and the date he had originally crossed into the United States, which had been about thirty years prior, or while he was still a child. When asked for the exact date that he migrated to the United States, he explained, "That I do not know, because my grandmother could not read or write." Convinced that his queries were getting him nowhere, the exasperated official eventually waved Moisés through.[87]

Until the second half of the twentieth century, Yaquis residing in Arizona simply lacked the legal clout to demand any kind of right to migrate, unfettered, across the U.S.-Mexico border. They were essentially landless, often, again, little more than squatters, well into the twentieth century. Most possessed an unclear citizenship status, along with an even more unclear tribal affiliation; they were not exactly American Indians, having originated in Mexico, but were undeniably *indigenous*. Officials, then, often could not help but wonder if that alone entitled them to certain rights. Further, the Yaquis had clearly established a permanent presence in the United States, venturing south only on occasion. Meanwhile, their Mexican counterparts evidently had no interest in immigrating, having long since stabilized their presence on lands to which they felt spiritually rooted. As one scholar observed, "According to the Indian's deep-seated beliefs, God gave the land to the Yaquis. As a result of this view, it is unlikely that any group of aboriginal Americans have protected their land more tenaciously or consistently."[88] Increasingly, however, the same could be said of Yaquis on the other side of the border. In the 1960s, tribal members in Arizona, with state government assistance, acquired yet another small plot of land, this time in a more formal fashion, on the outskirts of Tucson. They used the land to create several farming cooperatives. The acquisition represented, from the tribe's perspective, yet another step toward forging a Yaqui homeland in Arizona. The following decade they would initiate a drive for federally recognized status, an effort that reflected the desire of many Yaquis to further formalize their presence in their adopted homeland, straighten out their citizenship status once and for all, and continue the process of negotiating the greatest possible degree of autonomy.[89] Their experiences with the federal recognition process would mirror, in revealing ways, those of the Kickapoo Indians, who employed a similar strategy in *their* search for stability.

Until then, true stability remained elusive, while the hard-won patterns of transnational migration, though somewhat modest in scale and scope, became more and more difficult to maintain, as tribal members crossing for the wake learned. And although there were those tribal members who insisted on living under the laws of the United States and devoting themselves to religion rather than self-government, Yaqui elders, especially, were quite vocal about the fact that they, in the words of one Pascua Yaqui, "wanted to be like they had been on the Río Yaqui, that is, a nation within a nation, living according to their own laws within the United States."[90] For the Yaquis, claims of sovereignty were not the product of a "we were here first" mentality. Rather, sovereignty was earned over time through an ever stronger connection to place that took effort and commitment to forge. As the scholar David Delgado Shorter put it, "The strongest [Yaqui] claim of sovereignty is not that they lived in a specific place the longest, but that they have been making that place their own through the human labor that constitutes all ritual activity." It is through ceremonial acts, in other words, that they "make the land significant" and "affirm the community's value."[91] Yaquis in Mexico have, from the Spanish colonial period on, behaved as, at the very least, a nascent nation. If the "essence of national belonging" is, as the historian Thomas Holt argued, the willingness to "kill or die" to further a collective cultural or political agenda, then the Yaquis have long expressed a keen understanding of what national citizenship often entails. They have had a seemingly innate ability to, as another historian put it, "mobilize large numbers of people for collective projects, military or otherwise," as well as a penchant for "establish[ing] dominance" through "spectacular displays of force" and "ostentatious collective discipline."[92] Later generations of Yaquis living in Arizona would express a similar understanding of national citizenship, though in a less aggressive fashion. As far back as 1930 they began employing the rhetoric of nationhood in helping establish their sovereignty, declaring the existence of a "Yaqui Nation in Arizona" in a display of unity while going through a change in tribal leadership. They went so far as to create a Yaqui flag, perhaps the ultimate symbol of nationhood.[93] Though some non-Indians found that assertion somewhat preposterous, a bid for federal recognition north of the border in the 1970s would find those Yaquis in Arizona closer to making it a legal reality.

4 Almost Immune to Change

The Mexican Kickapoo

In 1948, the anthropologist Edward Spicer wrote a letter to a friend, presumably an immigration official, in which he relayed an interesting story about a Kickapoo Indian named Pesiskea Matapulla. A graduate student of Spicer's encountered Matapulla while traveling in Sonora, and Matapulla quickly volunteered a great deal of information about himself. He had been born near Shawnee, Oklahoma, to Kickapoo parents and migrated to Mexico as a child. Since then, he had visited Oklahoma only once. Matapulla was about fifty years old, the husband of a Mexican woman and the father of five. He claimed to have lost any documentation that might have confirmed either his U.S. citizenship or his affiliation with the Kickapoo tribe, however, and immigration officials repeatedly denied him reentry to the United States. Even though Matapulla occasionally received money from Oklahoma authorities in connection with his deceased father's estate, he had been unsuccessful in convincing U.S. authorities to wave him through. He asked the graduate student for assistance in getting himself and his brother, Namarsik, across the border. Evidently, the two wished to relocate to the United States permanently. "What should Matapulla do," Spicer asked, "to return to the United States? Could you help him in any way? If there is anything that can be done to establish his citizenship, could you get in touch with him? Does he appear in the agency records?"[1] Whatever became of Matapulla is unclear, but his story is emblematic of the awkward position in which transnational Kickapoos found themselves, a position made all the more awkward by increasingly rigorous efforts to control transborder traffic.

Spicer relayed the story of Matapulla in 1948. As the century progressed, the Kickapoos watched their right to migrate on a transnational scale steadily erode, much like the Yaquis. Still, contrary to what Matapulla's story suggests, the tribe retained a remarkable degree of freedom to pass and repass the border, a degree of freedom few North American tribes enjoyed and one that required a great deal of tenacity on the tribe's behalf to maintain. Even more so than the Yaquis, the Kickapoos exploited holes in the immigration system and capitalized on their uncertain citizenship status and tribal affiliation, all in the interest of solidifying their hard-won transnational presence. Although the parallels between the two groups are myriad, one distinction merits mention. The Kickapoos, throughout the twentieth century, were among the most mobile indigenous groups in North America. They forged a vast migratory labor network throughout the American West, Southwest, and Midwest that covered thousands of miles; founded a sort of transborder way station literally on the northern banks of the Rio Grande that the tribe increasingly considered home; and maintained a ceremonial center, a sort of spiritual homeland, in a remote pocket of Mexico at Nacimiento, Coahuila, where Kickapoo culture and religion could flourish in the open. The tribe also hammered out an arrangement with the Mexican government in the mid-nineteenth century that not only helped secure their land base, but also specifically allowed them to preserve and practice their unique culture. Thus, unlike Mexico's other indigenous peoples, the Kickapoos did not have to live with the threat of forced assimilation. They would also prove notoriously suspicious of and resistant to any government initiative that looked like an attempt to undermine their cultural autonomy, however well-intentioned it might have been.[2] But perhaps most significantly, while the Yaquis had essentially split into two groups, connected only by periodic sojourners, the Kickapoo tribe managed to move, with only a few exceptions, as a tribal whole, pouring into Nacimiento during the winter months, filing out en masse during the spring months, merging with and nearly disappearing into the migrant labor stream, and periodically regrouping in Eagle Pass, all the while encountering surprisingly few obstacles.

Efforts by immigration authorities to more meaningfully govern transborder traffic, however, threatened this delicate balancing act. As a case in point, in early 1966, Kickapoo Indian Pancho Salazar Garza and his brother were returning to Mexico following their annual trek to various harvests throughout the western and central United States. Prior to his departure from Mexico the previous spring, Garza had acquired a six-month tourist permit and a secondhand automobile. While in the United States he acquired a .32 automatic pistol, a nonfunctioning .22 rifle, a hunting knife, and several boxes of ammunition. Also on his person was a card, issued by the U.S. Immigration and Naturalization Service (INS) to the Mexican Kickapoos, which read as follows: "Member of the Kickapoo Indian tribe, pending clarification of status by Congress." Stamped across this document was the word "Parolee," a misleading classification that could, and did, lead uninformed authorities to assume these men were somehow parolees from prison. About ten miles north of Lamesa, Texas, a highway patrol officer stopped Garza and his brother, searched their vehicle, and then promptly took them to police headquarters for interrogation.[3]

Apparently, the officer had reasonable cause for suspicion. First of all, Garza claimed Mexican residency, but possessed a Utah driver's license. He initially claimed to have been en route from Utah, but later claimed to have been working in Brownfield, Texas. Second, one of Garza's documents, presumably his tourist visa, appeared to have been altered, the date of issuance having been changed from 1962 to 1964. Finally, the Garza brothers were unable to establish ownership of the firearms, obliging the officer to confirm whether or not they were stolen. After interrogating Garza and his brother, the officers finally confirmed both their identity and their ownership of the firearms. Authorities released Garza and his brother shortly thereafter, and for reasons that are unclear forwarded their firearms to the tribe's attorney in Austin.[4]

While the officer's concerns may have been valid given the series of red flags, among officials along the border it was evidently common knowledge that the Kickapoos did, in fact, spend part of the year in Utah (where they picked cherries) and part of the year in Brownfield (where they manned the cotton harvest). They also typically harvested apples and onions in Colorado and worked the beet-thinning period in Montana and Wyoming for part of the year. Thus, Garza could accurately claim to have been en route from Utah, or Texas, or any other of the many stops along their annual migratory route. Further, it was not unusual for an American employer to assist tribal members in purchasing automobiles and acquiring driver's licenses, since they valued their services. In this instance, while Garza was not a year-round resident of Utah, his employer, who was, took it upon himself to make sure Garza had all the proper documentation.[5]

For much of the twentieth century, the Kickapoos participated in this seasonal migratory cycle, one that usually began in the month of May and terminated in the month of October. Only the elderly or ill stayed in Mexico, charged with caring for the tribe's cattle, so Nacimiento could appear deserted for months at a time. Tribal members organized themselves into patrilineal family groups, with the father acting as a crew chief of sorts. They typically traveled nonstop from Mexico in camper-equipped pickup trucks, reportedly dispensing with road maps because of their knack for remembering landmarks, and carried little more than bedding, clothing, and cooking utensils.[6] The migrants typically stayed in communal housing provided, free of charge, by the farmers. One reporter provided a detailed description of Kickapoo housing on a farm in Brighton, Colorado. It was a former dairy barn, partitioned off into several "apartments" by whitewashed plywood. The quarters contained a single window, a single lightbulb, and "fly strips thick with insects." As for furniture, each unit contained nothing more than a few mattresses, a stove, and a refrigerator. "When it comes time to pick apples," he said, "it's time to go home." Even as late as the 1980s, most Mexican Kickapoos continued to participate in the annual migration, with many expressing a general contentment.[7]

American employers were typically enthusiastic accomplices in helping the Kickapoos maintain these seasonal migratory patterns. A rancher in Big Bend colorfully expressed an attitude shared by many Kickapoo employers: "They're the greatest barbed wire fence builders and repairers I've ever had. You just tell them what to do, or rather tell their leader. And they'll start building fence like a bunch of Swedes laying railroad track."[8] However, although their livelihood depended on seasonal employment, the Kickapoos would not tolerate an overly demanding or unsympathetic employer, nor would they neglect their ceremonial duties for employment obligations. "Last year I was unable to go to work for you," wrote Pancho Jiménez to George Schuman of Clearmont, Wyoming, "as you did not help me out when I wrote you for a small allowance of $40.00." He expressed a desire to return to work for Schuman, but only if he received a *sixty-dollar* advance. "We do not work in the winters," he explained, "and money gets very scarce around here about this time of the year and our *employers usually give us a hand.*"[9]

The anthropologist Dolores Latorre, who, along with her anthropologist husband Felipe, lived near the tribe's Mexican settlement for several years, elaborated on the difficulties faced by Kickapoos during the winter months, difficulties stemming in part from the tribe's ceremonial commitments. "The Kickapoos are very busy with their New Year ceremonies," she wrote to one planter, "and there is little time left for them to attend even to the essentials of earning a living." She described these tribal customs as "more important to them than anything else," even making a living. Kickapoo women constructed a new winter house each year, beginning usually around November, and maintained the winter residence until the end of the New Year ceremonies, which typically corresponded with the first week of March. Next, they tore down their winter houses and then repaired and, finally, reoccupied their summer residences. "If a Kickapoo woman owns a house," Latorre wrote, "she is duty bound to observe these rules and nothing will keep her from carrying them out." Meanwhile, the husband was not allowed to leave the village, even for employment, until the family had fully transitioned from the winter to the summer house. There is some evidence, however, that the Kickapoos did not entirely ignore their nonceremonial responsibilities during these periods. For example, Latorre revealed that due to some early work-related commitments among the men one season, the Kickapoos' chief, Papikwano, was "rushing the ceremonies."[10] Interestingly, the Kickapoos often relied on their employers to directly fund their ceremonial observances through payday advances. "Now we have to give a fiesta for one of our relatives," wrote Fernando Jiménez to his employer, "and we would like very much for you to advance us about $50.00 US in order that we can be able to perform that important ceremony which should be before the 12 of March."[11] As the Latorres once wrote to some acquaintances, "These people will do nothing until they finish their ceremonies and let's face it!"[12]

The Kickapoos' letters to various employers, a great many having been written by Dolores Latorre on their behalf during the 1960s, also reveal that the tribe had a certain rapport with their bosses, a rapport that went much deeper than an employer-employee relationship and even bordered on friendship. In early 1965, Jesusita Valdes wrote a C. S. Dawson in Provo, Utah, requesting fifty dollars to pay for groceries purchased on credit. "Through Lonnie Salazar," she wrote, "I was supposed to receive part of the money he received from you, but Lonnie drank it up, so I got nothing." Thus, she requested that Dawson "not send the money through anyone, but send it directly to me at [Múzquiz]."[13] Another Kickapoo, named Margarito Treviño, asked S. C. Carranza of the Holly Sugar Company in Sidney, Montana, for fifty dollars "to buy cigarettes."[14] Their employers evidently granted the Kickapoos' requests more often than not, and also commonly expressed a more personal interest in their well-being. "Thank you for sending me the money I requested," wrote Pancho Valdes. "My wife is better," he continued, "and I hope she will be almost completely well by the time we get to your country."[15] John Mohawk wrote to a Mrs. Dick Burr of Provo that he and his family were fine except for his wife, who was "suffering considerably from her knee as water accumulates in it and is painful." He requested that she fill his wife's prescription for pain medication, sending it to Eagle Pass, since, he explained, "the Mexican customs might stop the medicine at the border like they have done for other Kickapoo." Tribal members were also in the habit of having employers acquire their automobile license plates. They insisted, however, that plates be sent to Eagle Pass instead of Múzquiz in order to, in the words of one Kickapoo, "avoid customs complications." On at least one occasion Mexican customs tried to charge a Kickapoo Indian a five dollar duty for plates shipped to Mexico, money that he did not have. He promptly returned the plates and asked his employer to reship them to an address in Eagle Pass.[16]

In addition to migrating for employment purposes, the Kickapoos also migrated to be near family. "Thank you for the $15.00 in cash which you sent me," wrote Kiehtahmookwa, or Cecilia Jiménez, to her husband, Jim Katakyaha, who was then residing in Jones, Oklahoma. "I am feeling much better," she continued, "and am brown as a nut from this wonderful sunshine in Mexico." She went on to request that her husband come to Mexico and take her back to Oklahoma. She concluded, "We shall all be very glad to get back to you and our home," suggesting that perhaps the family maintained their Mexico residence strictly for seasonal, ceremonial purposes.[17]

The Kickapoos, thus, had a long history of crossing the U.S.-Mexico border unfettered, only occasionally encountering problems like Matapulla's at ports of entry. If questioned by immigration authorities, at least prior to the 1950s, they simply presented to guards at border crossings copies of a document that read as follows: "This is to certify that the families of the Kickapoo Indians, thirty seven in number, are to be protected by all persons from any injury whatever, as they are under the protection of the United States and any person violating shall be punished accordingly." A "Wm. Whittlee, Mj., 2nd Inft., Fort Dearborn" signed the document on September 28, 1832.[18] Although there are regular references in the historical record to the Kickapoos' knack for acquiring "passes" or "permits" from "Commanders of ports," Indian agents, or other U.S. officials in order to remain relatively footloose and fancy-free, the 1832 document in particular became a kind of tribal institution unto itself.[19] In fact, the tribe continued, in the words of one report, "cling[ing] with a childish faith to copies of a document which [they] cannot read, and which has been handed from father to son" well into the twentieth century. Border guards, meanwhile, made a habit of honoring the document, probably not so much out of a fear of being "punished accordingly," but because they had gradually developed a familiarity with and a respect for the Kickapoos' work habits.[20] Whether or not the document still carried the force of law was evidently a question no one bothered to ask, though the tribe certainly considered it a treaty, negotiated government-to-government, which exempted migrant Kickapoos from immigration regulations. Thus, the tribe's unfettered movement appears to have been an unwritten rule along the border.

Still, tribal members were careful about keeping certified copies of the document handy. In fact, one Eagle Pass notary claimed to have made at least a hundred certified copies from a *copy* of the original in his fifteen years in the business. One can imagine his surprise, then, when a young Kickapoo wandered into his office with the *original*. It was a development that, according to one report, touched off a "flurry of speculation and lightning research," since those familiar with the document had often wondered if the original still existed. "When questioned," the article continues, "[the Kickapoo] said his 'abuelito' in Nacimiento had given it to him. It was tattered and worn, and mended with cellophane tape." The notary made the copies, but not before cautioning the young man that great care should be taken with the document.[21] At midcentury, however, the document had been copied by both Kickapoos and non-Kickapoos alike so many times that immigration officials increasingly began calling its validity into question. Their suspicions were understandable, since, as Dolores Latorre explained, "Mexicans began to avail themselves of the many times copied document and were crossing as Kickapoos and not as Mexican nationals whose entry into the U.S. is very complicated."[22] And more trouble was on the horizon for Kickapoo migrants.

Under Operation Wetback, which was a 1953 legislative initiative designed to curtail undocumented Mexican migration northward, the tribe faced increasing scrutiny. For the first time, the issue of the tribe's nationality began to preoccupy and even trouble officials within the INS. After reviewing the Kickapoo case in the mid-1950s, the INS concluded, "The Service must, on the basis of the situation known to it, take the position that Kickapoo Indians residing in Mexico are to be treated the same as other persons residing there and that they are not entitled to any special rights or privileges under the immigration and naturalization laws because of their tribal membership." Thus, in 1957 the INS designated the Mexican Kickapoos "aliens," which would complicate, if not completely curtail, their transborder movement. This development evoked protests from a contingent of sympathetic Eagle Pass residents, who urged their local congressman to challenge the ruling. After taking the tribe's case to the INS in San Antonio, the local representative returned to Eagle Pass with encouraging news. After considering the Kickapoo case, the immigration service concluded, "A review of all available information would indicate the Kickapoo should be permitted to cross and recross the Mexican border." They cited the 1794 Jay Treaty, signed by the new United States and Great Britain, which protected *all* Indians' right to migrate across the U.S.-Canada border, as justification. Although local officials predicted that the INS's decision would not sit well with Congress, it ultimately went unchallenged.[23]

The invocation of the Jay Treaty may seem anachronistic and, given its focus on the U.S.-Canada border, irrelevant. Article 3 of the treaty states, "It shall at all times be free to His Majesty's subjects, and to the citizens of the United States, and also to Indians dwelling on either side of the said boundary line, to freely pass and repass by land or inland navigation, in the respective territories and countries of the two parties on the continent of America." The United States and Great Britain reaffirmed the provisions of the Jay Treaty in the 1796 Explanatory Article in the wake of the Treaty of Greenville. In fact, it mentioned the Kickapoos, at this time only precariously established in the Great Lakes region, by name. Along the U.S.-Canada border, Indians passed freely until the 1924 Immigration Act. After its passage, immigration officials in the United States required Canadian Indians to register as aliens and obtain immigrant visas or else face deportation proceedings. A few years later, and in the wake of a series of legal challenges, officials adopted a provision stating that the 1924 act "shall not be construed to apply to the right of American Indians born in Canada to pass the borders of the United States; *Provided*, that this right shall not extend to persons whose membership to Indian tribes or families is created by adoption." The 1952 Immigration and Nationality Act altered this provision somewhat, establishing a 50 percent blood quantum requirement for those claiming an exemption from the usual rules governing immigration.[24] Still, taken collectively, these developments seemingly affirmed, in a somewhat convoluted manner, the Kickapoos' right to traverse the northern border at will, so long as they could prove tribal membership. The question remains, though, if the Jay Treaty applies to the southern border, as the Kickapoo claimed. The legal scholar Richard Osburn argues that while "Indian interaction between tribes separated by America's northern border is safe," along the southern border it is not, with the exception of the Kickapoos and Tohono O'odham (with the latter experiencing somewhat less freedom than the former, especially in recent years). These exceptions, however, have nothing to do with the Jay Treaty and everything to do with those anomalous aspects of their histories discussed herein, including, especially, historical precedent.[25]

At midcentury, the INS implemented a new system designed to govern the tribe's movements in a more formal fashion, one that was more "official" in nature but still comparatively lax. They began issuing the Kickapoos what immigration officials called "annual parolee papers," which migrant tribal members had to renew from year to year. "Paroling Kicka-poos," one official clarified, "is an immigration term. It's not a criminal thing. The Immigration Department is not sure of the citizenship of these Indians." According to the enrollment records of the Oklahoma Kickapoos from this period, about half of their Mexican counterpart was likely born in the United States, an understandable figure given the fact that the tribe spent most of the year migrating within U.S. borders. However, few Mexican Kickapoos bothered to record births, partly because the tribe had never considered such official documentation important and partly because of a characteristic reluctance to register themselves anywhere. Thus, for decades their citizenship status remained unclear, and mostly by design. Until officials clarified that status, they had little choice but to con-sider the Kickapoos American citizens when in the United States and Mexican citizens when in Mexico—a far from ideal arrangement unless you were a Kickapoo.[26]

Migrating Kickapoos considered themselves, variously, either dual citizens or citizens of neither country. A 1957 INS study included a telling conclu-sion that perhaps best summed up the Kickapoos' sentiments. "It is a con-sensus," the report contended, "that the Kickapoo consider their tribe a nation unto itself." When uninformed authorities forcibly detained Kicka-poo migrants, as in the Garza case, the official response could be surpris-ingly swift. For example, in the 1960s, an immigration official asked a Kickapoo from Múzquiz, who was attempting to cross into Mexico, for his papers. Since the Kickapoo was unable to produce sufficient proof of his citizenship status, authorities detained him. "The U.S. government was in-formed of this," reported a journalist from Eagle Pass, "and there was a tremendous fuss in Washington. They even sent a high immigration official from Washington to the Texas border." Oddly, that same official seized the reporter's file on the Kickapoos, in what was likely an attempt to keep the incident out of the news.[27] Evidently, the U.S. government, as surprising as it may be, had no objection to tribal members asserting their right to mi-grate, a right that, at least from the tribe's perspective, went back to 1832.

The Kickapoos also enjoyed a host of notable legal and political excep-tions while living in Mexico. First of all, the Mexican government recog-nized the tribe's right to govern itself. The Kickapoos' government has traditionally consisted of a "chief," or *capitán*, who serves as the civil, po-litical, and religious leader of the group, and, at least until the late 1930s, when they evidently stopped meeting, a council of elders that worked closely with the chief. Mexican officials have historically interfered with the workings of the Kickapoo government only when serious crimes were committed, such as manslaughter, robbery, and cattle rustling. Government officials also excluded the tribe from several national censuses. They counted the Kickapoos for the 1930 and 1970 censuses, but not for those conducted in 1940, 1950, 1960, or 1980. Their exclusion was apparently at the urging of local officials, who were uncertain whether or not the tribe could properly be considered Mexican citizens, since, put simply, they were not treated as Mexican citizens, particularly when it came to the favoritism they received at border crossings. Immigration officials also did not inspect their vehicles upon their return from the United States, nor did they require that the Kickapoos pay duties on items brought back from the United States. Finally, the Mexican government did not require that tribal members register their vehicles in Mexico.[28] The Kickapoos honored the terms of their arrangement with the Mexican government, and Mexican officials, in turn, allowed their very unusual relationship to persist.

This is not to imply, however, that the Mexican government ignored the Kickapoos when it came to broader discussions of Indian assimilation, discussions that, as detailed earlier, had become commonplace by mid-century. For example, writing in the 1960s for an official publication, the anthropologist Miguel León-Portilla lumped the Mexican Kickapoos together with other Mexican tribes, including the Yaqui and Tohono O'odham, that he considered among the least acculturated of Mexico's Indians, or those who had witnessed only "sporadic attempts to raise their living conditions or to scientifically study their [language]." However, he nonetheless considered the Kickapoos a special case. He explained, "Note should be taken, as a case of almost complete isolation, of the Kikapoo [sic] group that lives on the 'ranchería' 'El Nacimiento,' located in the Municipality of Múzquiz, Coahuila." Unlike other Mexican Indian groups, he continued, the Kickapoos "form a part, from an ethnic and linguistic point of view, of the Algonquin family" from the United States, and had only comparatively recently established a presence in Mexico. Still, although León-Portillo differentiated the Kickapoos from other Mexican Indians, he did not imply that this distinction meant anything when it came to the question of acculturation. In other words, Indigenistas would not exempt the Kickapoos from their nationalizing project.[29] He also singled out the Mexican O'odham as a special case. "It should be explained," he wrote, "that the Papagos, located near the U.S. border where there are also individuals of said group, receive certain influence from the United States, principally because some of their children attend Papago reservation schools in the state of Arizona." Yet again, however, he did not imply that their unusual history and/or orientation exempted them from the Indigenistas' larger mission to acculturate Indians living within Mexico's borders.[30]

Regardless, Mexican policy as applied to the Kickapoos has generally been one of noninterference, leaving them with considerably more autonomy than their Oklahoma relatives. And much as in the Yaqui case, the Cárdenas administration had a lot to do with institutionalizing this hands-off approach to managing the tribe's presence. In yet another presidential decree, Cárdenas "officially" recognized Papiquano and Minonina as chiefs of the Kickapoo tribe, and in 1939 he amended the decree, directing that their hunting rights be recognized without the oversight and interference of government authorities. They were permitted to hunt, unfettered by federal or state hunting laws, in the Sierra Madre nine months out of the year. It further allocated a small salary for the tribal chief from the Mexican government (though successive leaders appear not to have received the same perk). Evidently, however, the tribe was not entirely comfortable with the sudden attention from Mexico City, and tribal elders, in turn, strongly discouraged tribal members from participating in Mexican politics and elections, fearing that doing so might make them vulnerable to an erosion of their rights and incursions on their lands. And unfortunately for the Kickapoos, the agreement struck with Cárdenas regarding hunting rights did not outlive his presidency. Over time the wilderness on their perimeters was subdivided and doled out as *ejidos* and ranches. The non-Indians who worked these parcels, not surprisingly, had little interest in the Indians' historic agreement with the Mexican government. President Carlos Salinas was the first to flat-out ignore the Kickapoos' hunting rights, and although they reached out to successive presidents to right these wrongs, as one Kickapoo put it, "Es perdido." It's lost.[31]

The hunting rights issue may seem to be a minor one, but the Kickapoos considered it a serious affront to the tribe's religious freedom. Put simply, the deer hunt is a sacred activity. As one journalist explained later in the twentieth century, "A father cannot baptize and bestow a tribal name on an infant unless he can contribute to the rite four slain deer." The animals were scarce around Nacimiento and "rare as polar bears" in Eagle Pass. Hunting regulations imposed by both private landowners and government officials became increasingly restrictive by the end of the century south of the border, and in Texas these restrictions were "unrelenting." With most Kickapoos earning only a few thousand dollars a year by century's end, few could afford seasonal hunting leases. Besides, a hunting lease would not have fully addressed the problem anyway. After all, babies are born year round, and leaving them nameless was simply not an option. Many Kickapoos thus turned to poaching, but were likewise unable to pay fines that could run into hundreds of dollars when caught. Thus, many ended up working these fines off on county road gangs.[32]

Still, relations between the Kickapoos and Mexican local and national officials have mostly been comparatively positive. One notable exception, however, concerned education. Efforts to provide a non-Indian education to the Kickapoos were rarely well received. In the early 1920s, for example, the administration of Alvaro Obregón installed a school and a teacher at Nacimiento. Fearing the impact that a non-Indian education could have on their culture, the Kickapoos burned down the school and purged their community of all government agents. Federal officials reached out to the Kickapoos again later that decade, and this time enjoyed the smallest of victories. After refusing a federal educator's request that they send five of their children to the aforementioned Casa del Estudiante Indígena boarding school in Mexico City, the Kickapoos, evidently trying to meet the officials halfway, agreed to allow a leatherworking specialist and an and agricultural adviser to settle among them. President Cárdenas also tried to bring the Kickapoos into the Mexican educational system. In a meeting with Cárdenas in 1938, however, Kickapoo chief Papiquano advised, "I am the head of my people; you are the head of yours. I don't interfere with you; you don't interfere with me." The Kickapoos' recalcitrance when it came to education persisted throughout the twentieth century. "As of the 1980s," the historian Andrae Marak observed, "only the parents of about twelve Mexican Kickapoo children were sending their children to school for fear that the education offered in Mexico (or in the United States for that matter) would lead to their children's acculturation."[33]

All the while, the Mexican counterpart of the Kickapoo tribe maintained a rather curious relationship with their Oklahoma relatives. The boundary between the two contingents actually remained quite diffuse throughout the twentieth century. Intermarriages were not uncommon; movement between the two locales was, of course, common; and it was actually relatively easy, though evidently uncommon, for a Kickapoo to "switch" from one group to another. Ceremonial visits to Mexico and Oklahoma from both sides were a constant, and a layover in Oklahoma while on the migratory trail was similarly common.[34] Yet barriers between the two Kickapoo contingents remained. Although the two groups always considered themselves products of the same tribal heritage, both recognized that those residing south of the border were considerably more culturally conservative. Then there was the fact that in 1937, under John Collier's Indian Reorganization Act, the Oklahoma Kickapoos adopted a form of government and constitution that their southern counterpart found somewhat stifling. Mexican agrarian law classified the Mexican Kickapoos' land as an *ejido*, a much less formal, looser designation that left the Kickapoos with considerably more freedom to govern themselves within their communally held lands as they saw fit. The *ejido* organization required only that the Kickapoos elect a *jefe*, or president, a treasurer, and a secretary, all serving three-year terms. Other positions included a judge, a post often held, at least among the Kickapoos, by a religious leader, and a *consejo de vigilancia*, or investigator, who dealt with livestock and other economic matters. Although the *ejido* organization sounds quite formal, the Kickapoos' broad interpretation of these requirements and posts left it considerably less so. Thus, they enjoyed a degree of freedom and independence that, at least in their estimation, their Oklahoma counterpart did not.[35]

The status of Kickapoo lands in Mexico, in fact, seemed to have gradually evolved over time in a way that granted the tribe even more freedom and independence. The Kickapoos' original designation upon their arrival was that of a "military colony," a classification that carried with it much less government interference than *ejido*, and thus more autonomy. Military colonies, however, have obviously become a thing of the past. Mexican officials have also, at times, referred to Kickapoo lands in Mexico as comprising a *ranchería*, a designation that carries with it economic connotations. But *ejidos*, which are still fairly common arrangements in Mexico, bring with them the maximum amount of autonomy available under contemporary Mexican law. In fact, the *ejido* distinction has throughout Mexican history been an exemption, and even a privilege, reserved, generally speaking, for Indian communities that possess some preexisting governing structure. However, although the Kickapoos' status, officially speaking, remained that of an *ejido* for most of the twentieth century, their original "military colony" designation, which implies an even greater degree of autonomy, may have more accurately reflected the reality. In fact, the Latorres gleaned that because of a failure to "comprehend the complicated laws" surrounding these various designations, some Kickapoos were under the impression that at least part of their lands still had antiquated *colonia* status under the Mexican government and thus considered themselves an "autonomous nation."[36]

Descriptions of Nacimiento by outsiders have tended to emphasize the freedom and splendid solitude in which the group evidently lived. A traveler later in the twentieth century recounted seeing a few houses made of cinder blocks, but "the dominant architecture was the traditional loaf-shaped wickiups made of cattail reeds." He observed the Kickapoos going about their daily activities, some strolling about, some reclining on straw cots under front porches, some clumped into groups engaging in conservation, all seemingly in a state of relaxation. It was "a scene of leisure," he wrote. The village itself, he noted, was surrounded by "dramatic rock cliffs" and mountains blanketed with oaks. It also boasted a stream, running cool and clear through the small cluster of houses and buildings. When asked if the "sacred stream" had a name, one Kickapoo replied, "No. We just call it river." As of the late twentieth century, the village did not have water pipes or a sewage system. In fact, electricity had only recently arrived in Nacimiento. The Kickapoo evidently were not looking to significantly alter this pattern of life. As one explained, "Texas is where we work. Nacimiento is where we go to live our lives as Kickapoo people."[37]

A third Kickapoo contingent, it should be added, resided in the state of Kansas, though in dwindling numbers. Originally established in 1832 and consisting of roughly 768,000 acres, the Kansas reservation had been subjected to allotment in 1887 and had dwindled to just under 4,000 acres of allotted land and just under 1,000 acres of tribal land by the end of the 1930s. The Kickapoo Tribe of Kansas organized under the auspices of the Indian Reorganization Act in 1934. As of 1962, the tribal roll listed 498 persons. In just seven years that number had fallen to 250 (though Bureau of Indian Affairs officials believed the number was more like 1,000, and were working with Kansas Kickapoos to produce a more accurate count).[38] They appear to have been left to their own devices by their relatives, however. "I've been waiting a long time for a Kickapoo from Oklahoma or Mexico to come up to Kansas," one told a reporter in 1973, "but none of the southern Kickapoos ever come to this part of the country." The result was that the Kansas Kickapoo had lost "nearly all" of their Kickapoo culture. It is unclear why tribal members bypassed Kansas, since the Mexican Kickapoos were known to venture as far north as Michigan to visit even more distant relatives.[39]

Those Kickapoos who permanently resided in the United States and enjoyed federally protected status often expressed and even acted upon an interest in strengthening ties with their Mexican counterparts. Yet their efforts did not always sit well with their southern relatives. In the 1960s, for example, Oklahoma Kickapoos initiated a drive to add Kickapoos in Mexico to their tribal rolls. Although motivated in part by the Oklahoma

Kickapoos' desire to receive the maximum amount of compensation for tribal lands lost earlier in the century, the enrollment drive may also have represented a sincere effort to help their relatives, then widely perceived as poverty-stricken and uneducated. The Latorres appear to have assisted the tribe in its efforts, claiming to have been, in Dolores's words, "up to our necks in work" in the process. Two representatives from the Oklahoma group visited Mexico in 1966, but managed to sign up only a "handful" of Mexican Kickapoos. The Latorres then took over. After a few days the Latorres had forty-nine signatures on applications for enrollment in the Kickapoo tribe of Oklahoma. However, the pair ran into a couple of serious obstacles. First of all, only a few Kickapoo children had birth certificates, namely, those who were born in the United States while their parents were on the migratory trail. Second, few could remember if they had already registered in 1937, when the tribe last formulated a tribal roll. A comparison of the current membership roll with the 1937 roll helped the Latorres solve the latter problem, which left only the birth certificate problem. They proposed a compromise with the BIA whereby, in lieu of a birth certificate, they would send an affidavit signed by two other tribal members confirming the individual's Kickapoo identity. The BIA, in the end, agreed to this somewhat unusual request.[40] The Latorres also assisted officials in estimating the age of tribal members, which proved to be no small task. Dolores explained:

> We have developed several "tricks" for estimating the ages of the Kickapoo by combining their personal estimation of their age (some actually know the exact date of their birth) plus certain historical "landmarks" such as the year they arrived in Mexico, McKenzie's raid, the coming of the Kickapoo group who arrived in 1907, the Mexican Revolution, "la gran gripa" (1918 Influenza epidemic), the big drought of the 50's when they began going stateside to work, etc. Then by asking them such personal questions as: "Were you a 'señorita' (had your menarche) when the flu epidemic came?" Or, "were you married when such or such an event occurred?" etc., we finally can approximate the age of a person within four or five years.[41]

However, the Latorres also encountered resistance from within the Mexican band, with one member confiding to Dolores her fear that enrolling in the Oklahoma tribe, in Dolores's words, "will mean that the Kickapoo from here have to return to the U.S. where their ways will be taken away from them as was tried before they came here." The tribe's distrust of the BIA also figured into their reluctance to register, even when the agency acted through fellow Kickapoos. After personally distributing BIA-produced applications to tribal members per the Latorres' request, Kickapoo Pancho Minacoa privately revealed that even he was afraid of "esa gente," or "those people."[42] The fact was that at the end of the day the Mexican Kickapoos trusted no one. Mexican authorities typically got the cold shoulder, the tribe repeatedly refused to allow church officials on their lands, and, as already discussed, they burned down two schools that the Mexican Department of Education constructed in their village earlier in the century.[43] Thus, their resistance to these latest overtures surprised no one, and the Latorres' efforts to register the Mexican Kickapoos, though well meaning, appear to have yielded little fruit.

Relations between the Oklahoma and Mexican groups, however, could also be quite positive. One Mexican Kickapoo, for example, extended an invitation to his Oklahoma-based brother-in-law to visit Mexico. "Would be very happy to have you come down to Mexico in February," he wrote, "but it is best if you come all the way to Muzquiz by bus as every time we cross the border, the Mexican customs make us pay $15.00 to get our cars back into Mexico." And in an interesting aside, the Kickapoo also promised to send his Oklahoma relative some peyote.[44] Mexican Kickapoos also remained bound to their Oklahoma counterpart for more pragmatic reasons. The availability of welfare checks, for example, depended on at least their periodic presence north of the border. Writing to Kickapoo Palo Trevino, the Oklahoma Department of Public Welfare warned that its policy allowed only two successive checks to be mailed to out-of-state addresses. The letter continues, "This means you may receive your February and March checks in Mexico, but you must return to Oklahoma by April 1st, to avoid a change in your welfare grant."[45] Another Kickapoo, forced onto disability due to an undisclosed medical condition, stood to receive aid to the disabled from the state of Oklahoma for the rest of his life, but with an important condition. "Our concern at present," a representative from the Shawnee Agency wrote to the Latorres, "is that [his wife] will not realize that he cannot be out of the state of Oklahoma for a period of more than three months and still maintain residence or eligibility for financial assistance." The agency requested the Latorres' assistance in stressing to tribal members that they must not remain in Mexico for longer than three months, lest the checks from Oklahoma cease.[46]

Despite occasional headaches, however, many Kickapoos appear to have valued their freedom, independence, and splendid isolation, whether at home in Nacimiento or on the migrant trail. Tribal member Aurelio García explained: "The Kickapoo are different than most American Indians. Most have their reservations. They stay there. Nowhere to go. These people, the Kickapoo, are free, like birds or whatever . . . They feel like they can go any-where."[47] Another Kickapoo echoed this sentiment, telling a reporter in the 1980s: "I don't like staying in one place too long. I get bored. I had a steady job in Oklahoma City. But I got tired of it." Much of the migrant work, he maintained, was temporary, easy, and lucrative. For example, harvesting asparagus, which required them to work only a few hours in the morning and a few hours in the evening, earned them up to $800 a week. He and his family typically stayed in communal housing provided, free of charge, by the farmers. While in Mexico, they inhabited housing some would con-sider substandard, but not the Kickapoos. They designed their winter homes to allow for quick assembly and disassembly, making their migratory life-style all the more convenient to maintain. "I just want to leave it that way," he concluded. "I don't want to change. Indians are not made to be rich . . . We work, pay taxes, that's it."[48]

It should be pointed out, however, that not all Kickapoos found life on the migrant trail fulfilling. As Kickapoo Margie Salazar put it in the 1990s: "As a child, I remember traveling with my parents on long difficult journeys. I worked in the fields, and we all chipped in to survive, but I knew there would be a better life. I worked very hard between trips to get my educa-tion and complete my GED. I did not want to keep working with my hands." Another Kickapoo mentioned having turned to migrant labor only reluc-tantly, and only when he was unable to secure a job as a roofer, his occupa-tion of choice.[49]

Regardless, their wages, in addition to providing subsistence, also funded ceremonial observances and a host of social obligations. This was no small matter, since the tribe believed that following through on their religious commitments protected not just the Kickapoos but the *entire* human race from calamity. As one Kickapoo put it: "A Kickapoo does not pray for him-self alone. He prays for all people. And if Kickapoo are not allowed to practice their traditions, this will be borne out in wars, disease, natural disasters."[50] According to one journalist, the Kickapoos believed they were living in the last of four worlds. He explained: "The first three were de-stroyed by air, rot, and water; this one will be consumed by fire. But their faith seems to be largely free of apocalyptic fret and doom. As long as they observe the tradition and conduct their lives honorably, at peace with na-ture, they will have an eternal reward in the western sky." Indeed, nature figured prominently in their ceremonial cycle. The springtime ceremonial season begins after two annual rites: the second thunderstorm of the spring season and the blooming of a specific species of tree. At that moment, the journalist added, "the tribe's spiritual leader summons the people, and at Nacimiento the holy season begins. For several weeks Nacimiento is closed to anyone who is not Kickapoo." Overall, however, it was impossible to partition off religion from other aspects of Kickapoo culture. One Kickapoo religious leader likened their culture to a human hand in which religion represented but one finger. Though significant on its own, it was very much interrelated with and dependent on other aspects of Kickapoo culture and, thus, impossible to isolate in its own category.[51]

Also important from the Mexican Kickapoos' perspective was the fact that their demanding migratory/ceremonial cycle enabled them to remain largely aloof from outside cultural influences. "Kickapoos Almost Immune to Change," claimed a 1977 headline from the *Austin American-Statesman*. "Kickapoos Are Living 400 Years in the Past," declared another. One article detailed a Kickapoo burial ceremony, whereby tribal members painted a purple streak across the face of the deceased so that his god, Pepazce, would recognize him. After placing him in a shallow grave, they left the deceased Kickapoo with a corn cake and the following words: "Go willingly to Pepazce; do not molest those of us who stay behind." The village then entered into a four-day period of mourning. The reporter marveled that, no, this was not Western historical fiction. "It is fact and still occurs only five or six hours' driving time from Austin near the Mexican town of Muzquiz in Coahuila," he wrote. He added that the tribe's original agreement with the government of Mexico, made the previous century and mentioned above, included a provision that read, "It is not demanded of them (the Indians) to change their habits and customs."[52]

But although subtle, changes were occurring. Less than a decade later, a headline read, "Kickapoo Indians Launch Longest Journey—Move into Modern Life." The purchase of automobiles and transistor radios became more common. Some Kickapoo young women began getting permanents and wearing nail polish. Some Kickapoo young men began wearing their hair in a style reminiscent of the Beatles. Younger tribal members also began studying the English language in increasing numbers. The tribe also began turning to modern medicine more frequently, particularly when it began to look like their medicine men were failing them. Still, their suspicion of outsiders remained. For example, the tribe turned down an offer of $100 per man per day, plus expenses, to appear in a Jimmy Stewart picture being filmed near

Three young Kickapoos, 1962. The caption, likely written by one of the Latorres, reads, "Kickapoo Youths Wearing Their Hair in Imitation of the Beattles [*sic*]." Nettie Lee Benson Latin American Collection, University of Texas Libraries, University of Texas at Austin.

Brackettville, Texas, most likely because of a preference to steer clear of such publicity.[53]

As mentioned above, the city of Eagle Pass, which is about ninety miles from Múzquiz, figured prominently in the Kickapoos' migratory cycle. While living with other tribal members beneath the international bridge in Eagle Pass, one Kickapoo reportedly told a journalist, "The Indian was here in Eagle Pass before it was a town." Indeed, they had been crossing the border near the present-day site of the city since at least 1848, when they camped out in the area just prior to their move to Mexico, and used the area as a crossing point for the remainder of the century. Immigration officials noted their appearance as early as 1862. In more recent decades, they have lived in cardboard huts while there, paid about eight dollars each month for water, and often bathed in the muddy Rio Grande. As of the 1980s, the tribe had some forty-nine dwellings that they built themselves, along with three trailer homes that, all told, covered about two and a half acres. The huts, one anthropologist noted, were "generally built out of a combination

Kickapoo couple weaving sotol baskets in "Kickapoo Village," which likely refers to their settlement near Eagle Pass, between 1965 and 1967. The caption reads, "Although this is women's work, in this instance the Mexican husband of this Kickapoo woman is giving her a hand." Nettie Lee Benson Latin American Collection, University of Texas Libraries, University of Texas at Austin.

of saplings, scrap lumber, cardboard, and sheets of black plastic, all held together by strips of the trimmed salvages [sic] of denim obtained from the local Wrangler jeans factory." On more than one occasion, several huts burned because of cigarette butts or burning matches carelessly tossed out of a car window by passersby. At one point a freak flood washed away most of the tribal members' personal belongings. Local assistance in these kinds of cases was usually not forthcoming. "One less Indian to worry about, says the government" seemed to be the consensus, according to one Kickapoo.[54] Such attitudes were perhaps not surprising, considering the fact that most Americans recognized the Kickapoos only through the popular *L'il Abner* comic strip, which included a Kickapoo character named Lonesome Polecat. His pastime was the production of a beverage called Kickapoo Joy Juice, an alcoholic concoction.[55]

Over time, however, the Kickapoos' ties to Eagle Pass became more and more substantial, and they reached a point where formalizing their presence in the city became yet another tribal imperative. The 1960s and 1970s would find the increasingly Texas-based Kickapoos pursuing formal recognition as an American Indian tribe and petitioning for a protected land base in their adopted home. In explaining their choice of Eagle Pass for the site of a potential Kickapoo reservation, one Kickapoo stated, "We refer to Eagle Pass because our grandparents and our forefathers are buried there. This is why we refer to that as our home ground." "Our forefathers came from the United States," another later told a congressional committee, "and we like the United States and are proud of the fact that we originated from here."[56] The tribe had evidently grown tired of the uncertainties that came with camping beneath the international bridge between stops along the migrant trail, and their transience was exacting an obvious toll. "The Kickapoo Tribe, Mexicans and North Americans at the Same Time," read a 1979 Mexican headline. The article characterized the group as "dead and forgotten, without a house or a home," facing their "inevitable extinction, which will probably occur within the next decade, more or less."[57] Such a lifestyle, as can be imagined, did not help persistent problems within the tribe, including alcoholism and a general lack of access to adequate health care. Still, they seemed to fear eviction from their Eagle Pass encampment above all other concerns. As one Kickapoo revealed, "Every day we go to bed with fears that tomorrow we are going to be thrown out of there."[58]

In the 1960s, the city of Eagle Pass granted the tribe a small piece of land, partly out of a concern for their safety and partly to keep them from being a nuisance. Like the Yaquis, the Kickapoos used the land to establish a variant stream of tribal tradition, a reconstituted tribal whole that drew from a specific indigenous heritage while adapting it to their new setting. Also like the Yaquis, they launched a campaign for federally recognized status to secure the greatest possible degree of sovereignty.[59] In short, they had officially begun nation building. Also like the Yaquis, however, they faced a serious obstacle in that they were claiming the right to nationhood in a region in which they were relatively recent arrivals. In other words, they were, in the eyes of many legislators, "Mexican" Indians seeking to become "American," or, perhaps more accurately, "Texas" Indians, even though they had actually originated well north of the present-day U.S.-Mexico border. These were all distinctions, however, that the Indians themselves simply refused to recognize. Like the Yaquis, the Kickapoos had long behaved as at least a nascent nation. Further, their unusual relationship with the Mexican government meant that they had grown accustomed to a certain degree of autonomy (along with a host of associated protections) and no doubt wanted—or perhaps even expected—the United States to honor the precedent set by its southern neighbor and legislate accordingly. Doing so, however, would be tantamount to ignoring over a century's worth of efforts to invest the U.S.-Mexico border with legal, diplomatic, and even cultural meaning, since a "special" relationship with the nation-states on both sides of the dividing line would effectively place the Kickapoos above the fray in their efforts to protect the border's hard-won integrity. And again similar to the Yaqui case, recognition north of the border could pose potentially troubling questions about national citizenship that might redirect broader conversations about indigenous nationalism and indigenous borders down troubling paths. In both regards, then, it looked like a potentially slippery slope. But although the Kickapoos' push for federally recognized status in the 1980s would appear rather audacious, to the tribal members themselves it was simply the logical next step in substantiating what they innately viewed as a perfectly legitimate claim to nationhood.

5 We Are Lost between Two Worlds

The Tohono O'odham Nation

. . . .

In a 1990 "open letter" to Tohono O'odham living north of the U.S.-Mexico border, those living south of the boundary communicated their fear that a rift was forming between the two halves of the tribal whole. While the letter expressed gratitude for their support in the form of "money, materials, and encouragement," it also described worsening conditions south of the boundary. "Our human rights and aboriginal rights have slowly been violated or disappeared in Mexico," the letter contends, "as more and more Mexicans have moved onto our lands. Sometimes there were gradual take-overs, other times deception/fraud were used and other times brutal and forceful takeovers." An inadequate, and ever shrinking, land base had increasingly forced southern O'odham to leave their communities for cities in Mexico such as Hermosillo and Caborca, as well as cities in the United States. By the end of the twentieth century, southern O'odham controlled a mere 1,800 acres, not nearly enough to maintain their generations-long tradition of subsistence farming. Migrating away from their communities was a compromise that, however necessary, "affected the continuity of the O'odham traditions, culture, and language." The letter was evidently meant to serve as a reminder that, as the authors put it, "as O'odham we are one people."[1]

Southern O'odham had been hopeful for a more secure existence when, in 1948, the Mexican government opened the aforementioned National Indian Institute to assist its indigenous people. In 1990, however, they complained bitterly that the office's efforts did not reach the O'odham until the 1970s. Even then, the O'odham alleged, the office was "weak" and "under-funded," working mostly in concert with "ranchers and dope traffickers to take more O'odham land." Thus, the problem was not a lack of rights under the Mexican government, but the enforcement of existing rights. After futile protests to the Mexican government, these O'odham now turned to their increasingly distant northern counterpart for assistance. In 1983, the O'odham nation established an office north of the boundary to investigate legal issues, census reports, and correspondence between southern O'odham and the Mexican government, but their efforts bore little fruit. The problem, from the southern O'odham's perspective, was simple to diagnose but difficult to treat. "To recover or reclaim the O'odham lands," the letter continues, "the people who left must come back to their lands, but in order for the people to stay on the land, they have to be able to eat and to find some way to sustain themselves." It would take economic development and educational and health facilities, all working hand in hand, to help "draw people back onto the lands." They claimed to have had the support of Sonora's Yaquis and Mayos, but needed firm support from their U.S.-based counterpart as well. Tellingly, they went on to assure their northern relatives that they intended to remain in Mexico, realizing that while O'odham north of the border had extensive property, they "need to preserve [it] for their children, grand children, and great grand children." "The Traditional O'odham Leaders of Mexico want to thank you," the letter concludes, "and express that we are willing and anxious to go to your community or district meetings and give you more information as we can not put every thing on paper now."[2]

The 1990 letter was just another in a long string of efforts by southern O'odham aimed at reclaiming lost lands. Early the previous decade, for example, seventy tribal members occupied the National Indian Institute offices in Caborca, Sonora. They did so to draw attention to the tribe's lack of educational and health facilities and to bring the land issue to the fore. O'odham governor David Santiago Manuel Lara explained to a Tucson reporter that while his tribe had resided in Sonora for centuries, they never actually possessed a legal title to their lands. "When others bought land in the area," he stated, "they received documents entitling them to it, even though Indians already lived there."[3]

By the end of the twentieth century, transborder ties between O'odham living in Mexico and O'odham living in the United States had weakened to the point that the southern contingent felt neglected, even forgotten. Once a way of life for the tribe, transborder movement became increasingly difficult as the twentieth century progressed, a lesson the Yaquis and Kickapoos had also learned the hard way. Sweeping changes along the U.S.-Mexico border, coupled with the dramatic development of the American Southwest's economy, appeared to be the culprit. In this light, the letter reads like a wake-up call for northern O'odham, a reminder, again, that the concerns of O'odham south of the boundary should be the concerns of *all* O'odham. Instead, both groups watched nervously as federal officials on both sides of the border gradually implemented rules and regulations designed to more closely monitor and control O'odham transborder migratory patterns. Consequently, the very practice began falling out of favor, and tribal interests began to diverge.

North of the border, the O'odham had gone through their own period of readjustment in an effort to maintain tribal cohesion and cultural continuity. One anthropologist noted in the 1970s, "While so many Papagos still reside in villages that appear at first glance to possess pristine aboriginality, the fact is that a century of American ownership of the Papaguería has resulted in increasing interpenetration of the American and Papago socio-cultural systems. The changes in Papago society have been continuous, cumulative, and transformative."[4] Religious observances that had long required transborder mobility became ever more difficult to maintain, while the O'odham's increasingly visible participation in, and increasing dependence on, southern Arizona's cash economy slowly eclipsed the importance of transnational economic networks. By the late twentieth century, then, movement between Tohono O'odham lands in the United States and Mexico had nearly ground to a halt, having lost nearly all of its cultural, political, and economic relevance. While the Yaquis and Kickapoos faced increasing restrictions on their movements during this period, the O'odham's migratory patterns had essentially become a thing of the past, effectively isolating their southern counterpart while simultaneously sending northern O'odham down a divergent economic, political, and even cultural path. In other words, forces beyond their control increasingly complicated and, in the end, prohibited the maintenance of the tribal whole as the twentieth century progressed, leaving the O'odham among the most divided of North America's Indian nations.

By midcentury it was becoming apparent to the O'odham that residing north of the boundary held notable advantages over residing south of the boundary. As the Indian agent at Sells put it at midcentury, it was proving difficult for O'odham south of the boundary "to remain content and satisfied . . . seeing that the O'odham in Arizona are improving in health, they have better education, and advance in everything having to do with their prosperity, while their brothers on the other side of the border lose what little they have."[5] In 1950, one anthropologist estimated that only a few hundred O'odham resided on the Mexican side of the border on a permanent basis, living primarily in *rancherías*, or "villages with houses scattered barely within sight of each other," while others who had long since lost their lands "eke out a parasitic existence around towns of Mexicans who have taken their lands." Somewhat hyperbolically, he claimed that these

O'odham had "given up their Indian heritage and are waiting passively to die."[6] This chapter will explore the historical roots of these disparities, highlighting moments when the barrier between these two halves of the tribal whole, long signified by the U.S.-Mexico border, began to appear insurmountable.

Unfettered movement in the present-day U.S.-Mexico border region had been of paramount importance to the tribe since well before the boundary's inception. As O'odham Josiah Moore recently explained, "The history of our people shows that they were migratory and that they moved seasonally on a north-south axis to various springs, wells, streams, grazing areas and religious and cultural sites between what now is Arizona and Sonora." U.S. officials had, from the very beginning of their relationship with the group, assured the tribe that their right to migrate would remain in place. Moore maintains that as U.S. and Mexican officials began implementing the 1848 Treaty of Guadalupe Hidalgo, Major W. H. Emory, who was one of four U.S. commissioners placed in the field, personally assured tribal members that they would "be able to visit back and forth across the border and carry on the usual relations between villages as though the boundary were non-existent." The Americans ultimately constructed fences along the border, but actually placed gates at those locations most commonly used by the tribe to move across their lands. The tribe also claimed to have an "informal" agreement with the Border Patrol that they would continue to move freely, but would keep officials apprised of those movements. By the end of the twentieth century, however, past assurances and informal agreements meant little.[7]

Subsisting in a desert environment has proved perennially challenging for the tribe, often necessitating unfettered mobility. As one scholar explained, "The movements of entire families or kinship villages to work for other people are of ancient vintage." After his arrival in O'odham country in 1692, Father Kino noted the O'odham practice of moving "from parts so remote, from the north, from the west, etc.," to capitalize on the regional economy and to attach themselves to developing settlements. Whether it was a mission, a mine, a cattle ranch, a cotton field, or any one of a number of economic enterprises over the next three centuries, the O'odham regularly reverted to a migratory lifestyle when their own farms and fields proved unproductive or inadequate.[8] And it was a subsistence strategy that the tribe had practiced, in some form or other, since well before the arrival of Europeans. Often referred to as the "two-village" system, it entailed a seasonal migratory cycle between winter villages in mountainous areas,

A Tohono O'odham man poses in front of his off-reservation home in the Sonoyta Valley, Arizona. No date given. Nettie Lee Benson Latin American Collection, University of Texas Libraries, University of Texas at Austin.

where the group had access to water sources, and summer settlements in the desert below near the deltas of washes, where they waited for the late-summer monsoons. They also maintained encampments near sources of saguaro cactus, the fruit of which the O'odham used to make wine for ceremonial purposes.[9]

As of the late nineteenth and even the early twentieth century, the two-village system still figured prominently in the O'odham's subsistence strategy. When the water dried up on their Arizona reservation, usually at the end of the summer, O'odham families simply packed up and headed south. "Over the mountains where you call Mexico," one O'odham woman explained, "there were more of our people who had water ditches in their fields. We worked for them and they gave us food." As for the trek south, O'odham women placed "the children and the bedding and a small grinding stone" atop horses while they ran alongside, carrying pots, nets, and other necessities. O'odham men, meanwhile, went "far up in the hills . . . running with their bows and arrows, looking for deer, and sometimes they met us with loads of meat on their backs." She also mentioned cutting wheat and even harvesting figs for Mexican farmers while south of the border.[10] As the economy of the American Southwest began booming, however, the O'odham found less and less incentive to venture into Mexico. North of the border, they worked as railroad laborers, nurserymen, truck drivers, cooks, and general construction laborers. They became increasingly skilled in the process, running tractors, bulldozers, and cotton-picking machines, while also taking responsibility for their maintenance. In fact, one Tucson official noted in 1957 that "there is more of a demand for Indian labor than there is a supply," and that area employers seemed to be "prejudiced in favor of the Papagos."[11] Accompanying this surge in off-reservation employment was a surge in O'odham population density on the reservation as O'odham realized they no longer had to travel quite so far afield for employment opportunities. In fact, reservation population figures, which had long been on the decline, witnessed a dramatic reversal between 1900 and 1950. Tellingly, however, population figures for those O'odham living south of the boundary remained stagnant, never deviating dramatically from estimates dating back hundreds of years.[12]

Sometimes their wholesale movement into the cash economy, particularly during the twentieth century, required a period of adjustment. One O'odham woman recalled the first time she witnessed a group of Apaches giving her husband cash, rather than food or clothing, in exchange for horses. She marveled at the fact that cash allowed him to "go to Tucson and buy any kind of food he wanted," a circumstance that eventually led to a condition unfamiliar to her. "I got fat," she revealed, and found that she was unable to stoop over and put on the new shoes he bought her. On one trip to Tucson, he even offered to buy her a sewing machine, to which she replied, "What would I do with it?" They left it in the shop window. She was also surprised when her husband took her to Tucson to work "for the white people" rather than into Mexico with the other O'odham when their water supply dried up. As further testament to the tribe's preference for mobility, she concluded about her husband: "He was good to me; he took me everywhere. I have been lucky in my husbands; I never had to stay home."[13]

Although leaving O'odham lands to participate in Arizona's cash economy at the expense of older economic networks had become the norm at midcentury, it was not a new phenomenon. For example, during the 1910s, a shantytown occupied predominantly by O'odham sprang up on the southwestern outskirts of Tucson. Concern for the Indian squatters' well-being steadily grew among locals in ensuing years, prompting the Bureau of Indian Affairs to construct a school for O'odham children nearby. A subsequent series of real estate booms, however, threatened this arrangement, as local entrepreneurs began subdividing and selling non-Indians the lands upon which the O'odham were camping. Some of these same entrepreneurs arranged to sell the O'odham plots of land at reduced prices, an offer many evidently could not refuse. Two small subdivisions resulted from these transactions, named, appropriately, Native American Addition and Papagoville. Some O'odham remained in these new neighborhoods, while others opted to move farther south onto public lands. Development followed them wherever they went, however, and by the 1920s the vast bulk of Tucson's O'odham had either purchased lots, moved in with area relatives, or left the city altogether. Still, by midcentury the O'odham had established a permanent presence in Tucson, and, little by little, replaced their once temporary structures with sturdy adobe brick houses.[14]

Aside from the lure of the burgeoning Tucson economy, other forces conspired to thrust the O'odham off the reservation and into the cash economy during the first half of the twentieth century. While drought had long catalyzed O'odham movement, the intervention of the U.S. government in the 1930s only complicated the tribe's latest bout with persistent dry weather by undermining one of their primary subsistence strategies. U.S. government officials, acting through the New Deal's Civilian Conservation Corps, arrived on the O'odham reservation with a livestock reduction plan early in the decade, a plan they hoped would counteract a recent surge in cattle deaths on tribal lands. As one O'odham remembered, "The government tried to tell the Papago cattlemen that cattle died on our ranges because of too many mesquite trees and too many rodents." They claimed that removing mesquite trees and eradicating rodents would encourage the growth of pasture grass that would, in turn, reverse a supposed trend toward overgrazing. Then, without consulting the tribe, officials proceeded to implement their plan.[15]

If they *had* consulted the tribe, they would have learned that the trees represented a key component of the tribe's subsistence strategy. First of all, in the absence of pasture grasses, O'odham cattle ate the mesquite beans. It was also not unusual for the O'odham themselves to eat mesquite beans. Second, the tribe depended on the trees for both firewood and fencing. As one O'odham explained, "Mesquite was weaved together to build corral fences. We didn't use wire . . . because the cattle would get cut up by it." He did concede that the reservation had witnessed environmental change over the course of the previous decade or so, and that the blue grama, common grama, and cotton grasses that had once grown four or five feet high were nowhere to be found by the 1930s. The culprit, however, was not the mesquite trees, but simply drought. He argued: "The Indians knew that it wasn't rodents or too many mesquite trees that caused the lack of grass. It was the lack of rain . . . If it rains, good. If not, then we are hurt. If the cattle are going to die, let them die. But they will die right here on their reservation." Although the O'odham tried to explain to government officials that regional droughts were cyclical and that the O'odham were accustomed to riding them out, in the end the "white man never understood."[16]

Overall, New Dealers had a difficult time implementing their programs in such close proximity to the U.S.-Mexico border. As one historian observed, "In Arizona's borderlands, the Indian New Deal included an extra layer of complexity." Since the border had essentially divided indigenous peoples of similar cultures, languages, and traditions, many of whom often worked side by side with and even intermarried with non-Indians, "decisions about who would or would not be eligible for reorganization seemed arbitrary."[17] But the era proved profoundly significant for the O'odham, since, because of their political reorganization under the auspices of the Indian New Deal, the group began to imagine themselves as a distinct political unit, separate from even close relatives like the Akimel O'odham. Ironically enough, then, the U.S. government was in no small way responsible for the Tohono O'odham's eventual adoption of the rhetoric of nationhood.[18]

At the same time, however, the early twentieth century also witnessed a growing schism between "progressive" and "traditional" O'odham on the reservation. In 1911 a group of O'odham founded the Papago Good Government League, which was essentially a group of "progressive" O'odham. They were mostly Presbyterians, had been educated at BIA schools, considered the allotment of tribal lands and the adoption of a ranching economy to be the keys to economic growth on the reservation, and overall favored assimilation into the American cultural and political mainstream. They also tended to live around Tucson and Sells, the area's two urban centers. More "traditional" O'odham, meanwhile, tended to be Catholics, opposed allotment, were much more likely to uphold tribal traditions such as the annual pilgrimage to Magdalena, and tended to have stronger connections with O'odham living south of the border. They also tended to live in the much less population-dense northern reaches of the reservation, and were more likely to take advantage of seasonal employment opportunities off the reservation. As the historian Andrae Marak put it, "The Tohono O'odham were thus caught between two nations, the United States and Mexico, and two religions, Presbyterianism and Catholicism . . . They were also caught between two worlds, the traditional and the modern."[19] But while "progressive" O'odham appeared ready to embrace assimilation and, especially, education north of the border, they nonetheless appeared committed to governing themselves. As one put it, "We want all of our children educated so that . . . we will have a strong country that the Americans respect."[20]

The schism between northern and southern O'odham was even more acute than the one that divided progressive and traditional O'odham, however. For example, southern O'odham were left out of debates over reorganization during the Indian New Deal era, since according to the Mexican constitution they technically possessed no special status and, thus, no right to a protected land base simply by virtue of their "Indianness." Sanctioning their participation with a "tribal" government was a nonstarter in a nation that does not, according to its constitution, recognize ethnic difference. They were also struggling, as mentioned earlier, with land dispossession. In 1920, for example, an O'odham governor based in Sonoita complained to officials that Mexicans had taken to planting wheat on lands the tribe had long regarded as their own. Shortly thereafter, Mexicans acquired lands on the reservoir side of the local dam and were hoarding the water for themselves. Another Mexican attempted to block O'odham access to one of their wells, while an American cattle outfit began building fences on O'odham lands. The O'odham's attempts to seek redress, as one historian put it, "generally resulted in inaction, the status quo, or their expulsion," while similar attempts north of the border "resulted in the creation of a reservation and governmental efforts to retrieve their property."[21]

This is not to say that *all* of the southern O'odham lands were vulnerable, however. In 1928, Mexican president Elías Calles designated lands around the O'odham village Pozo Verde (amounting to roughly 7,675 acres) an *ejido*. As previously discussed, although the designation implied communal use of the land, it was not what those familiar with U.S. Indian policy would consider a reservation. In fact, when the Mexican government granted the O'odham *ejidos*, they were designated *dotaciónes*, or endowments, rather than *restituciones*. The latter designation would have represented an acknowledgment by the Mexican government that the land had once belonged to indigenous communities, which would have invested the *ejidos* with at least a degree of sovereignty. The former designation, meanwhile, meant that officials would treat the Indians no differently than peasants and farmers in the region. Further, despite the designation, O'odham numbers continued to dwindle dramatically. An American traveler, for example, counted 900 O'odham scattered across twenty-three villages earlier in the century, and by 1930 perhaps as few as 500 individuals living in Sonora identified themselves as O'odham. From here, O'odham *ejidos* near the border found themselves increasingly surrounded by and steadily losing ground to large cattle ranches and other economic interests. The O'odham claimed that outsiders were dividing and selling off O'odham land, enclosing those lands in barbed-wired fences, diverting O'odham water sources, blocking the O'odham's access to grazing lands, and even rebranding O'odham cattle. Then, during the Depression-era repatriation campaign north of the border, Mexican officials began establishing agricultural colonies for recent deportees on lands claimed by the O'odham. Although the O'odham complained constantly, the fact that their complaints appeared to fall on deaf ears led them to conclude that the Mexican government had abandoned them. The end result was that many Sonoran O'odham were simply absorbed into nearby Mexican towns. After surveying the Sonoran O'odham in 1957, one Mexican anthropologist concluded that non-Indian encroachment on O'odham lands had reached crisis proportions, which he considered to be a "grave injustice."[22] By 1930, then, it was clear that the geopolitical border meant something to these Indians, if it had not before. And since it would be decades before northern O'odham would take action on behalf of their relatives living south of the boundary, the line separating O'odham communities from Mexican communities would only continue to blur.

Other problems southern O'odham encountered were religious in nature. The years between 1931 and 1934 were a time of extreme anticlericalism at the highest levels of the Mexican government. What followed was a "defanaticization" campaign designed to secularize, especially, Mexico's educational system and indigenous peoples and communities. The campaign climaxed, at least in Sonora, in 1934 with the ransacking of the O'odham church in Magdalena, in which books, religious icons, and the San Xavier statue itself were burned. The incident convinced many southern O'odham that their children would be better off attending schools in Arizona, where, as one scholar put it, "they would be free to worship as they saw fit, and where, in fact, Tohono O'odham religious beliefs and education were closely intertwined." Thus, anticlericalism served as yet another impetus to migrate north, at least for those who had the means, and connections, to do so.[23]

It should be pointed out that O'odham south of the boundary were not alone in seeming to merge with non-Indian communities. By midcentury a significant number of northern O'odham had permanently moved their residences off the reservation to compensate for general housing and employment shortages on the reservation. Although some returned periodically for social and/or religious occasions, a significant number did not. Many, therefore, further removed themselves from not only their southern contingent's social, political, and economic orbit, but also that of their U.S.-based contingent. This increasing number of off-reservation O'odham began attracting less than flattering press during the 1940s, when several newspaper articles appeared asserting that tribal members were in dire need of assistance. A 1947 article, for example, contended that between 400 and 500 O'odham near and around Tucson were practically destitute. Another article put that figure at 7,000, while yet another cited seventy-five families. While the articles did not agree on numbers, they did agree that the tribe was undergoing a serious economic crisis that was impacting off-reservation O'odham, and also shone a light on deteriorating conditions on the reservation. The O'odham did not entirely welcome the recent press coverage. "What we resent," one O'odham responded, "is the implication that the Papagos as a tribe are a charity case. The morning after the first newspaper story appeared, our Papago children didn't want to go to school. They were embarrassed, as we all were." The tribe quickly began receiving calls and visits from concerned neighbors and charity organizations, including the Red Cross. A tribal representative denied charges of widespread starvation, citing the fact that the tribe possessed 6,000 head of cattle and were typically able to grow enough beans, melons, squash, and other vegetables to support themselves, with some left over. They also pointed out that they had recently donated 200 pounds of clothing to needy Navajo children. "We still are an independent and proud people," he stated, "but . . . acknowledge that larger appropriations for health care, education, roads, and irrigation would vastly improve reservation conditions."[24]

What followed was yet another temporary surge in non-Indian interest in the O'odham's well-being. In 1951, Congress proposed a bill to "rehabilitate" the O'odham reservation. The purpose of the bill was to "establish the members of this tribe on an economic level comparable to that of the rural population of the area; to facilitate their integration into the social, economic, and political life of the Nation; and to hasten the termination of Federal supervision and control special to Indians."[25] As Tribal Chairman Thomas Segundo put it in hearings surrounding the bill:

First, the productivity of the reservation at the present time is so low that it cannot support the population, but the Papago people found the answer when between 10 and 20 years ago this area surrounding the Papago Reservation came under subjugation. When it came under irrigation farms began to develop all around the Papago Reservation. It served as an outlet for the Papago people, because where they could not subsist on the reservation, they went off the reservation, hired out as farm laborers, and still do that. This year 4,500 Papagos, or over 50 percent of the population, left the reservation and went into the cotton fields to pick cotton from about September through January. Some went clear through February into March . . . They had to. For many of them there was nothing to subsist on on the reservation. For many of them that was the only income they were getting . . . That would have to tide them over until the next cotton chopping and picking season.[26]

Segundo went on to remind Congress that the O'odham had been staunch allies of the United States for nearly a century by this point, serving as scouts and guides for the U.S. military during the late nineteenth-century "uprisings in the Southwest" and sending young O'odham to fight—and often die—in both world wars. In fact, they had only recently buried an O'odham soldier who had died in Korea. "We have not gotten much, either," he added. "As an ally of the United States we would have expected better treatment, more assistance from the Federal Government, but we did not get it." This being a point in time when Congress was actively debating the withdrawal of federal responsibility for Indian reservations, Congress was largely unsympathetic. Arizona senator Ernest W. McFarland expressed a troubling, though increasingly pervasive, attitude regarding the Indian presence in the United States: "Don't you think that is one of the troubles here? We have been treating these people as foreign nations too much. We have to treat them more like white people and like everybody else both in expenditures of money and everything else."[27] Despite having the support of the Department of the Interior and various Indian welfare organizations, the rehab bill stalled.[28]

Thus, in 1952 Pima County officials attempted to fill the void left by federal inaction, organizing the Association for Papago Affairs to combat the tribe's economic and health problems. However, non-Indians underestimated the ability of the tribe itself to address internal economic difficulties. Rather than attempt to capitalize on Anglo sympathies, the O'odham, as always, simply altered their subsistence strategy. The new strategy involved maintaining the tribe's land base under the BIA's protective auspices while also forging economic links with surrounding Anglo communities.[29] It should be added, however, that since the 1930s the U.S. government had been encouraging O'odham participation in the larger economy through a series of programs designed to move them off the reservation and into wage work; then relocation programs implemented during the 1950s proved equally influential in thrusting the O'odham into the cash economy. Thus, while the O'odham characteristically took the lead in forging new economic networks and identifying new subsistence strategies, outside pressures often served as an additional impetus. Regardless, at midcentury the tribe turned to southern Arizona's booming cotton industry, a development that ultimately touched off another major set of changes in the tribe's migratory habits.[30]

Perhaps fortuitously, problems on the O'odham reservation corresponded with dramatic changes in the regional economy. In his 1950 study of the Tohono O'odham's work habits, entitled *Papagos in the Cotton Fields*, the anthropologist Henry Dobyns observed that the population of the American Southwest, once quite modest, had grown more than 50 percent over only the course of a decade. "Now most Indians are no longer isolated," he concluded. It was a development that had a decisive impact on the O'odham. Dobyns noted that thousands of O'odham left the reservation each year to work the irrigated valleys and flood plains of the Santa Cruz and Gila Rivers, areas, incidentally, where they had "gone to harvest for centuries," but which they now no longer controlled. He also observed that very few O'odham actually sought employment; instead, employment most often found them. Farmers, foremen, and contractors had long since caught on to the fact that the O'odham were particularly capable and reliable workers (although Dobyns claimed that the Yaquis had the best reputation among Arizona's non-Anglo labor force), and would actually visit the tribe's reservation to recruit laborers. In an interesting parallel to the Kickapoo case study, Dobyns noted that the O'odham typically traveled as family units, with the father, mother, children, and sometimes extended family members all remaining together throughout the harvest season. Although they lived in less than ideal circumstances while on the migrant trail, or in mostly substandard cabins with inadequate floor space, few windows, and poor ventilation, they managed to distinguish themselves in the eyes of employers and fellow workers by making the best of a bad situation. As Dobyns observed, "If cleanliness is next to Godliness, the Desert People living in southern Arizona labor camps are amazingly close to their deity."[31] And the O'odham were not averse to pursuing less conventional employment opportunities. Many appeared as extras in the 1940 Columbia Pictures epic *Arizona*, a film that, as one scholar put it, "not only foreshadowed the Southwest's rise as an iconic film location and tourist destination but also offered a snapshot of racial and cross-border dynamics in Arizona." Some local O'odham, along with local Mexican Americans, signed up for six months of employment at a wage of ten dollars per day, choosing a job as an extra over one as a field hand, however temporarily.[32]

Thus, the need to migrate on a transnational scale for subsistence purposes waned as the tribe learned to take advantage of its proximity to what was in the early to mid-twentieth century one of the fastest-growing economies in the United States. "Papagos have been truly migratory," one scholar explained in 1957, "only so long as there has been a need for it." "I believe," he further speculated, "that we can expect further stabilization of population in the future as the trend continues." Although the Arizona reservation remained an important religious, political, and social center, many O'odham recognized benefits in living outside its boundaries and, to a greater or lesser degree, forfeiting their freedom of mobility. Officials had long operated under the assumption that O'odham living in Tucson were merely "temporary sojourners," but by midcentury they increasingly came to realize otherwise. Non-Indians generally welcomed the O'odham into the urban fold, while the O'odham themselves, as the twentieth century progressed, participated more visibly in southern Arizona's political and economic spheres. But unlike the scenario south of the boundary, the cultural divide between the O'odham and their non-Indian neighbors remained fairly distinct throughout the twentieth century, much as it did in the Yaqui and Kickapoo cases. One local official called this "cultural dualism," meaning that the O'odham had, in a sense, satisfactorily resolved their Indian way of life with that of the larger community where they resided without feeling to need to fully assimilate.[33]

The anthropologist Jack Waddell echoed this sentiment, explaining that the O'odham, although widely distributed in space, remained steadfastly committed to seemingly ancient tribal and kinship responsibilities. He described O'odham tribal and kinship ties as "sentimental domains" linked together over extensive spatial areas, domains that required a great deal of flexibility on the part of the tribe. "A long history of geographical mobility within an extensive but spatially limited area," he concluded, "has produced a somewhat malleable form of family organization that is capable of adapting to a number of economic situations and still provides meaningful relationships with kinsmen." Although O'odham culture remained far from static, it nonetheless retained a profound relevance among tribal members, one whose pull did not weaken even as tribal members fanned out from the tribe's geographic core.[34]

Unfortunately, the O'odham's participation in the cotton industry peaked relatively quickly. During the second half of the twentieth century, O'odham workers began losing this predictable and lucrative source of seasonal employment as more and more cotton growers in the area mechanized. Consequently, migrating for seasonal employment entered a twilight phase. Migrating for religious purposes, however, did not. In fact, the act of migrating for ceremonial observances remained widespread long after economic networks had fallen by the wayside. Further, these ceremonial migratory patterns represented the last of the tribe's transnational networks, or the last link between the two halves of the divided Tohono O'odham nation.[35]

Migrating on a transnational scale for religious reasons had a long history by the mid-twentieth century. Writing in 1894, a non-Indian observer described one ceremony that included a ten-day period before the festivities even began during which O'odham from all over Arizona and Sonora made their way to Santa Rosa, Arizona, bringing produce of all kinds for a feast, which they followed up with a dance. Crossing the border during this period, of course, posed little challenge for the tribe. Still, this same observer, while accompanying tribal members to an O'odham village south of the international boundary, wrote of a prophetic encounter with a Mexican customs official, one that hinted at difficulties to come. "At Sasabé," he explained, "the [Mexican customs] collector explained that he was sorry, very sorry to turn us back, but—. I there issued an ultimatum to the effect that we were going to Altar. The collector looked surprised . . . He desired us to wait until he could send a message to Nogales, but I declined to wait." The expedition continued across the border despite the official's objection, which, as of 1894, evidently lacked any real authority.[36]

Much like Kickapoo migrant laborers, O'odham migrant laborers in Arizona refused to budge on the issue of ceremonial observances, even if they conflicted with their employment obligations. At the peak of the picking season, the O'odham would drop whatever they were doing for the sake of these commitments. Among their most important religious occasions was (and in many cases remains) the Fiesta of St. Francis Xavier, a tradition that likely began in the eighteenth century under the direction of Franciscan missionaries. It started in early October (once the summer's heat and rains had subsided) and sometimes lasted for several weeks. One anthropologist observed, "Many [non-Indian] farmers throw up their hands then, and gripe loudly about families that leave for two or three weeks or a month."[37] The site of the fiesta was the small Mexican town of Magdalena, which is situated about sixty miles south of the U.S.-Mexico border and just west of Mexico's International Highway 15. The main attraction there was a small chapel containing, as mentioned earlier, a statue of San Francisco Xavier, who was, as one scholar describes it, a kind of "composite saint," or a blending of the identity and influence of several religious figures whom the tribe reveres and celebrates for various reasons. He explains: "The story centers around the lives of three men, two of whom died long before Europeans arrived in this region. The first is Father Eusebio Kino, the Jesuit missionary who labored in the Pimería Alta between 1683 and his death in 1711, and who lies buried in the Magdalena plaza. The second is Saint Francis Xavier, a Spanish Basque who died off the coast of China in 1552, and whose body lies in the former Portuguese colony of Goa, on India's west coast. The third is Saint Francis of Assisi, a medieval Italian who founded the Order of Friars Minor or Franciscans. All three have touched our region in a number of ways; the presence of all three is still strongly felt."[38] The O'odham believed that this "composite saint" works miracles on behalf of his adherents and generally watches over the Sonoran Desert. "In some ways he acts more like a local deity than a Catholic saint," one scholar concluded.[39]

The trip to Magdalena alone could take a week or more depending on one's point of origin. And not only were these pilgrimages time-consuming, they were also expensive. In fact, O'odham families would often spend all of the money they had earned up to that point over the course of their stay. According to one observer, they factored in $90 for transportation, food, and lodging for an average-sized family, then would set aside an additional amount for new boots, gifts for relatives, a donation to the saint, beer and mescal, and enough money to, if necessary, "get out of jail the next morning." They also often returned from Magdalena with sacred objects such as religious pictures and statues. Thus, they could easily spend $125 in the space of a week. As for the actual border crossing, he noted that while U.S. tourists had to obtain "tourist permits," this rule proved more difficult to apply to migrating O'odham. Many O'odham spoke neither English nor Spanish, possessed no proof of citizenship, and were often unsure on which side of the border they had been born. "The migration of the Desert People," he concluded, has "given many virtually duel [sic] citizenship."[40]

In 1947, a Tucson-based reporter accompanied tribal members who were en route to Magdalena. "In past years," the article claimed, "the wagon caravans have stretched out for 10 miles," containing as many as 2,000 O'odham. The journey typically took four to eight days, and covered between 140 and 200 miles, depending on the route. The O'odham did not mind the grueling trip, since, according to the article, "it is a holiday, a time for recalling when the Sonora lands belonged to their ancestors, and for telling old tales." As for the border crossing, the article contended, "For years the Immigration regulations of the United States and Mexico have been swept aside by this annual tide of Indians." The World War II years were somewhat different in that immigration authorities required the Indians to obtain a special permit from the Selective Service board to temporarily cross into Mexico.[41] That exception aside, the O'odham appear to have had an informal agreement with immigration authorities that permitted their unfettered transborder movement. This could be attributable, in part, to the fact that, again, the pilgrimage had such deep historical roots. John Russell Bartlett of the United States and Mexico Boundary Commission visited Magdalena during the fiesta in 1851 and estimated that the population of the town had swelled by some 10,000 individuals. He described a lively scene, complete with orchestras playing polkas and waltzes, roadside booths selling food and liquor, and public gambling. And a more recent attendee contended that not much has changed since 1851.[42]

One anthropologist explained that the trip south of the border was "as important to the Papagos as Christmas to Anglos." The meetings were a time for performing baptisms, praying to the saint for cures, and giving thanks for past good fortune, while also a prime opportunity to socialize. Another lure, he contended, was liquor, "the sale of which is not restricted in Mexico, as in the U.S. for Indians." In maintaining these ceremonial obligations, the O'odham typically enjoyed the assistance of their employers, again nearly mirroring the Kickapoo experience. Although some employers scoffed at the O'odham's request, most apparently sympathized with and tolerated their cultural convictions. Growers in the region evidently prized O'odham workers over Mexican and Jamaican contract labor, German and Italian war prisoners (at least during wartime), and inexperienced town laborers, and thus happily contracted them at high wages. And when their workers increasingly began requesting that the growers not only allow them to make their annual ceremonial trips, but also provide transportation, growers often complied. While it typically meant a significant financial loss for the growers, they realized that their crops would likely not get harvested at all without the O'odham's cooperation. Thus, growers could devote a day to transporting tribal members to Mexico via automobile and a day returning from Mexico, and thereby lose much less money than they would have had they allowed the tribe to go by wagon, a more traditional mode of transportation that could mean a three- or even four-week absence.[43]

There have of course been efforts to supplant the annual pilgrimage. Some religious leaders viewed it as simply an opportunity to drink to excess and spend what little money tribal members managed to earn, while taking them away from their responsibilities for up to a month at a time. Father Tiburtius Wand, who administered to O'odham at San Xavier in the 1920s, attempted to offer an alternative to the Magdalena trip by installing a statue of Christ (the origins of which remain shrouded in mystery) in an elaborate case at the mission, where it remains today. Although the statue failed to wean the O'odham off the expensive and time-consuming Magdalena trip, it nonetheless attracted a number of devotees who today often decorate it with metal milagros (a type of devotional object), hospital bracelets, and handwritten notes.[44] Additionally, it is likely no accident that of the thirty-six mission churches constructed by the Franciscans on the Papaguería between 1912 and 1976, only one was placed south of the boundary. Clearly the O'odham homeland was being reimagined on their behalf in light of new border realities.[45]

Although deeply rooted in O'odham tradition, the Magdalena pilgrimage was not without its hazards. The O'odham, much like the Yaquis and Kickapoos, never really had a good relationship with their Mexican neighbors. O'odham Salvador López, for example, relayed an uncomfortable experience during an early twentieth-century pilgrimage to Magdalena from Sells, Arizona. On his way back to Arizona, he made camp with a group of O'odham. Suddenly, a mounted Mexican man entered the camp in pursuit of two Mexican girls. The O'odham men came to the girl's aid, and the Mexican escaped on foot. López pursued him, whereupon the man shot him in the hip. López's companions took him to a Chinese doctor, who treated him with herbs, while another group of O'odham caught up with the Mexican shooter. Mexican authorities ultimately fined the man 500 pesos, while the injury left López disabled. The brush with death discouraged López from returning to Magdalena. Instead, he simply visited yet another saint the tribe had recently acquired specifically for those residing in Sells, a move that further suggests that the tribe was gradually becoming less and less interested in maintaining even religiously motivated transborder migratory patterns.[46]

As noted above, O'odham living in Mexico have been only peripherally affected by what could be considered Mexican Indian policy currents, if at all. This does not mean, however, that the Mexican government neglected them completely throughout the twentieth century. Beginning in 1921, for example, Mexico's Education Ministry targeted the O'odham for assimilation, which in the minds of officials entailed, especially, an embrace of Mexican citizenship. One way to accomplish this, they reasoned, was to force "proper" gender roles on the O'odham, fund schools for O'odham children, and encourage O'odham men to become yeoman farmers. All three goals, it turned out, were unrealistic. Put simply, the O'odham had lost too much land to become farmers, and the fact that fewer and fewer lived on traditional O'odham lands and more and more lived in or on the outskirts of nearby cities and towns made any investment of the Mexican government's time and resources in the O'odham's collective future seem unwise. In fact, one scholar asserted that the 1930s was the last decade the southern O'odham lived in their traditional desert villages in significant numbers, and by the 1960s they could be described as "more or less fully incorporated" into nearby urban areas.[47]

Like their northern counterpart, O'odham on the Mexican side of the boundary also underwent a dramatic period of change near midcentury, though, as mentioned above, not always for the better. Illustrative of the southern O'odham's ongoing woes was a conflict over the placement of fencing near their lands. In 1937, a commission of O'odham arrived at a government office in Hermosillo to file a complaint. They claimed to have suffered "abuses and attacks" that interfered with "the tranquil and peaceful possession of their lands and cattle." Writing to the mayor of Altar, Sonora, Sonoran governor Ramón Yocupicio urged the mayor to "grant them the protection and guarantees which the law grants them, and arrange that they shall no longer be molested in their peaceful occupancy of their possessions and other interests." He encouraged the mayor to consider the U.S. example in "carry[ing] out the foregoing instructions," arguing that the reservation system had helped immeasurably in the "conservation and . . . development of [the Indians'] way of life."[48] The following year, a military official reported directly to the "Constitutional President of the Republic" concerning the arrival of another O'odham commission with a similar complaint, namely, that "their Mexican neighbors have fenced [their lands] in and persecuted them so that they have been obliged to abandon the few lands they have." He urged the president to, essentially, put an end to such injustices and give them the lands "to which they have the right."[49]

From here, however, the situation appears to have deteriorated considerably. The O'odham singled out a single perpetrator—local farmer Jesus

María Zepeda—who they alleged had been erecting fences and trespassing on O'odham lands "from time immemorial."[50] Shortly thereafter, local law enforcement apprehended a group of O'odham whom Zepeda had accused of destroying a section of his fence. State officials ultimately informed the O'odham that Zepeda had already proved to their satisfaction his ownership of 20,000 hectares near O'odham settlements and had their authorization to erect a fence around his property. They also chided the O'odham for resorting to violence rather than "defend[ing] their rights in legal form and manner." Still, the state's governor agreed to revisit the matter and once and for all establish ownership of the disputed lands in order to end the "conflict which has existed for many years."[51] President Lázaro Cárdenas, champion of the Yaqui Indians, had actually already demanded that O'odham in Mexico be given free and clear title to their lands, but the order was apparently not carried out. This was most likely because of the obstructionist tactics of private landowners who stood to lose lands they claimed as their own, but which were known to be the "traditional" lands of the O'odham. In fact, during the presidency of Manuel Avila Camacho (1940–46), a group of Sonoran property owners began pressing the government to relocate the O'odham to lands nearer the coast in an effort to get them out of the way. The O'odham refused to be dislodged, however, despite mounting pressure to move.[52]

As mentioned above, the Mexican government was not completely unresponsive as the O'odham aired their grievances. In March 1943, for example, officials from both sides of the border gathered in Sells in part to discuss persistent land-related difficulties, like those with Zepeda, long experienced by Sonoran O'odham. Among those in attendance were representatives from Mexico's Department of Indian Affairs, a representative from the Ministry of Foreign Affairs, Mexico's chief of animal medicine from the Ministry of Agriculture, various U.S. officials including the superintendent of the Sells agency, and the O'odham tribal council. Much of the meeting concerned the Arizona reservation. They discussed issues related to the regional economy, livestock husbandry, drought/rainfall levels, and irrigation. Interestingly, an official from Mexico's Department of Indian Affairs asked how the tribe determined eligibility for the tribal roll, a question that should have seemed irrelevant in a nation that does not recognize distinctions between Indians and non-Indians, at least officially. According to the meeting's minutes, "The response was that when the Roll was first made the only proof required was simply the fact that people then living on the reservation and [who] had been born there, were considered members of the tribe if they had Papago blood. In case anyone's citizenship was questionable, word of reliable Papagos was required as to that person's eligibility." Post-Indian New Deal, however, tribal members relied on the criteria laid out by their constitution: individuals who appeared on their group's first official census (January 1, 1936), their children, and children from off the reservation who were of one-half or more Indian blood and whom the tribal council agreed to adopt were all included.[53] The meeting, however, showed that officials on both sides of the border were not only attempting to find solutions to persistent problems within indigenous communities, but also beginning to consider these problems within a transnational context.

In this spirit, they also addressed the southern O'odham, ultimately producing a resolution that they hoped would help combat deteriorating conditions south of the boundary. First of all, the resolution created a commission composed of soil conservation experts, an irrigation technician, and a veterinarian, along with representatives from Mexico's Ministry of Agriculture, Department of Indian Affairs, and, interestingly, Ministry of Foreign Affairs. The commission would be charged with locating "the zone in which the Papago Indians of Sonora should reside definitely." Once the commission determined this site, the Department of Indian Affairs was to "deliver the lands in defined property to the Papagos, with all treatments necessary to guarantee them against any plundering," and encourage cattle raising and agriculture among tribal members.[54] Officials made clear, however, that they had no intention of establishing a "reservation" for O'odham south of the border. Yet while they vowed not to segregate the Indians, they also vowed not to force their acculturation. Finally, they also made clear that only O'odham of Mexican nationality could reside on the Sonoran lands; otherwise, officials feared that the presence of "North American Papagos" would compromise Mexico's territorial integrity.[55] This plan evidently failed to materialize, however, as evidenced by the southern O'odham's repeated pleas for assistance from their northern counterpart. O'odham south of the border would continue to struggle mightily with a largely unresponsive Mexican government.

It appears that O'odham in Mexico were not alone in their feelings of neglect. In 1948, Dr. Hector Sánchez, then head of Mexico's Department of Indian Affairs, delivered a speech in which he characterized *all* Mexican Indians as "geographically and socially disconnected," with only "marginal contact with national culture." In short, they often lived beyond the legislative reach of the Mexican body politic and the cultural orbit of Mexican society, which complicated efforts to improve their material circumstances.

And little seems to have changed in many spots around Mexico, with the Sonoran O'odham emerging in recent decades as a prime example. Experiencing disappointment when appealing to the Mexican government, then finding that their entreaties increasingly fell on deaf ears north of the boundary, many simply resigned themselves to a life of uncertainty on the margins of two nations. O'odham Clemencia Antone perhaps best summed up this predicament. Although born in Mexico, she never considered herself a Mexican, nor did she even bother to learn the Spanish language. She had no personal attachments to the Mexican nation per se, only those O'odham lands that happened to be situated within its borders. And yet because of her place of birth, U.S. officials denied her the privilege of citizenship and unfettered movement north of the boundary, as well as access to the same forms of governmental assistance that "American" Indians, including her fellow O'odham, today enjoy. Thus, she exists beyond the political and cultural purview of one government, and does not fulfill the requirements to live under the auspices of the other. "To me both governments see everything in black and white," she said. "There are no gray areas and that is where I am, in the gray area."[56] It was a familiar predicament for each of the indigenous groups discussed herein, but one perhaps most acutely felt by the O'odham.

While the second half of the twentieth century witnessed a gradual stabilization of the O'odham population, this did not mean that they completely abandoned their migratory tendencies. It did mean, however, that O'odham movements had become far more predictable and, most significantly, overwhelmingly confined within each half's respective borders. In 1962, census takers indicated that although approximately 60 percent of the northern O'odham population remained mobile, their movements consisted of little more than a seasonal shift between on-reservation and off-reservation homes, with the latter most often in Tucson. About two-thirds of the tribe engaged in seasonal and part-time wage work, while some of these people also maintained small herds of cattle and subsistence agricultural plots on the reservation. Others subsisted primarily on welfare payments.[57] This pattern appeared irreversible. After all, the tribe had moved full force into the regional economy, first as agricultural laborers, and eventually as prominent participants in the more general occupational structure of the American Southwest. Although a minuscule number of O'odham families (one anthropologist estimated about six or seven) still eked out a living raising cattle on the reservation near Sells, the vast majority of the roughly 11,000 O'odham had entered a new phase in their collective history. It was a phase that would require what one scholar described as a "more dynamic process of adaptation" than the tribe had mustered up to that point.[58]

By the end of the 1960s it was clear that Arizona's economy was transitioning from one based on farming, ranching, and mining to one based on high-tech and service industries. Off-reservation jobs that allowed the O'odham to live on O'odham lands at least part-time became harder and harder to find, thereby forcing the O'odham to focus on creating on-reservation jobs and, when these proved inadequate, seeking out permanent employment elsewhere. Nearly 40 percent of the O'odham population would end up settling everywhere from Tucson to Chicago to Los Angeles. Tucson, not surprisingly, had the largest off-reservation O'odham community anywhere. Although individual O'odham appeared to have proactively assumed control of their economic destinies, the reality was that they were growing increasingly dependent on the tribal government, the federal government, and large corporations.[59] The historians Andrae Marak and Laura Tuennerman summed up the predicament facing the O'odham, arguing that "the shift from self-sufficiency to engagement in a larger economy" placed the O'odham, along with other minorities, "in a particularly precarious position during national economic downturns." "It is ironic perhaps," they continue, "that as self-sufficiency was shed in favor of inclusion into the larger society, it was the problems of American society—rather than its benefits—that the Tohono O'odham often experienced."[60]

A subsequent breakthrough for northern O'odham occurred in 1970, when they began seeking compensation through the Indian Claims Commission (ICC) for lost lands. Created by the federal government in 1946 for the purpose of resolving outstanding disputes involving Indian land, the ICC was a thinly veiled attempt to legally abrogate Indian claims once and for all so that the government could continue terminating Indian tribes and relocating Indian peoples. Although the O'odham submitted their petition to the ICC in 1954, it would take more than ten years for the commission to hear the case, then another decade or so to dispense the O'odham's settlement money. The ICC ultimately concluded that the tribe had at one time legally possessed aboriginal title to much of southern Arizona, including the site of the city of Tucson, and had been unjustly divested of those lands by non-Indians. It agreed to award the O'odham $26 million. More important than the monetary award, however, was the symbolic significance of the judgment. As the historian Eric Meeks explained, "In the future the tribe would use this as state-sanctioned evidence for the expansion of its autonomy," making the ICC award "yet another building block in the construction of the Tohono O'odham nation."[61]

In the late 1970s, then, the Tohono O'odham tribal council began using some of its expanded power to address persistent problems faced by its southern counterpart. According to Mexico's National Indian Institute, by 1979 the number of O'odham living in Sonora had dwindled to about 200. Such figures can admittedly be misleading, since those O'odham who temporarily worked and/or lived elsewhere were likely excluded. Nonetheless, at the top of their list of complaints, not surprisingly, were non-Indian encroachments on their lands. Although the Mexican government, as previously mentioned, had designated lands around Pozo Verde an *ejido*, those Indians who remained migratory, or who moved seasonally between their home villages and various places of employment, had a difficult time protecting the territorial integrity of their *ejido*. While they were on the migratory trail, their lands fell little by little into the hands of private ranchers. Once made aware of this trend, the Mexican government proved surprisingly responsive, ultimately setting aside another 50,000 acres of land for communal use by the O'odham. Northern O'odham also responded to this crisis, passing a series of resolutions in 1979 that collectively condemned the Mexican government for not doing more to protect O'odham lands, calling on a joint Mexican, U.S., and United Nations investigation of continuing encroachments on O'odham lands in Sonora. They also demanded the guarantee of "free access across the international Border and freedom to worship through ceremonials and traditional rites at all Papago sanctuaries and religious sites." By the end of the 1970s, then, Tohono O'odham on both sides of the U.S.-Mexico border had a clear sense of themselves as first and foremost tribal citizens whose own nation's borders just happened to overlap those of surrounding nation-states. That awkward orientation, however, would prove increasingly consequential as the century progressed, and that sense of tribal citizenship would suffer as a result.[62]

Broader fears that conditions along Arizona's southern border were deteriorating began attracting widespread official attention, which ultimately served to blunt the O'odham nation's renewed attempts to extend its sovereign reach into Mexico. In 1977, one newspaper account characterized the southern border of the O'odham reservation as a "'no border' border." The seventy-five-mile fence separating Arizona and Sonora was so full of holes by this time as to render it meaningless, and the author easily located unlocked gates across dirt roads that crossed the boundary line. The article continues, "And there are no signs proclaiming: 'Welcome to the United

Two Tohono O'odham crossing a fallen section of border fence in southern Arizona. Photograph by John Malmin. Copyright 1977, *Los Angeles Times*, used with permission.

States' or 'Bienvenido Mexico.' There is nothing, in fact, to indicate that you are crossing from one country to another, just the barbed wire fence with its myriad openings." The area had no border station and no agents checking for documents or questioning anyone's citizenship. "Officials of both countries," the author adds, "pay no attention to people moving back and forth—so long as they are Indians. For this is Papago country." "It is the strangest section of the 1,966-mile line separating the two nations," the article concludes.

Even stranger were some of the practices the reporter uncovered. Mexican O'odham seeking medical attention simply crossed into Arizona and were apparently "never turned away" at the government-run hospital in Sells, as had long been the custom. Further, many of these same O'odham regularly crossed into Arizona to collect welfare checks, which could be easily acquired by simply giving officials the home address of an American O'odham accomplice. O'odham children typically went north of the border for schooling. In a profoundly telling claim, one O'odham told the reporter, "You can be what you want to be when you are Papago—either a Mexican or an American." Another put it a little more mildly, stating, "We Papagos have dual citizenship. We are citizens of both nations whether we live on the Arizona side or the Mexican side of the border. That is why we can go back and forth with no papers."[63]

However, dynamics along the Arizona-Sonora border were changing rapidly, and the scenes this reporter witnessed would soon be a thing of the past, as would the O'odham's already tenuous claim to dual citizenship. The same article characterized the reservation as "a funnel through which thousands of illegal aliens have entered the United States." Drug smugglers were also increasingly drawn to the isolated reservation and its often unguarded crossing points. U.S. officials responded to these alarming changes by establishing the first all-Indian U.S. Customs force in the country, consisting of fifteen men and headquartered at Sells. It was an unprecedented attempt to address an unprecedented problem in what one customs official characterized as a "most unusual place." "Both sides of the international boundary have always been the land of the Papagos," he explained. "Before Mexico. Before America. And so it is today." The O'odham enthusiastically echoed the sentiment. "For us the border is an artificial barrier," explained one O'odham, "a meaningless symbol that cuts through the heart of the age-old Papago nation."[64] But by the late twentieth century, the "meaningless symbol" could no longer be ignored.

All of this is not to imply that the border did not have practical implications for the O'odham prior to the 1970s. Although the evolving regional economic dynamics discussed above had a lot to do with the abandonment of more traditional transnational migratory networks, the border itself was not blameless. For example, in the 1940s Sonora was riding out an epidemic of hoof-and-mouth disease, prompting officials on both sides of the border to carefully monitor, and in many cases halt altogether, transborder traffic. It was during this period that O'odham Henry José crossed into the United States to volunteer for the U.S. Army. After he was turned down by the military, U.S. immigration officials detained him because of the epidemic. He was not allowed to return to his ranch in Mexico for several years, which proved disastrous. "When I got home," he later explained, "my house was gone, my land was fenced, and my cattle were mixed in with someone else's herd." He then filed a complaint with the Mexican government. However, because he lacked official documentation attesting to his ownership of the land, authorities dismissed the complaint. "My father was born on the land," he said, "and I think his father, too. And they told me I couldn't live there and if I cut any fences or took any of my cattle back, I'd be arrested and sent to jail. I lost everything. I had to hire out as a ranch hand and I had to pick cotton on the other side."[65] But whereas problems like José's were, once upon a time, essentially anomalous, similar violations of the rights of individual O'odham became far more widespread in the 1970s as the O'odham reservation once again began attracting unwanted news coverage and the wrong kind of official attention.

The O'odham's ability to come and go at will continued to deteriorate, ultimately prompting the publication, in 2001, of a book entitled *It Is Not Our Fault: The Case for Amending Present Nationality Law to Make All Members of the Tohono O'odham Nation United States Citizens, Now and Forever.* In it, they explain: "Our Nation is divided. Our people are no longer free to live, work and travel. Our families are separated. We cannot visit the sacred places where our ancestors rest . . . Under present law, some of us are subject to arrest, prosecution, incarceration, and deportation because we do not have documents . . . Our vehicles have been seized." Although many O'odham were born in the United States, few had documents attesting to that fact. "If I do not really exist," queried O'odham Johnson José, referring to his inability to acquire a birth certificate, "how come I am paying taxes?" Further, no birth certificate meant no retirement benefits, even after a lifetime of hard work. Roughly 1,400 O'odham lived south of the boundary as of 2001, and often expressed sheer puzzlement as to why they now had to obtain permission to travel across their own tribe's lands. "We live in fear," they poignantly concluded. O'odham Art Babachi went so far as to propose the seemingly impossible, writing, "I ask Congress to take away the border. Make the land to the north and the land to the south all O'odham land again.[66]

Aside from problems with undocumented immigrants and drug traffickers, the tribe had also confronted an increasingly aggressive border patrol that often seemed determined to curtail tribal movements. "Recently," one O'odham claimed, "incidents have been reported in which members of this nation were prohibited from entering the U.S. . . . in order to meet hospital appointments at the Indian Health Service hospital in Sells, and their hospital appointment records and tribal membership cards were confiscated." Tribal members with tuberculosis, diabetes, and other life-threatening illnesses have been denied care to which, according to O'odham law, they are legally entitled, and forced to return to Mexico by non-O'odham agents operating on O'odham land.[67] "Even though I am a great-grandmother," wrote Ruth Ortega, "the U.S. Border Patrol still chases me . . . Now when [they] stop me, I am tired of talking to them and answering their questions so I only talk O'odham to them and they let me go." Rita Bustamante, who census takers included on the 1937 trial roll compiled by the Bureau of Indian Affairs, also encountered constant obstacles any time she tried to cross. Unable to conceal her frustration, she argued, "All of these lands are O'odham lands. It should not be so hard to cross." "The boundary has hurt me," explained María Jesús Romo-Robles, "because I cannot see my children. They cannot come and see me because they cannot safely return north." Those born in Mexico and attempting to live in Arizona were subject to arrest, prosecution, and deportation, an irony not lost on George Ignacio. "My father told me that in 1937 the United States recognized my Nation . . . as a sovereign government . . . Although my father was Chairman of the Tohono O'odham Nation, in your words, he was an 'illegal alien.'" "They do not want to recognize that we have been here for millions of years," he added, concluding, "We are a Nation. It makes me feel bad when we are called 'illegal aliens.' It is degrading."[68] Living near the border is one thing, but living *on* the border, the O'odham were learning the hard way, was another. Their geographic orientation had virtually guaranteed the perpetual omnipresence of non-O'odham authorities and an environment of heightened (and often mutual) suspicion.

Stepped-up efforts on the part of the Border Patrol made casualties of key O'odham traditions for more than a few tribal members. Alejandro Velasco explained, "The last several years I have been unable to attend the St. Francis ceremony in Magdalena. When I try to cross the boundary, the Mexican officials tell me that my Tohono O'odham membership credential is worthless and they turn me back." As a consequence, the O'odham have instituted what one scholar referred to as a "floating" Fiesta of San Francisco, meaning that it is held at a different village each year, but always north of the boundary. "I just do not even try to cross anymore," Mary Anita Antone stated, lest she risk getting "stuck on the other side." "We are lost between two worlds," added Francisco Velasco, perfectly summarizing the tribe's predicament.[69] "Our People and our Nation," *It Is Not Our Fault* succinctly concludes, "cannot continue to suffer the consequences of a series of historical oversights."[70] Thus far, however, officials north of the border have shown an unwillingness to act on the O'odham's behalf, with perhaps one exception. In 2001 Congress was preparing to pass a bill that would have granted U.S. citizenship even to those O'odham living in Mexico, but the 9/11 terrorist attacks meant that the bill ended up on the back burner.[71]

Meanwhile, despite the Mexican government's efforts to shore up the southern O'odham's land base, their dispossession continued, and perhaps accelerated, as the twentieth century began winding down. One historian explained:

> *Mestizo* farmers in Sonora continuously encroached on their settlements, leasing them or poaching them outright. In the mid-twentieth century, Sonoran O'odham lived in some twenty settlements, but by the end of the century they only inhabited eight. Moreover, only a single family lived in each of these localities, whereas between two and five families had lived in them in the mid-twentieth century. The vast majority of Sonoran O'odham had left their rural villages to work on Arizona's Sells Reservation, or in cities such Tucson, Caborca, or Hermosillo, where they sold bread and tortillas, worked on ranches and mines surrounding these cities, or performed manual labor. To survive, some worked for Mexican drug cartels, which benefitted from their family connections on both sides of the border and their familiarity with the routes and terrain of the Arizona-Sonora border region.[72]

Population figures are telling. From the mid-twentieth century to 1990, Arizona's O'odham population went from about 7,200 to over 17,000, while Sonora witnessed a decline from 400 to less than 50 during the same period. And although some no doubt remained, the 1990 Mexican census did not count any O'odham at all.[73] Perhaps more so than the Yaquis and Kickapoos, then, the Tohono O'odham have struggled mightily to reconcile tribal boundaries with those of the two nation-states within which historical circumstances beyond their control placed them. The twenty-first century found the Tohono O'odham nation hopelessly divided. While many southern O'odham weathered the long string of assaults and emerged with their culture and identity intact, they appear to have, as Andrae Marak and Laura Tuennerman put it, "a culture and identity different from that of the Tohono O'odham living north of the border." They also struggle with often acute poverty. Those in the north, meanwhile, enjoyed the benefit of BIA-administered health, social, and educational benefits. But although a small number of northern O'odham landowners have prospered by leasing their lands to mining companies, and an even smaller number have prospered as ranchers, problems on the reservation abound. By the second half of the twentieth century, the O'odham's average family income was only a fifth that of whites, many did without electricity and running water in their homes, hundreds of O'odham children did not attend school because families relied on their labor, 25 percent of children born on the reservation did not survive their infancy, and more than 50 percent did not survive to the age of eighteen. One can understand, then, the need to remain mobile, to migrate off-reservation on a temporary or, increasingly in recent decades, permanent basis.[74] But perhaps the unforgiving desert environment should share the blame with the seemingly arbitrary international boundary. As the anthropologist Ruth Underhill concluded in the 1970s, "The desert has scarcely changed. Unless some modern miracle can make it livable, its people must still move back and forth. Now they travel farther and stay longer. But they come back."[75] It was a fitting observation, and one that retains a particular resonance to the present day.

Still, like the Yaquis and Kickapoos, the Tohono O'odham have refused to forfeit their hard-won transnational way of life. As discussed above, the annual Magdalena pilgrimage remains on the ceremonial calendar for many O'odham, representing what one scholar considers "the continuation of a process of mediation between the regional and the international, a process that has been going on since Father Eusebio Kino started work [there] about three hundred years ago."[76] And there is recent evidence that the sense of neglect felt by southern O'odham discussed at the beginning of this chapter is perhaps beginning to abate. For example, in 1993 a mining company set up shop on *ejido* land that contained Quitovac, one of nine O'odham villages in Sonora. O'odham living near the mine gradually grew troubled by the mine's presence and suspicious of its claims that its operations were environmentally sound. Soon the O'odham began blaming the company's unfenced cyanide leach pit for a host of disturbing environment-related developments, such as the poisoning of animals and the contamination of a nearby sacred spring. Northern O'odham soon joined their southern counterpart in protesting the mining enterprise. O'odham leaders from both sides of the border held a series of community meetings to devise a plan of action, and from this renewed spirit of cooperation emerged two key things: a petition, which the O'odham submitted to Mexico's agrarian attorney general, demanding the revocation of the mine's permit, and the recognition, for the first time, of the authority of traditional O'odham leaders south of the border. In doing the latter, O'odham north of the border made clear their desire to reverse the pattern of political and cultural estrangement from the tribal whole that had proved so detrimental and disorienting to southern O'odham. Their actions also suggested a desire to make whole again what was at least a nascent O'odham nation, one that the U.S.-Mexico border divided before it had the opportunity to fully coalesce.[77] Although regular transborder movement has more or less ground to a halt among the O'odham as a consequence of what might be called the militarization of the border, they have time and again proved adept at pursuing tribal agendas and maintaining tribal imperatives in the face of seemingly insurmountable odds. The situation may appear grim in some respects, in other words, but certainly not for the first time.

When the O'odham produce images of their creator, I'itoi, whether in jewelry, baskets, or other works of art, he is very often situated in a kind of circular labyrinth or maze. In some stories, the maze represents a map either to or from his cave, which, as mentioned above, is said to be beneath Baboquivari Mountain. In other stories, as the historian José Antonio Lucero explains, it "represents the choices one encounters along the journey of life." He continues, "As religious, imperial, and state practices divided the O'odham people along multiple lines, they made the O'odham vulnerable to threats from many sides." Thus, the image provides "an apt metaphor for the twists and turns of the collective history of the Tohono O'odham people and nation," since, like I'itoi's maze, these divisions ultimately "created new paths for O'odham politics." These paths may have been intermittently bumpy, but any adversity seems only to have strengthened the O'odham as a collective. It is fitting, then, that the so-called man in the maze appears on the "unofficial" O'odham nation flag.[78]

6   All the Doors Are Closing and Now It's Economic Survival

Federal Recognition

∙∙

Before I built a wall I'd ask to know
What I was walling in or walling out,
And to whom I was like to give offence.
—Robert Frost, "Mending Wall"

Writing to Arizona congressman Morris K. Udall in 1964, Tucson attorney A. Turney Smith aired his objection to a proposal to carve out a Yaqui reservation on the city's outskirts. "These so-called Indians are not Indians in the proper sense of the word," he wrote. "They are a mixture of several breeds—they have no nationality—no home and are not citizens of any country." Granting the Yaquis land, Smith argued, would amount to planting a "Leprosy colony" near Tucson. "When these Yaquis get hold of liquor," he claimed, "they get wild and will do most anything even to killing." Udall's response, though diplomatic, was terse. Evidently unwilling to dignify Smith's allegations with a defense, Udall simply wrote, "I don't quite know what I can do with your objections." Another local attorney, however, wrote Udall with a more measured objection. "The defining of a Yaqui," he argued, "is almost an insurmountable task. What we have done is taken in a very broad class of persons as eligible for [tribal] membership . . . I do not believe there would be any way to know definitely the names of all the individuals we desire to benefit."[1] He had a point. Even as late as the 1960s—more than half a century after Yaquis began filtering into Arizona from Mexico— officials had yet to clarify their status or determine if they were Mexican nationals, Mexican Americans, Mexican Indians, or American Indians.

Initially, few Yaquis living in Arizona bothered applying for U.S. citizenship, primarily because of the relatively steep twenty dollar application fee. With an unclear citizenship status, however, they could not formally own land, and thus often remained, decades into the twentieth century, little more than squatters of uncertain nationality. Furthermore, status issues increasingly impeded their transborder movement as the twentieth century progressed, complicating (if not thwarting altogether) efforts at maintaining open lines of communication with their southern counterpart. In short, by the mid-twentieth century Yaquis in Arizona were more vulnerable to the whims of outsiders than those living along Sonora's Yaqui River. They enjoyed none of the legal protections afforded "American" Indian groups nor the economic safety net enjoyed by American citizens, and evidently never failed to recognize the precariousness of their situation.[2]

The fact was, however, that by 1964 the tribe had stabilized its presence in Arizona, and tribal members had little intention of abandoning their adopted homeland. Since transplanted from the Yaqui River valley in the late nineteenth and early twentieth century, Yaquis living in the United States had made remarkable strides in rebuilding Yaqui society and culture, or at least a "variant stream" thereof. Although some locals may have doubted the "legitimacy" and/or "authenticity" of the tribe's claims to Indianness, those most intimately acquainted with them had little reason to question their commitment to tribal life. The Arizona contingent of the Yaqui tribe had long maintained an elaborate ceremonial schedule, particularly at Easter; had remained distinct from surrounding Mexican communities; and had remained firmly committed to educating all tribal members in the Yaqui language, tribal customs, and tribal history.[3] Still, in order to secure their presence in Arizona, tribal members needed to convince outsiders of not only their legitimacy and authenticity (which, if the letters to Udall were representative, was a tall order), but also their commitment to their adopted homeland. Ultimately, the tribe decided to undertake the federal acknowledgment process, or to seek a status as "American" Indians, even given the glaringly obvious fact that they had not originated within the borders of the United States. As the self-appointed arbiter of Indianness in an era when Indian policy currents were again shifting, the U.S. government would ultimately have no choice but to carefully consider a case that, at least on its surface, could not have seemed more open and shut (of *course* they were not "American" Indians). In characteristically audacious fashion, however, the Yaquis would force all involved to reconsider even basic definitions and assumptions that had long guided not just American Indian law and policy but also national citizenship. However preposterous a bid for recognition might have seemed in the eyes of many Arizonans, the tribe's determination to assert its sovereignty was becoming difficult to ignore.

At roughly the same time, the Kickapoo Indians hit upon the same strategy. Frustrated with living beneath the international bridge when not on the migrant trail and weary of being plagued by status issues while on the move, the tribe sought, once and for all, to negotiate a protected land base in its adopted home of Eagle Pass, Texas. Like the Yaquis, the Kickapoos ultimately turned to the federal acknowledgment process, thereby leaving them open to similar lines of criticism, namely, that they were either a "foreign" or "Mexican" tribe, that they simply did not meet the criteria of an "American" Indian tribe, or that they did not have substantial enough historical ties to the state of Texas. But given the peculiar nature of the federal acknowledgment process, at least in the late 1960s and the 1970s, the evidence could, in the right hands, be made to suggest otherwise. Put simply, the Mexican counterpart of the Kickapoo tribe, although significantly smaller and seemingly cut off from the primary center of Kickapoo life in Oklahoma, had a long-standing reputation as militantly separatist and profoundly conservative, even among fellow tribal members. Over the course of the twentieth century, Yaquis in Arizona gradually acquired a similar reputation. While it was difficult to question both groups' "Indianness," the question of their nationality, as this chapter shows, proved far stickier.

The federal acknowledgment process, then, became a sort of litmus test, a way to determine if their hard-won transnational patterns of life, their right to migrate on a transnational scale, and their right to forge, maintain, and even strengthen transborder tribal ties would ever acquire more formal acceptance. It became a test of the degree to which indigenous groups residing in North America were independent, sovereign political entities, or whether the policies of surrounding nation-states would forever trump tribal agendas and initiatives. It also became a test as to whether the powerful, omnipresent nation-states that the United States and Mexico had become would tolerate the existence of these anomalous indigenous nations. After all, both tribes boasted a long history of evading and/or resisting state authority, while also steadfastly refusing to remain confined within non-Indian borders. Thus, far more than serving as the strategy of choice in legitimizing their claims to Indianness, to some sort of authenticity as indigenous peoples, federal acknowledgment, at least north of the border, would also legitimize their right to govern themselves *wherever* they chose to reside. It would come at a price, however, since convincing U.S. officials to grant them a status as "American" Indians meant distancing themselves from at least a portion of their transborder counterparts. In other words, they were forced to downplay the extent to which they remained mobile and/or maintained transborder political, economic, and social ties. Thus, the indigenous nations that had coalesced in the U.S.-Mexico borderlands would, near century's end, emerge diminished versions of their former selves. Given their tumultuous and violent histories up to this point, however, a little stability and security likely seemed worth the trade-off.

This final push for stability and security would propel these tribes into legal and political circles for the first time, where they would demonstrate an impressive level of resourcefulness and political sophistication as well as a surprisingly all-encompassing commitment to tribal life. They found willing accomplices in a host of scholars and educators, sympathetic legal professionals, and, perhaps most importantly, politicians. This chapter examines first the federal acknowledgment process itself, then these tribes' late twentieth-century experiences with the process. Taken collectively, their experiences reveal a refusal to compromise certain tribal imperatives along with a reluctant willingness to share power with surrounding political entities in the interest of peaceful coexistence. While the Yaquis and Kickapoos, in only a few years, went a long way in clarifying their statuses with both the U.S. and Mexican governments, explication of the Tohono O'odham's status, particularly that of its southern counterpart, remained elusive. What emerged as the twentieth century closed, then, was not a story of unqualified triumph, but rather of difficult compromise and ongoing struggle. Still, the late twentieth century marks a watershed moment, when these transborder indigenous peoples finally forced officials on both sides of the border to confront, sometimes in concert, a host of troubling issues posed by indigenous claims to nationhood that directly challenged their own, claims that clearly were not going away.

"Recognition" and Its Evolution

The federal acknowledgment process has a long history. Problematic to the core, it essentially represents an attempt to place legal parameters on the concept of "culture." While the concept of culture is shaky enough on its own, when it has been introduced into legal idiom, the results have typically been baffling, leaving lawmakers, as well as those placed in the unenviable position of interpreting their laws, with more questions than answers. Yet, as the historian Richard White wrote, "Cultural conventions do not have to be true to be effective any more than legal precedents do. They only have to be accepted."[4] Thus, the two are not all that different. After all, both are essentially political constructs, both develop and evolve in response to external stimuli, neither can exist in a vacuum, and, perhaps most significantly, only through popular acceptance can either acquire any measure of legitimacy and relevance.

U.S. Indian law has never been known for consistency. According to the legal scholar Sidney Harring, "U.S. Indian law lacks historical vision because it is so policy oriented and so full of contradictory objectives."[5] Major precedents have often arisen out of singular, isolated events, while legal policy currents have not exactly been immune to the influence of popular political movements. And its traditional status as "judge-made law" has frequently subjected it to all manner of prejudices, political agendas, and questionable ideological commitments.[6] Yet the foundation of Indian law has remained unchanged since the Supreme Court handed down three landmark decisions, *Cherokee Nation v. Georgia* (1831), *Worcester v. Georgia* (1832), and *Crow Dog* (1883). These decisions, respectively, established the idea of Indian reservations as "domestic dependent nations," introduced the concept of tribal sovereignty, and ultimately gave birth to a "pluralist" legal tradition in the United States, meaning one set of laws for Indians and one set of laws for everyone else.[7]

We should not attach too much significance to the role of case law in defining the character of U.S. Indian law, however. As Harring astutely observes, "The record of Indian peoples' attempts to protect their sovereignty defines the legal concept of sovereignty more accurately than does a long line of ambiguous federal cases, and the history of this struggle is a vital part of the U.S. legal tradition."[8] Although all three tribes under consideration here fought vigorously to protect their tribal sovereignty, they ultimately realized that there were limits to what they could achieve without forfeiting at least some of that sovereignty through compromise with the dominant political entity or, in the case of these transborder tribes, entities.

Although tribal sovereignty remains the linchpin of Indian law, in practice, at least north of the border, the concept falls apart without federal acknowledgment of an Indian group's right to "tribal" status. The emphasis placed on tribalism in Indian law, however, became increasingly problematic throughout the early twentieth century as more and more Indian groups living within U.S. borders began demanding federal acknowledgment of their sovereign rights as a "tribe," and the federal government found itself unprepared to respond to the question of what exactly constituted a tribe in the first place. The Yaqui and Kickapoo cases introduced additional variables in that these groups only relatively recently (in the

Yaquis case), or only occasionally (in the Mexican Kickapoo case), called the United States home. Attorney William Quinn Jr. has proposed perhaps the most helpful framework in examining the development of the federal acknowledgment process in an effort to address these complicated questions in a systematic way. He describes the evolution of the federal acknowledgment concept as a shift from "cognitive" recognition, meaning that federal officials simply "knew" a tribe existed, to "jurisdictional" recognition, whereby federal officials legally acknowledged a tribe's status as a "domestic dependent nation" to be dealt with on a government-to-government basis.[9]

Formal recognition most often took place when the federal government began granting reservations during the nineteenth century. Although the concept of recognition had not been formally articulated, officials nonetheless "cognitively" acknowledged the legitimacy of tribal organizations based on their history of relations with the federal government as well as their physical location on a federally sanctioned reservation. Treaties existed as another avenue to acknowledgment, but the federal government discontinued the practice of treaty making in 1871, leaving unrecognized tribes seeking to change their status with little recourse. Other less common methods of acquiring federal acknowledgment included executive orders, unilateral statutes, and approval of a request for recognition by the secretary of the interior.[10] Thus, since the U.S. government handled the acknowledgment process largely on a case-by-case basis and through a confusing array of methods, unrecognized groups that sought to obtain the benefits of federally acknowledged status, such as government-financed health, education, and other developmental programs, as well as recognition of their sovereign rights as a political entity, had no clear idea where to begin. Moreover, the development and evolution of federal acknowledgment from abstract notion to articulated legal concept was a painfully slow process, plagued by linguistic and conceptual ambiguities, legal setbacks, and often alarming policy shifts.

Still, for tribes seeking to recreate a relatively autonomous tribal existence in the United States in the twentieth century, acquiring federally recognized status represented a quantum leap in the right direction. The Yaquis and Kickapoos both found themselves embroiled in the struggle to change their status with the U.S. government in the second half of the twentieth century, as did many other tribes. What makes these tribes' experiences unique, however, is the fact that they had to overcome the additional burden of often being labeled "Mexican," as opposed to "American," Indians. Not being "native" to the immediate areas within which they resided, these tribes had difficulty convincing local and federal officials that they were entitled to lands and federal benefits typically reserved for those groups who had established a relatively stable presence within the current boundaries of the United States centuries earlier. From these tribes' perspectives, however, the fact that circumstances beyond their control either encouraged or forced them to assume a transnational orientation was of little import and should not be held against them.

Perhaps they were not "native" to the regions they currently inhabited, but they could still accurately claim to be "tribal" peoples. Or could they? The question of what constitutes a tribe, at least north of the border, has been endlessly debated. For example, during the 1898 case *Dobbs v. U.S.*, the Court of Claims tried to define the term "tribe," and concluded that "a nation, tribe, or band will be regarded as an Indian entity where the relations of the Indian[s] in their organized or tribal capacity has [sic] been fixed and recognized by treaty . . . [and where there is no treaty] the court will recognize a subdivision of tribes or bands which has been recognized by those officers of the Government whose duty it was to deal with and report the condition of the Indians . . . [and] where there has been no such recognition by the Government, the court will accept the subdivision into tribes or bands made by the Indians themselves."[11]

The "tribe" designation acquired increasing complexity as it relates to the acknowledgment process in the 1901 *Montoya v. U.S.* case, which established a distinction between being "recognized" by the federal government and being "in amity" with the federal government. In this case, the Supreme Court found that while the federal government had, in fact, recognized the Chiricahua Apaches as a band, their status differed from that of other tribes owing to the fact that they were not "in amity" with the United States at the time. While the implications that this case had for authorities' conception of the term "tribe" were significant, legal scholars still discuss the case for different reasons altogether. The case marks the first articulation, however vague, of not only what constituted a tribe, but also *how* a group might go about changing its status with the federal government to "recognized."

In fact, the legal scholar William Quinn refers to the *Montoya* decision as the "Montoya test," meaning that it had become the new standard in defining "tribe."[12] Here the Supreme Court concluded, "By a 'tribe' we understand a body of Indians of the same or similar race, united in a community under one leadership or government, inhabiting a particular though sometimes ill-defined territory."[13] The decision would have far-reaching implications for the acknowledgment process, essentially plotting the future trajectory of its development. Its emphasis on a stationary, distinct tribal community and a functioning tribal government, in other words, represented a big step forward as the process began taking shape. For the time being, however, debate continued. In his 1892 annual report under the subheading *What Is an Indian?*, Commissioner of Indian Affairs T. J. Morgan admitted, "One would have supposed that this question would have been considered a hundred years ago and been adjudicated long before this. Singularly enough, however, it has remained in abeyance, and the Government has gone on legislating and administering law without carefully discriminating as to those over whom it has a right to exercise such control."[14]

Perhaps the first case in which federal courts directly addressed the issue of federal acknowledgment came in *United States v. Sandoval* (1913), which represented an attempt by the Supreme Court to limit the "plenary power," or essentially absolute power, of Congress over Indians. The Court argued against the perceived congressional right to extend its authority over a group or community by "arbitrarily calling them an Indian tribe." Rather, the Court insisted that only after a group was formally identified as a "distinctly Indian community" could Congress determine "whether, to what extent, and for what time they shall be recognized and dealt with as dependent tribes requiring the guardianship and protection of the United States."[15] However, the parameters of "Indianness" that officials became more and more conscious of establishing through this long succession of related court cases became less distinct as the concept of "culture" came to the fore during the John Collier era of Indian affairs (1933–45). The so-called Indian New Deal, with the Indian Reorganization Act as its centerpiece, attached a great deal of importance to federal acknowledgment by establishing that only "recognized" tribes would receive BIA-related benefits. It contained the clearest statement yet: "The term 'Indian' as used in this Act shall include all persons of Indian descent who are members of any recognized tribe now under Federal jurisdiction, and . . . all other persons of one-half or more Indian blood."[16] Collier then listed all formally acknowledged tribes, some 258 Indian groups, including the Tohono O'odham but not the Kickapoos or Yaquis, in order to determine voting eligibility in approving or rejecting the IRA. The issue then became, "How, then, can an unrecognized Indian group *establish* recognition?"[17]

Between the enactment of the IRA and the mid-1970s, this question would occupy government officials and scholars alike. In his seminal *Handbook of Federal Indian Law*, published in 1942, the legal scholar Felix Cohen stated, "The question of what constitutes tribes or bands has been extensively con-

sidered in recent years by the administrative authorities of the Federal
Government in connection with tribal organization effected pursuant to section 16 of the Act of June 18, 1934."[18] Cohen then attempted to outline five
criteria that the Interior Department generally considered when making
such a determination:

(1) That the group has had treaty relations with the United States.
(2) That the group has been denominated a tribe by act of Congress or
    Executive order.
(3) That the group has been treated as having collective rights in tribal
    lands or funds, even though not expressly designated a tribe.
(4) That the group has been treated as a tribe or band by other Indian
    tribes.
(5) That the group has exercised political authority over its members,
    through a tribal council or other governmental form.[19]

Following a period of substantial progress in the development and articulation of the federal acknowledgment process, the U.S. Congress fell
silent on the issue in the postwar years, and remained so until the 1970s.
Instead, Congress began the 1950s with the termination policies, which, as
discussed earlier, essentially relegated governmental responsibilities for Indians in the areas of social welfare, education, law enforcement, and economic assistance to the individual states, thereby effectively severing tribal
ties with the federal government and abolishing some reservations.[20] The
new legislative trend made federal acknowledgment seem like a moot point.

It was not until the Johnson and Nixon administrations that the issue of
federal recognition came to the fore once again. These administrations over-
saw the production of perhaps the most exhaustive survey of the history of
federal Indian policy ever written. The congressional commission in charge
of the study, known as the American Indian Policy Review Commission, issued a two-part overview in 1977 that contained separate recommenda-
tions from eleven task forces. The volume produced by Task Force #10
examined "Terminated and Non-federally Recognized Indians," and contained a long list of unacknowledged tribes. The task force concluded by
suggesting the establishment of federal acknowledgment criteria and procedures in an attempt to address the needs of these unrecognized tribes. It
was not long before the BIA began receiving petitions from groups interested in obtaining federally recognized status. In fact, by the mid-1970s the
Interior Department had over forty on file. The Interior Department immediately issued a temporary set of guidelines until an official system could

be developed, and within ten months, on September 5, 1978, the department finalized and implemented the revised procedures.[21]

The seven criteria established by 25 CFR 83, the "Procedures for Establishing That an American Indian Group Exists as an Indian Tribe," state that an Indian group's petition must

- a) establish that they have been identified from historical times to the present on a substantially continuous basis as an American or aboriginal;
- b) establish that a substantial portion of the group inhabits a specific area or lives in a community viewed as American Indian, distinct from other populations in the area;
- c) furnish a statement of facts which establishes that the group has maintained tribal political influence or other authority over its members as an autonomous entity throughout history until the present;
- d) furnish a copy of the group's present governing document . . . describing in full the membership criteria and the procedures through which the group currently governs its affairs and members;
- e) furnish a list of all current members . . . based on the group's own defined criteria. The membership must consist of individuals who have established, using evidence acceptable to the Secretary of the Interior, descendancy from a tribe which existed historically or from historical tribes which combined and functioned as a single autonomous entity;
- f) establish that the membership of the group is composed principally of persons who are not members of any other North American Indian tribe;
- g) [demonstrate] that the group or its members are not the subject of congressional legislation which has expressly terminated or forbidden the Federal Relationship.[22]

Fulfillment of these provisions in petition form is only one aspect of the acknowledgment process. Because the entire process comprises several stages, it is often quite lengthy. At least more recently, from the time that the BIA receives the petition, three months typically elapse before it reaches the BIA's Branch of Federal Acknowledgment (BFA, later renamed the Office of Federal Acknowledgment). The BFA then notifies the petitioner of any readily apparent deficiencies and extends the petitioner the opportunity to revise and resubmit the petition if the problems can be easily remedied. The petition then languishes for approximately one year until it is given "active consideration" status. Often referred to as the "waiting period," the one-year span is the result of a tremendous backlog of petitions awaiting review. During the active consideration period, BFA staff carefully examine the petition section by section, often taking up to eighteen months to do so, as this stage requires site visits, a verification of genealogical claims and documentary evidence, and a search for any additional evidence. The BFA then produces a written decision concerning whether to tentatively approve or reject the petition, which is then published in the *Federal Register*. After the decision's publication, the BFA requires another 120 days to elapse to allow for any rebuttals or other objections from government officials. In the event that the BIA has no further objections, it publishes the finalized decision and extends federally recognized status.[23] Recent estimates put the number of unrecognized Indian enclaves in the United States at well over 200, while the BIA currently recognizes approximately 332 Indian tribes, bands, or other entities (a number that does not include Alaskan natives). Within less than a decade after implementing the procedures, the BIA had already received 91 petitions, and by 2004 had received more than 250.[24] Anthropologists believe that a pattern of geographic distribution among these unrecognized tribes exists, namely, that they have largely been found on either the Eastern Seaboard or the western coast, or in the Deep South.[25]

A broad and fairly common complaint among tribes that have undertaken the acknowledgment process is that the procedures do not allow for the pressures of acculturation, which are easy to succumb to without previous government protection.[26] As the historian Alexandra Harmon has observed, "People who profess to be Indians have had to defend their claims with a frequency and rigor seldom demanded of people in other ethnic or racial classes."[27] Herein lies an inherent flaw in the recognition process. Legal precedent has gradually established the notion that Indian rights are not racial, but political. In other words, the tribe is viewed as a political unit rather than as a collection of individuals from a common ancestry.[28] However, the U.S. government still has not developed a satisfactory definition of "tribe." Does the designation require documented lineage from a historic tribe, a history of community-based political organization, or the recognition of a tribe's claim to "Indianness" by the surrounding community, or is it simply a question of cultural retention in the face of pressures to assimilate? In practice, the procedures require all of these things and more. Furthermore, scholars generally agree that Indians have, since long before contact with whites, viewed themselves as nations, or at least some form thereof, until having the label "tribe" foisted on them by non-Indians. The phenomenon of the "tribe," then, is little more than the product of colonialism. Still, the U.S. government insists, up to the present day, that petitioning Indians exhibit at least some of the characteristics of nations, such as consistent territorial claims, some degree of political organization, and at least an informal legal code, without allowing for the fact that policies emanating from imperial powers and, later, nation-states have, for the most part, had as their primary objective the elimination of all of these things.[29]

Nevertheless, the BIA, shortly after implementing the procedures, estimated that approximately 30 percent of petitioning groups would ultimately be granted federally acknowledged status. And as the anthropologist Susan Greenbaum asserted in 1985, "The BIA's interpretations [of the petitions] thus far have exhibited considerable flexibility with respect to limitations and adaptations imposed on the unrecognized tribes by virtue of their status." She adds that recent decisions have placed little emphasis on cultural retention but have instead looked for proof that the group has "retained sufficient internal organization and stability of membership to be able to reasonably enter into a government-to-government relationship." In this regard, Greenbaum concludes, the BIA has been more than fair.[30] Furthermore, the BIA revised its regulations in 1994 to lessen the burden on petitioning groups. Among the more notable changes were ones concerning the hopelessly vague provision requiring Indians to prove that non-Indians had identified them as Indians "from historical times to the present." After 1994, petitioning groups only had to go back to 1900. The BIA also qualified the provision calling for evidence of self-government. Instead, petitioning groups had only to prove that a distinct community existed at key moments in the group's history.[31] But criticisms of the process still abound. Some contend that the BIA's Office of Federal Acknowledgment (OFA) has not been consistent in the application of the criteria, to the benefit of some petitioners and the detriment of others. Others have characterized some OFA staff as incompetent and/or unqualified, too secretive about their methods and findings, and too bound to rigid and even outmoded notions of "authenticity." Still others argue that the office has been too generous, and has thus recognized too many tribes in too hasty a fashion. The fundamental problem with the process, however, seems to be that federal bureaucrats have become, in one historian's words, "colonially empowered voices in Indian identity debates," while the acknowledgment process itself has become just another form of "white paternalism" and another means of "exerting colonial power." It is no wonder, then, that for petitioners the process has tended and still tends to stoke "anxiety, shame, anger, grief, and feelings of inadequacy over cultural loss."[32]

Regardless, as the Yaqui and Kickapoo cases demonstrate, the acknowledgment process could exhibit a great deal of flexibility, particularly since these groups undertook the process while it was still in its formative years. In retrospect, and in light of the number of tribes who have failed in their efforts to achieve recognition, these groups' bids for a status change seem improbable and their success almost like a strange oversight.[33] After all, a quick glance at the acknowledgment criteria is enough to lead one to conclude that these tribes were not eligible by a long shot. Yet a look at their experiences reveals a dizzying array of factors working to their advantage. Simply put, the right people came together at the right time and place. The tenacity on the part of the tribes and the sympathy and even indignation on the part of influential neighbors, coupled with the peculiar cultural and political dynamics within the U.S.-Mexico borderlands region during the mid- to late twentieth century, combined to make their recognition a reality. Put another way, these groups had located within the U.S.-Mexico borderlands what one historian called "clandestine social spaces," spaces beyond the purview of officials within which their cultures could flourish and their collective identity could remain intact. Another historian referred to these spaces as "forbidden landscapes," or regions that are often "at the crossroads of empires, nations, markets, and cultures," where corporations, states, and regional entrepreneurs have often tried, and have often failed, to assert control. When the time came to convince both locals and local officials north of the border of their "Indianness," then, they were ready.[34]

The Yaquis and Federal Acknowledgment

For the Yaquis, that opportunity came in the 1960s. Since migrating, the tribe had long relied on non-Indians for assistance as it sought to stabilize its presence in Arizona, but it was during the 1960s that tribal members found their most powerful advocates. Writing to Arizona congressman Morris Udall in 1962, Robert Roessel, then director of Tempe's Indian Education Center, discussed interesting parallels to the Yaqui situation elsewhere in North America. He wrote, "It is very interesting to compare the present situation of the Yaqui to that of the Rocky Boy Cree and Chippewa, and Indians of Montana during the 1900s." These Indians were at one time residents of present-day Canada, and gradually migrated into the present-day United States, where they remained. "After being a political football," Roessel continued, "finally justification prevailed and these Indians were assigned a reservation and placed under the Bureau of Indian Affairs." A local attorney, in a letter to Udall, added two more names to the list: the Metlakatla Indians of Canada, now residing in Alaska, and the Cocopa Indians of Mexico, now residing in Arizona. The Yaquis faced a similar predicament, and Roessel could not help expressing his desire for a similar outcome. He concluded, "Each of us, I am sure, can think of dozens of rational reasons why the Yaqui are not entitled to the service of the Bureau. At this point I am more interested in the humaneness of the situation and trying to find what can be done to help this destitute and forgotten group." Another attorney put it more succinctly: "Recognition is and probably will continue to be a determination of the merits of each case. In my opinion, the case of the Yaquis is indeed meritorious." Another local, cutting through the legalese, argued, "With all of the acres of sunshine available in Southern Arizona, there must be a place for them on federal land."[35] Those familiar with the Kickapoos expressed similar sympathies. "I'm not only willing, but I'm very eager to help you secure justice," vowed one official to a contingent of Kickapoos assembled at a congressional hearing, adding, "History tells us, certainly, that more than enough terrible injustices have been heaped upon the American Indians and I think whenever we have a remedy before us to undo some of that injustice and secure justice for you, we should use that remedy."[36] Since these kinds of attitudes pervade the history of Indian-white relations in the United States only once in a while, the spirit of the times, so to speak, seemed to be on the Indians' side.

Sudden local interest in the Yaquis likely stemmed from unwanted press coverage. On February 2, 1970, an article appeared in the *New York Post* entitled "The Plight of the Yaquis, Our Invisible Indians." "Fearful of deportation," the article begins, "one of the strangest groups of expatriates in history has been 'hiding' in the U.S. since the late 1800s. They live in some of the worst slums in America and have never sought citizenship." It quotes twenty-seven-year-old Virginia Balthazar, allegedly "one of few Yaquis to graduate from high school," as stating, "My people have always been afraid that if they speak up and ask for help they will be deposited on the other side of the border." The article describes Pascua as "a collection of tin, scrap wood and cardboard shacks" with "no indoor toilets, running water, electricity, sidewalks or paved streets." Its inhabitants, it continues, were habitually unemployed, unskilled, and illiterate. But things were changing, the article goes on to explain, since Morris Udall had sponsored a bill, still moving through Congress, to grant "those 'foreign' Indians" 200 acres of federal land near San Xavier Mission. Further, the Office of Economic Opportunity (OEO) and other relief organizations were taking notice of the Yaquis, providing assistance with housing and education. "Fear of recognition is starting to disappear," Balthazar told the article's author, concluding, "Not all Yaquis are accepting the old ways—the belief that it is better if nobody knew they existed."[37]

Though well meaning, the article understandably upset the Yaquis. Three weeks later, they mailed a letter to Udall requesting his assistance in pressuring the paper to issue a retraction, and enclosed a petition, containing fifty Yaqui signatures, in support of the action. "We don't know where this so-called journalist got his information," the letter reads, "but it is clear that he turned this half-hearted attempt to get a story into an oversimplification, and if that weren't enough, at least half of what he said was just plain bunk." The tribe evidently feared becoming a stereotype, and wanted the world to know that they, in fact, paid gas and light bills and were more than just unskilled, illiterate squatters, and that the deportation fears the author described were "ancient history." "We wrote to you," the letter concludes, "because of your prominence and interest, hoping that you will act on our behalf."[38] While the tribe apparently never received the retraction it requested, it did receive an encouraging response from Udall. In it, Udall calls the article "grossly inaccurate." He adds, "The suggestion that the Yaquis are fearful of deportation is ridiculous, since most Yaquis today are American citizens." Udall then promised to send along a copy of his and the Yaquis' letters to the author to make their objections known.

The article might have applied to an earlier generation of Yaquis, but by the second half of the twentieth century, those Yaquis north of the U.S.-Mexico border had come far in solidifying their presence in their adopted home and were poised to take the next step in fully realizing Yaqui nationhood in the United States. In this effort, Udall and his political associates proved invaluable assets. The tribe's push for federally recognized status began in earnest in the early 1960s, with a proposal to resettle the Yaquis at a new village site. By the mid-1950s, the city of Tucson had grown to the point that it very nearly surrounded the Yaquis' neighborhood. As the city began demanding property taxes from the group, Yaqui families began losing their lands to foreclosure. They found temporary assistance through the Marshall Foundation, a charitable trust that assisted the tribe in meeting their new tax burden while also helping tribe members acquire additional plots.[39] At the same time, however, the Yaqui community was itself expanding, and its present village site, due to space constraints, did not permit further growth. "At present," one newspaper reported in 1963, "some 600 Yaquis are crowded on a tract of land located west of Oracle Road and just south of Grant Road. Suffering from extreme overcrowding and substandard housing conditions, the area is corroded with poverty and many families live in dwellings so poor they are not adequately protected from the winter cold." According to the tribe, three and even four Yaqui families at a time often shared a single house due to overcrowding. It was around this time that Yaqui Anselmo Valencia, who would spearhead their push for recognition, visited Black Mountain in the Sonoran Desert and had a prophetic vision. He saw the tribe living peacefully on a plot of land far from Tucson's bustle, or far from the warehouses, nightclubs, and brothels that abutted their present village site. Shortly thereafter, Valencia began exploring his options and, most importantly, developing a relocation plan. With the assistance of the anthropologists Edward Spicer and Muriel Painter, Valencia ultimately selected a 202-acre plot of federal land one mile south of Valencia Road and roughly ten miles southwest of downtown Tucson. The plot, all involved agreed, held a great deal of promise.[40]

The plan may not have gotten off the ground without the help of Morris Udall. Udall, a former student of Edward Spicer's, vowed to assist the tribe if elected to the congressional seat just vacated by his brother Stewart, who had recently begun his tenure as secretary of the interior. To Udall, the undertaking was a good idea not only from a humanitarian standpoint, but also from a political one. As expected, the largely Democratic district elected Udall, and Udall, staying true to his campaign promise, went to work on the Yaquis' behalf. In May 1963, he introduced a bill that would allow the transfer of federal land to the tribe free of charge. It also called for the creation of the Pascua Yaqui Association, a nonprofit corporation headed by tribal members and charged with administering to the tribe.[41]

Earlier that year Udall had told a group of Pascua Yaquis that he expected the land conveyance to occur within six months. "It will be your land," he reassured them; "you can do what you want with it." One article reported that "good natured laughter" erupted when Anselmo Valencia added, "And it won't be on a reservation." The differences between the legal status of the Yaquis' land grant proposal and that of reservations were myriad. First of all, the nonprofit, Indian-run corporation, not the Bureau of Indian Affairs, handled the allotment of individual plots to individual families. In fact, the BIA would not be involved at all since the Yaquis, as of yet, did not have a legal status as American Indians. Second, the lands, once allotted, were subject to taxation and state and county jurisdiction in legal matters.

Finally, officials imposed an important ground rule, one typically reserved for recognized tribes. In order to occupy the new village site, Yaquis had to be at least one-quarter Yaqui, married to a Yaqui, or affiliated with the Yaqui religious order. They also had to have resided in the old village for at least a year. These provisions, one can assume, were designed to prevent a sudden influx of Yaquis, or even persons claiming to be Yaquis, from Mexico.[42] The Yaquis themselves, meanwhile, bristled at the provision. "Any Yaqui knows who is a Yaqui," one tribal member contended. Still, these provisions remain largely intact today.[43]

The Yaquis also launched a public relations campaign of sorts, enlisting Muriel Painter to help the tribe prove their "Indianness" to members of Congress. With the use of Painter's 1962 brochure, *Faith, Flowers, and Fiestas*, with its portrayal of Yaqui ceremonial observances, the tribe hoped to remove all doubt as to their authenticity by appealing to popular conceptions of Indianness. They also tried to fashion an image of themselves as humble, grateful refugees, committed to a colorful culture that was undeniably worth preserving, and pointing out that a small piece of federal land was the surest route to achieve those ends. Interestingly, Anselmo Valencia also adopted the practice of referring to himself as "chief," even though the title had little meaning to the Yaquis themselves.[44]

Resettlement of the Yaquis to a new village site was not without controversy. One local educator called it "a violation of every principle upon which this nation was founded" and "discrimination of the worst kind" in a country where every effort was being made to end segregation. Another local educator put it more bluntly, stating that the Yaquis "need new homes and would love to have better housing—but not at the expense of being buried alive way out in the country. You cannot motivate people to move forward when the only image they have is of the past." Some Yaquis, too, were uncertain about the benefits of the move, and felt that other Yaquis and local officials were placing undue pressure on them to relocate. Eventually, then, a small group of tribal members began adding their voices to the chorus of detractors, claiming that transportation problems would hinder Yaqui employment and that the schools nearest the new village site were already too crowded.[45]

Still, Udall proceeded to steer the relocation bill through the House Committee on Interior and Insular Affairs in 1964, and ultimately met with little opposition. President Johnson subsequently signed the legislation in October of that year. The Pascua Yaquis' initial elation at this surprising turn of events proved short-lived, however, when the tribe learned that realizing Valencia's dream of a Yaqui settlement on Tucson's arid outskirts would require a great deal of funding, which the Bureau of Indian Affairs was in no way obligated to provide. Again with the assistance of Edward Spicer, the tribe began seeking out alternative sources, and ultimately succeeded with President Johnson's newly founded OEO (which was designed to help wage his War on Poverty), to the tune of $433,000 over four years. The Pascua Yaqui Association, with Valencia now serving as its executive director, managed the federal funds, pouring them into services such as adult education classes, vocational training, welfare assistance, and summer youth programs, while also funding a number of new construction projects, including a Yaqui church. Meanwhile, the bulk of the region's Yaquis still resided at Old Pascua, as the original site came to be known, and remained suspicious of Valencia and the new community, resentful of its economic progress, and unsure of the wisdom of relocating to the still relatively isolated locale. In fact, tensions festered to the point that the two communities temporarily severed ties.[46]

Although New Pascua initially prospered, its success depended on OEO funding. Richard Nixon's 1972 presidential victory, however, spelled disaster for the fledgling program. Nixon almost immediately dismantled the OEO, and along with it the Pascua Yaquis' primary source of funding. The tribe, now facing a serious financial crunch, temporarily considered pursuing state recognition as an American Indian tribe, but backed down in the face of overwhelming opposition from Arizona's other Indian tribes. As one Arizona Indian explained, "We don't want them to dip into funds which are already inadequate," adding, "The Yaquis are from Mexico, outcasts from Mexico."[47]

In the mid-1970s, then, the Pascua Yaquis decided to push for federally recognized status. One newspaper editorial admitted that the request was problematic. "The Yaqui is considered to be a Mexican tribe," the article states, "but so, at one time, was the Papago Indian tribe." While most considered southern Arizona largely O'odham territory, the article contended, anthropological evidence suggests that the Yaquis' territory once extended well north across the U.S.-Mexico border. Still, the article raised concerns about whether the group possessed the requisite degree of internal organization to pass as a "tribe." "Indeed," the article continues, "the Yaqui people in Arizona have never had what could be called a tribal structure in the traditional sense. Their history in this country has been primarily as wards— of the state, of religious groups, of private organizations and foundations and well-intentioned philanthropists who helped, fought over and with the Yaqui people." By the mid-1970s, their unclear status had left the Yaquis in a difficult position. Their village needed a new sewer system, yet the fact that the land was under federal trust meant that the county could not build one. Officials denied the tribe access to federal Indian programs because they had not been formally declared American Indians. The tribe's village had little, if any, police protection, and financing for additional housing was becoming increasingly hard to come by. The editorial, in the end, recommended federal recognition, but opined that any legislation should include a stipulation forbidding further migration from Mexico. Perhaps not surprisingly, it also reported strong opposition from other Arizona tribes, tribes that felt that "the federal pie for Indians" was "already cut too thin." Indeed, the eight Arizona Affiliated Tribes ultimately expressed opposition, as did the Colorado River tribes and the White Mountain and San Carlos Apaches, while the Hopi reportedly lent "informal" support. As for the O'odham, they were, according to one Yaqui, "pretty quiet and still thinking about it."[48]

Meanwhile, the proposal sent at least one contingent of Yaquis, in the words of one reporter, "on the warpath." These Yaquis, most of whom lived at Old Pascua, feared the loss of "their rights as individuals and their freedom of choice" if they submitted to a status as "wards of the federal government." Some had an "intense aversion" to the prospect of being referred to as "American Indians" rather than "Yaquis." "There is a strong feeling," one Yaqui claimed, "that we are 'Yaquis' first and 'Indians' second." Further, they feared that a status as "reservation Indians," with all the term connoted, would demean the tribe, whether or not they chose to live on the reservation. Finally, they feared that reservation status for New Pascua would all but cut off aid to nonreservation Yaquis, or those living primarily in Old Pascua, South Tucson, Marana, which is just northwest of Tucson, and Guadalupe, a town fifteen miles south of Phoenix. "After they get all the money for their reservation," one Yaqui speculated, "maybe we won't get any, and every bit of money coming in we might be fighting them for." Still other Yaquis, however, feared the complete dissolution of Arizona's Yaqui community should the federal government not come to their aid. In Valencia's words, "Without their help, New Pascua would become a deteriorated community with no administrative function for running our own village." Another popular sentiment among tribal members was that the new status was the last hope for ensuring the preservation of *any* vestige of

Yaqui culture and traditions in Arizona. "We've been independent of the government all these years," one Yaqui concluded, "but all the doors are closing and now it's economic survival."[49]

The momentum the proposal initially garnered proved short-lived. "After being held in a House subcommittee on Indian affairs," editorialized one local paper in 1976, "a bill giving the Yaqui Indians tribal status hasn't moved an inch. But meanwhile, the problems of the Southwest Indians continue to grow, and will keep increasing until the bill is rescued from Congress' legislative jungle." Local officials and tribal members alike feared the bill was dying from "inaction," a fate that would threaten "the hope and livelihood of the Indian group with little chance of preserving their history for the future."[50] Their fears proved well founded. In 1977 that inaction forced tribal members to place their drive for federal recognition "on the back burner," in the words of one local reporter.[51] Another blow came later that year, when Ramon Ybarra, then director of the Pascua Yaqui Association, died of an "undetermined illness." Ybarra, who, interestingly, participated in the 1961 Bay of Pigs invasion during the Kennedy administration, worked tirelessly on behalf of the tribe to promote its cause, and his death hurt morale and left a leadership void.[52]

May of the following year witnessed a renewed and more aggressive move on behalf of the Yaquis to gain federally recognized status. With the aid of the Native American Rights Fund, the tribe sent a spokesperson directly to Washington to discuss the proposal face to face with the House Subcommittee on Indians Affairs. The committee ultimately agreed to at least consider legislative federal recognition.[53] Congressional hearings regarding the Yaqui request for federal acknowledgment commenced during September 1977. Arizona senator Dennis DeConcini was the first to testify on the Yaquis' behalf, stating, "There is no doubt in my mind that this recognition is both earned and needed. The assistance that could be extended through existing federal programs, services, and facilities, although a minuscule portion of the resources of this great country, would be a tremendous boost to these Native Americans who have struggled alone for so long."[54] In response to questions regarding their claim to "Indianness," Edward Spicer lent his considerable expertise in the form of a letter to the committee. He wrote: "The native Indian language continues to be spoken by the Yaquis in Arizona. The distinct Yaqui customs which have been uniquely their own since before the time of European discovery continue to shape and influence their way of life. This central core of Yaqui culture is highly prized by the Yaquis and has been maintained through the whole course of their unique and difficult historical experience."[55]

By March of that year the tribe could say with some confidence that federally recognized status would be forthcoming. "We are somewhat assured it will pass," stated Valencia, further noting that the tribe had, thus far, encountered little or no organized resistance, having easily garnered the support of other Yaquis, anthropologists, community leaders, and national Indian groups. The bill included an important stipulation, however, namely, that federal benefits would apply only to members of the Pascua Yaqui Association, which numbered roughly 2,500, those who could prove at least one-quarter Yaqui blood, and, perhaps most significantly, those who had proof of U.S. citizenship. Residence at New Pascua was not a prerequisite; the bill also included Yaquis living in South Tucson, Old Pascua, Marana, Guadalupe, and even Los Angeles.[56]

Valencia clearly recognized, however, that their efforts to push the bill through Congress would likely fail without addressing the fact that a large number of Yaquis still lived along the Yaqui River in Mexico and regularly migrated into the United States. More specifically, Valencia felt it important to establish the fact that recognition would protect the future of only American-born Yaquis, stating, "Out of approximately 2,500 members of the Pascua Yaqui Association, about 20 were born in Mexico. They are people from 60 to 98 years old; unfortunately, they will not be with us for too many more years."[57] The Yaquis also carefully noted that they would not be "campaigning" for additional Yaquis to add to the tribal rolls, even though about 6,000 Yaquis called Arizona home.[58] A Yaqui nation that truly transcended the U.S.-Mexico border, Valencia seemed to realize, simply could not survive the recognition process. His appeal convinced Congress, and in 1978 it approved Public Law 95-375, which provided federally recognized status to the Pascua Yaquis and made them eligible "for all Federal services and benefits provided to Indians because of their status as Indians."[59] Interestingly, the Yaquis claim the distinction of being the last tribe to obtain federally recognized status prior to the promulgation of the formal Federal Acknowledgement Process. Had they pursued recognition through the Bureau of Indian Affairs rather than through the legislative process, their bid very likely would have failed. The latter route was simply too rigorous and, one could argue, inflexible, at least when addressing an anomaly like the Yaquis.[60]

It is important to note, however, that the bill passed in a compromised form. Rather than grant the tribe unconditional federally recognized status, a modified version of the bill gave the state continued civil and criminal jurisdiction over the tribe's village site. Still, it retained the most important features of the original proposal, including the recognition of the Yaqui tribal government, reservation status for the New Pascua site, and unfettered access to federal Indian programs. The final bill, however, contained no provisions limiting membership or establishing any requirements for future membership. This task ultimately fell to the Pascua Yaquis themselves, and in ensuing years Yaquis living throughout Arizona would gradually settle in New Pascua, swelling the ranks of Arizona Yaquis to about 15,000 by the end of the 1990s.[61] Though the Carter administration initially objected to the tribe's recognition, it ultimately relented, since, according to a House staff member, Udall was handling Carter's civil service reform bill, and the administration wanted to avoid "get[ting] Mr. Udall mad."[62]

The battle over the tribe's status, however, was not over, and difficulties and resentments would fester in ensuing years. The 1978 recognition bill officially classified the tribe as an "adult Indian community," and not a "historic tribe." The differences between the two are far from negligible. A historic tribe enjoys the full range of powers granted to federally recognized Indian peoples, including the right to enroll new members, control inheritance laws, create and enforce a civil and criminal justice system, and determine population size, without BIA oversight, when applying for federal benefits. A nonhistoric tribe, or adult Indian community, does not have unconditional control of its tribal rolls (although the Yaquis were an exception), and policy changes within the tribal government require the approval of the BIA. Further, these tribes cannot levy taxes, condemn property, or maintain law and order on their reservation. Finally, these groups carry the unfortunate label of "created tribe" in the eyes of the federal government. Thus, in 1993, the Yaquis, this time with the assistance of Ed Pastor, Udall's congressional successor, pushed for a final clarification of their status, a status that would entitle the tribe to full sovereignty. Not surprisingly, the BIA objected on the basis that the tribe did not originate in the United States. "I don't think we're saying that the Pascua Yaquis are not a tribe," stated a BIA representative, "but it's not just 'a tribe is a tribe is a tribe.' There are historical differences. It may seem like hairsplitting to Congress, but we have a procedure . . . and there are many groups that don't qualify under the law. It's very dangerous to set a precedent that says all Indian groups are the same." Interestingly, it had taken the BIA all these years to call the tribe's pedigree into question. A historic tribe, the spokesperson continued, "has existed since time immemorial and its powers are derived from its in-

extinguishable and inherent sovereignty." The BIA looked for direct ancestral links between Arizona Yaquis and the mother tribe, but claimed, after
having researched the matter, only to have uncovered a "series of unrelated
lineages." The Yaquis understandably felt that the BIA was misrepresent-
ing their history, and answered with an assertion that the tribe has "roamed
since pre-Columbia days across Arizona and the rest of the Southwest." One
Yaqui elaborated, "Yaqui clans and customs would not have survived if only
individual Yaquis had crossed the border, but did survive because the tribe
came across as villages, clans and as a tribal group." While the state recognized a government-to-government relationship with the tribe, the federal
government held out, and has yet to revisit the issue.[63]

The Kickapoo Bid

As was the case with the Yaquis, the Kickapoos' problems, many of which
stemmed directly from their unclear legal status within the United States,
worsened as the twentieth century progressed. "The Kickapoo Tribe, Mexicans and North Americans at the Same Time," read one Mexican headline.
The 1979 article went on to characterize the group as "dead and forgotten,
without a house or a home," and simply waiting for their "inevitable extinction, which will probably occur within the next decade, more or less."[64]
An earlier article, again of Mexican origin, placed the Kickapoos on a short
list of Mexico-based tribes heading for extinction (incidentally, the list also
contained the Yaquis). It counted only one hundred Indians residing in
Nacimiento, and claimed that their economic circumstances were increasingly forcing tribal members into the United States on a more permanent
basis. It concluded that the few remaining Indians stubbornly refused to
abandon their land solely because their children were born there.[65]

Numbering between 600 and 700 people, the Mexican Kickapoos were,
in fact, increasingly calling Eagle Pass, Texas, home, despite the fact that
conditions there were less than ideal, to put it mildly. The tribe's living conditions did not go unnoticed by their non-Indian neighbors. As previously
noted, the city of Eagle Pass granted the tribe a small piece of land on an
informal basis during the 1960s. The small plot, however, proved woefully
inadequate for ceremonial observances, and some Kickapoos evidently continued to live beneath the international bridge. Thus, the tribe adopted the
habit of migrating north of the border to work, then south of the border to
meet their ceremonial obligations, while making their home in between.
Over time, the group's ties to Eagle Pass grew stronger and stronger. In

explaining their attachment, one Kickapoo stated, "We refer to Eagle Pass because our grandparents and our forefathers are buried there. This is why we refer to that as our home ground." "Our forefathers came from the United States," another Kickapoo later told a congressional committee, "and we like the United States and are proud of the fact that we originated from here." Yet the specter of forced removal still loomed. As another Kickapoo revealed to the committee, "Every day we go to bed with fears that tomorrow we are going to be thrown out of there."[66]

The first action on the tribe's behalf came in April 1977, when the Texas Senate unanimously voted to legally recognize the Kickapoo Indians living under the international bridge in Eagle Pass. Senate Bill 168 acknowledged the "traditional Kickapoos" as a Texas Indian tribe, adding to a roster that included El Paso's Tiguas and East Texas's Alabama-Coushattas, while also authorizing the Texas Indian Commission to provide economic assistance to the beleaguered group. While tribal members retained dual citizenship, they were now eligible for state aid for Indians. "Texas is always known as a big state," the Kickapoos' chief told the state senate's Human Resources Committee, "always doing things big. Let this be one of the big things you do for a group that is wandering around looking for a place to live."[67] The tribe applied for and received a $1.5 million Community Development Block Grant from the Small Cities Program, which operated under the auspices of the U.S. Department of Housing and Urban Development. The Texas Indian Commission, in the wake of recognizing the Kickapoos as Texas Traditional Tribe, sponsored the grant proposal, then watched in frustration while the Texas attorney general almost immediately revoked the grant, claiming that the federal government had not authorized the Texas government to interact with the tribe. The move generated a great deal of media attention, which the Kickapoo handled with aplomb.[68]

As mentioned, the state of Texas had two Indian reservations as of this point in time: El Paso's Tigua and East Texas's Alabama-Coushatta. Texas had no state-level equivalent of the BIA and only a small "relocational" office in Dallas, which officials had designated to assist Indians from other states who had come to Texas seeking job opportunities. The Alabama-Coushattas, though federally recognized in 1927, lost that status in 1954 during the termination era, while the Tiguas had entered into a trust relationship with the state for the first time in the 1960s. Shortly thereafter, however, the Texas attorney general announced his opinion that the state simply could not favor any race over another when appropriating funding. Therefore, he concluded that the activities of the Texas Indian Commission had to be reconsidered. The implications of the attorney general's opinion made the state's indigenous peoples understandably nervous. A representative from the Texas Indian Commission pointed out that following this line of reasoning would leave one with the impression that only the federal government "has authority to discriminate between races." While he agreed that Indians should be entitled to the same level of assistance as any other Texans, he also insisted that their needs were quite different, particularly since they were so "unassuming." "They won't put themselves forward," he argued. "In turn, they don't receive the assistance without somebody . . . taking them before the authorities and saying, look, we need help. They won't ask for it." It was a concern that the attorney general had evidently failed to consider.[69]

In the 1980s, then, the tribe, with the assistance of sympathetic officials, took its case to the federal government. It was an effort to both gain federally acknowledged status and protect itself from the legal and bureaucratic morass it had been wading through while functioning under the auspices of the Texas Indian Commission. Understandably, the bid was problematic from the beginning. One official from the Texas Indian Commission admitted that the stigma of being a "Mexican tribe" still followed the Kickapoos around at both the federal and state level and could potentially derail their efforts. It was an assumption that had led to constant red tape as the tribe sought security and stability. "I don't think there is any question," he asserted in a display of support, "that they are U.S. citizens."[70] Such attitudes regularly put the Kickapoos on the defensive, necessitating constant reminders that, in the words of one Kickapoo, "we are not Mexican people. We are Kickapoo Indians." During congressional hearings concerning the tribe's fate, one congressman queried, "So far as the bureaucracy is concerned, your members in this century are only of the Kickapoo Nation. You are not clearly U.S. citizens nor are you considered to be Mexican citizens. This is an impediment for you to get the kind of assistance that you desire and need; is that correct?" Their reply, not surprisingly, was a resounding yes.[71]

Another sticking point in deliberations over the tribe's request for federally recognized status was the fact that they controlled a large tract of land in Mexico. "I understand the Government of Mexico," one congressman noted, "in gratitude for service that the Kickapoo provided to that Nation, has given you land in Mexico. If that is accurate, how was the land held? Who owns it really at this point, and what is the magnitude of that holding? I understand that it is many thousands of acres. Is it clearly owned by the Kickapoo, and, if so, how do you own it?" The Kickapoo delegates anticipated this line of inquiry. They explained that the Mexican government, out of sympathy for the tribe, granted them 23,000 hectares upon their arrival in Mexico with the understanding that it would be held jointly and that it would not be sold. "So we're there temporarily," one Kickapoo explained. "Really our home is on the border because that is where we took up permanent residence." He added that the Mexican land was very poor and lacked an adequate water supply. Further, the use of the Mexican land as a ceremonial site by Oklahoma Kickapoos seems to have bothered the Eagle Pass contingent, which only strengthened their resolve to obtain a place where they could "worship in privacy and conduct our ceremonies and rites" separate from their Oklahoma counterpart. As in the Yaqui case, the Kickapoos appeared cognizant of the fact that claims to nationhood that completely ignored the reality of the U.S.-Mexico border would not survive the recognition process. But unlike the Yaquis, the Kickapoos managed to maintain the all-important transnational lifeline linking Nacimiento and Eagle Pass. Officials were receptive when the tribe requested the legal protection of their right to hold land in Mexico, and decided to include the Mexican government in their deliberations over Kickapoo recognition.[72] It was a revolutionary step for the U.S. Congress, one that finally acknowledged the fact that transnational tribes should be treated as such.

In 1982, then, the Inter-American Indian Institute, on behalf of the Mexican government, submitted a Declaration of Principles to the congressional committee overseeing Kickapoo recognition. The institute expressed its opinion that the tribe should be granted U.S. citizenship, largely because it would ease their passage to and from Mexico. It also felt it only fair that the Mexican Kickapoos enjoy the same rights enjoyed by tribes living along the U.S.-Canada border, rights that stemmed from the aforementioned Jay Treaty. The Declaration of Principles also recommended that the tribe receive an adequate, nontaxable land base that was "subject to federal restraints against alienation." The last "principle" was perhaps the most significant. The institute opined that any legislation should not only "explicitly recognize the tri-cultural status of the Kickapoo," but should also "direct all appropriate federal officials, when providing education and other special services to the Kickapoo, to consult and cooperate with the appropriate Mexican Government officials in regard to the delivery of such services, in order to meet the special tri-cultural circumstances of the Kickapoos."[73]

The Oklahoma Kickapoos, meanwhile, seem to have recognized the desire of the Texas band to remain separate from the larger tribal entity. They did not object to severing at least some aspects of their relationship with their Texas- and Mexico-based counterpart. One committee member reminded the Oklahoma Kickapoo representative that the legislation under consideration contained a provision granting the Texas band complete autonomy, which meant that it would be recognized as a separate political entity from the Oklahoma tribe. Further, the provision required that the Oklahoma Kickapoos amend their tribal constitution, giving those Kickapoos included in the current bill a separate status within the tribe, though they would remain on tribal rolls in Oklahoma. In other words, their southern counterpart wanted to remain united under the "umbrella of the tribe of Oklahoma," or wanted to maintain some measure of political influence while guarding their access to sources of state and federal forms of assistance. But they also wanted a *legal* separation between the two groups, a separation that the Mexican Kickapoos viewed as symbolic more than anything. "You people in Oklahoma, the tribal leaders," another committee member asked, "are willing to amend your constitution to accommodate them?" The representative's response was a simple "yes sir." The Oklahoma contingent also agreed to allow the Texas band to participate in tribal elections and even, if elected, serve on the tribal council. They seemed to recognize the fact, painfully clear to the Texas band, that in addition to the family and cultural ties that kept the two groups united, the Texas band had traditionally relied on the Oklahoma tribe's "expertise" in dealing with the U.S. government. They relied on their relatives' education, ability to speak English, and knowledge of the financial aspects of maintaining a tribal land base.[74] While they wanted to remain distinct from their Oklahoma counterpart, in other words, they were not yet prepared to sever their relationship. It was an unusual arrangement for an unusual tribe.

The other key issue in deliberations surrounding the tribe's request for federal recognition concerned their right to cross the border. "The act must do nothing," one committee member demanded, "to jeopardize their right to pass across the border in both directions that they presently enjoy." Attorneys working on behalf of the Kickapoos went to great lengths to ensure that the pending legislation did not curtail this right. They worked closely with the Mexican State Department and other Mexican officials, and even retained an attorney in Mexico in order to be "absolutely certain" that their right to migrate would not be curtailed by the pending legislation. One member of the Kickapoos' legal team went so far as to attend the fortieth anniversary meeting of the Inter-American Indian Institute in Mexico City, during which officials from both the United States and Mexico agreed to cooperate on the issue of border passage of indigenous peoples. Mexico, in turn, sent its own delegate to the Kickapoo hearings in Washington to testify that the two nations had reached a preliminary agreement. He assured committee members that since the Kickapoos' lands in Mexico enjoyed *ejido* rather than reservation status, a land grant in Texas would not affect their status in Coahuila. "Something that would be important here," he continued, stressing the significance of Mexico's Declaration of Principles, "will be to recognize in the bill the fact that the Kickapoos have a tricultural element and this should be . . . [taken] into consideration." He further highlighted a fact that may have eluded the committee, stating, "The existence of Indian groups, along border areas, is not unique to the United States and Mexico. There are more than 70 ethnic groups in the Americas that face similar problems, in some cases, more severe problems than the ones that concern us today." He pointed out that following independence, the developing nations in Latin America drew their borders with little regard for indigenous and ethnic groups that called these regions home. Finally, he expressed the hope that the legislation under consideration would help open doors for other Indian groups occupying other border regions by encouraging the committee to think more broadly, or to develop a hemispheric consciousness when it came to indigenous peoples.[75]

Aside from the transnational implications of Kickapoo recognition, all involved in the federal acknowledgment effort recognized that the Kickapoos sorely needed a protected homeland, and the practical reasons were myriad. "Many of our people suffer from illnesses," one Kickapoo explained. "There is much T.B., asthma, headaches, pink eye, measles, and whooping cough." The tribe had no outhouses and no stoves, and instead of investing in such fundamentals of daily existence had to spend their meager earnings on food. Put simply, life had become a struggle for the tribe. They lived on what was essentially borrowed land in Eagle Pass, afraid of improving it because it could be taken away at any moment. Their children did not take well to education because of their inability to speak English and the fact that, as Kickapoos, they were conspicuously different from the other children of Eagle Pass.[76] They battled, on a daily basis, stereotypes of Kickapoos as, in the words of one scholar, "a people who are relentlessly stubborn, excessively aggressive, overly suspicious, and collectively ignorant." These stereotypes had evidently even penetrated academia. One scholar, testifying before the congressional committee, claimed that a colleague cautioned him about testifying on the tribe's behalf, contending that the Kickapoos were "mean as hell" and "just no damn good."[77]

Woman hanging laundry in the Kickapoos' makeshift village near Eagle
Pass, Texas. Photograph by John P. Filo. © 1980 The Associated Press.

In 1981, Congress passed H.R. 4496, a bill granting federally recognized
status to the Kickapoo "Band." It included provisions that placed lands in
Maverick County, Texas, in federal trust and made the tribe eligible for federal services available to other federally recognized tribes. Then, in the
mid-1980s, the tribe pushed for an additional clarification of their status.
"Holdout Kickapoo Indians Relent, Become U.S. Citizens," read one headline. Describing the Mexican Kickapoos as a "renegade band," the article
explained that immigration officials granted 143 Kickapoos certificates that
bestowed upon them "permanent alien status." Interestingly, the recognition
bill gave the tribe the option of acquiring either U.S. or Mexican citizenship, yet another unique twist in the Kickapoos' recognition saga. While
U.S. officials expressed pride that "so many of them have chosen to become
U.S. citizens," federal recognition actually was not dependent on which
country they chose for citizenship status. It did, however, affect their eligibility for state and federal welfare programs that fell outside of BIA auspices, which for many made U.S. citizenship a no-brainer.[78]

Federal recognition, from the tribe's perspective, was just one more con-firmation of its right to nationhood. In legitimizing this right to others, the Kickapoos have long cited the 1832 document discussed earlier, which the tribe used to cross the U.S.-Mexico border and which the tribe character-izes as a government-to-government treaty. But the tribe also possesses what it feels is an even more powerful confirmation of their sovereignty: a coin-like medallion, dated 1789, that bears the profile of George Washington on one side and a pair of clasped hands and crossed pipes on the other side, along with the inscriptions "Friendship" and "The Pipe of Peace." It was a gift, according to the tribe, from President Andrew Jackson. One Kickapoo explained its significance this way: "It is, in essence, the cornerstone of the tribe's relationship with the Americans . . . It's a commitment, government to government."[79] Couple this conviction with the outcome of their recog-nition bid, then, and it is no wonder that one writer who interviewed Kick-apoo tribal members in the 1990s observed, "[They] do not perceive the border to be nearly the impediment that other borderlands tribes do."[80] After all, it had failed to contain their claims to sovereignty. Yet embracing recognition entailed compromise. Although the Kickapoos now had a pro-tected homeland in their adopted city of Eagle Pass, reservation status has not always delivered on the promise of that sovereignty. The historian Jef-frey Shepherd argues that while reservations are often viewed as safe ha-vens in which indigenous groups can assert their autonomy and practice their cultures, they have historically been "targets of colonialism and racial transformation." Venturing outside of reservation borders, meanwhile, has historically meant inhabiting "a liminal space where they were racialized others at the bottom of the sociocultural hierarchy of America."[81] Yet retain-ing the right to migrate in a transnational fashion meant retaining a safe haven of a different sort, one well beyond the reach of agents of the U.S. government.

The Tohono O'odham's Status Woes

While the Yaquis and Kickapoos had more or less stabilized their commu-nities on both sides of the border by the end of the twentieth century, emerg-ing from centuries of tumult with a secure land base and at least some degree of sovereignty, status woes still plagued the Tohono O'odham. Con-sidering the degree of interaction between the Tohono O'odham tribe and the U.S. government over the course of the twentieth century, the tribe re-ceived federally recognized status surprisingly late in the game (though much earlier than the Yaquis and Kickapoos). As previously discussed, the United States had given reservation status to O'odham lands in southern Arizona early in the century, and since then had charged an Indian agent in the area with hearing their grievances and implementing reservation-based economic, health, and educational programs. Still, the tribe had little in the way of internal political organization, making the government-to-government relationship, which distinguished recognized from nonrecognized tribes, essentially impossible. In the 1930s, then, the Bureau of Indian Affairs, acting under the auspices of John Collier's Indian Reorganization Act, encouraged the tribe to formulate and implement a tribal constitution and replace their council of elders with a majority elected tribal council.[82] The tribe cooperated. Forty-eight percent of those O'odham living on the reservation voted on the matter, with 88 percent voting in favor. They submitted a tribal constitution to Secretary of the Interior Harold Ickes in May 1936, and the department took only a few months to approve it. In 1937 the tribal council began to meet, though it would take some time for it to gain anything approaching reservation-wide acceptance as a central authority. Regardless, once the tribe was unified under a single, federally sanctioned government, its sovereign status was effectively guaranteed. It was a significant development since, again, the Tohono O'odham had never really had a central government. As in the Yaqui case, authority tended to flow from the village level up. Individual villages tended to be politically autonomous, with decisions related to agriculture, ceremonial obligations, and hunts made during nightly meetings. Political alliances across villages, meanwhile, tended to be temporary and typically were formed only in the event of war. Under the new arrangement, various district governments gradually emerged to provide representation for village-level governments, thereby mimicking the older, more familiar arrangement, while a tribal chairperson and legislative council assumed governing power over the reservation as a whole.[83]

The absence of a formal governing structure prior to the New Deal is perhaps understandable. The reservation, the anthropologist Ruth Underhill explained, "was on the very land where the Papagos had always lived and there were no treaties or payments connected with it. It was simply marked off so that Papago could continue to have their own country, without fear that White ranchers would fill it up." Thus, there was simply no need for any kind of central authority. The Spanish had earlier attempted to organize the tribe into a coherent political whole, with little success. In fact, tribal members were unable to even pronounce the word *gobernador*, since their own alphabet lacked an "r." Instead, when necessary, they employed the word *gobenal*, a practice that actually persisted well into the twentieth century.[84] Then, when the BIA conducted a census of the O'odham population during the New Deal, it included tribal members on both sides of the U.S.-Mexico border, even though the reservation technically ended at the international boundary. These individuals were all included in the 1937 "base roll," which, as mentioned earlier, is submitted along with the constitution as a condition for formal recognition. At least at some point, then, the U.S. government appeared poised to accept the reality of the tribe's transnational orientation. Otherwise, why include "Mexican" O'odham in the base roll? Further, in the years following their recognition, the BIA continued to treat all O'odham the same, regardless of where they were born or where they currently resided. The tribe explained, "Federal buses picked up our children living south of the boundary and transported us to schools in the north. Some of us born south of the boundary served in the military. Some of us went to war. Still, we were not guaranteed United States citizenship." Those born north of the boundary, meanwhile, were. The base roll then, would cause considerable confusion later when those members residing south of the border increasingly found their tribal and citizenship status called into question.[85]

Whether or not southern O'odham have any kind of legal status north of the border remains unclear up to the present day, and related challenges still abound. Even though BIA officials might have led them to believe otherwise in an earlier era, the BIA had made clear by the end of the century that the O'odham's status as a federally recognized tribe stopped at the border. "Tohono O'odham Seek Sovereignty" read a 1989 newspaper headline, illustrating the fact that federal recognition in the United States had not solved the political, economic, and, perhaps most importantly, legal issues still confronting the tribe. It was yet another case of federally recognized status failing to deliver on the promise of sovereignty. That same year the tribe made the audacious move of taking its grievances to the World Court, claiming that it was on the verge of extinction due to repeated human rights violations at the hands of both the U.S. and Mexican governments as well as the steady erosion of tribal autonomy. In their request for unconditional sovereignty, including total exclusion from the laws of both nations, the tribe first challenged the legitimacy of the Gadsden Purchase, which initially divided the tribe in 1853. The O'odham went on to argue that "illegal" immigration restrictions curtailed a slew of basic rights and freedoms covered by the Universal Declaration of Human Rights, the 1948 document that created the World Court, including, especially, Article 15, which maintains that all human beings are entitled to an inalienable nationality. Further, U.S. and Mexican laws, they claimed, were hastening the loss of O'odham lands on both sides of the border. These lands were often being taken "fraudulently and violently," according to the tribe, by developers and ranchers. The losses amounted to roughly 93 percent of the 60,000 square miles occupied by the tribe at the time of the Gadsden Purchase, leaving them with 4,450 square miles in the United States and a mere 12 in Mexico.[86]

They had a point. Though, as detailed earlier, O'odham land losses in Mexico accelerated around midcentury, they actually began early in the twentieth century, when the Mexican government began encouraging the settlement of "vacant" lands in northern Sonora. Suddenly, significant numbers of newly landless O'odham were either relocating to Mexican cities or being conscripted into the Mexican military. In fact, evidently at least some enlisted in campaigns against the Yaquis. The tribe's attorney explained: "They would wait for the O'odham, traditionally nomadic in their ways, to head north to Arizona for religious ceremonies or for the yucca harvest. Then the ranchers would bring government inspectors out to the lands and say, 'See, this land is abandoned.' Then they would file a land claim, tear down the O'odham houses, incorporate the O'odham cattle into their own herds and put up fences."[87]

Involved in the 1989 claim to sovereignty was the noted Indian activist and scholar Vine Deloria Jr., who began characterizing it as "the prime test case" and argued that its outcome would have enormous implications for all tribes whose communities overlap North American borders. Further, the strategy of using the World Court, if successful, would place tribes making similar claims on equal footing with large nation-states such as the United States and Mexico. Southern Arizona, then, was starting to look like a potential "proving ground" in a new direction in Indian policy, one that might ultimately be hemispheric in scope. Lest the World Court seem an unlikely avenue for the pursuit of an Indian policy goal, the *Tucson Citizen* maintained, "it would not be unheard of for the World Court to establish a separate nation for a group of people. The court has broken off several parts of South Africa to establish new independent nations." One Tucson attorney, however, was pessimistic. When the Nicaraguan government appealed to the World Court after the United States began mining its harbor, the court ruled in the small nation's favor. The United States, however, refused to recognize the validity of the ruling or the jurisdiction of the court, claiming that the World Court cannot rule on cases involving sovereignty or national security. Thus, even if the O'odham were successful, Mexico and the United States would likely contest the decision or simply refuse to recognize it.[88] Ultimately, all such speculation proved irrelevant. World Court officials in the end refused to hear the case.

This was not the first time a North American group had appealed to the international community when grievances went unaddressed at home. In the 1920s, the Mohawk Indians were battling the Canadian Department of Indian Affairs over fishing and hunting rights. After reaching an impasse, Mohawk chief Deskaheh left his home in Akwesasne, Mohawk Territory, to present the matter to the League of Nations in Geneva, Switzerland. Similar to the O'odham's attempt to appeal to the World Court, however, Deskaheh's efforts did not get far. Although he managed to enlist the support of King George V of Great Britain as well as the government of the Netherlands, in the end the league refused to hear Deskaheh out. Instead, the league insisted that any issues between the Mohawks and the Canadian government were strictly domestic, not international, concerns. Although unsuccessful, Deskaheh's strategy to enlist the international community in a dispute between a Native nation and a nation-state was a completely new one as of the 1920s.[89]

The next avenue the O'odham pursued was the United Nations Commission on the Rights of Indigenous People. In 1989, with the assistance of University of Arizona law professor Robert A. Williams, the tribe submitted a list of alleged human rights violations. These violations, they maintained to the Geneva-based organization, arose directly out of their struggles over land. This latest effort, again, evidently failed to significantly advance their cause.[90] However, perhaps sensing the pressure being placed on them by ever more resourceful indigenous groups such as the O'odham, the Mexican government did respond. Late in 1989, government officials announced a proposal for a constitutional amendment that would act as a sort of Indian Bill of Rights. "If passed," explained the head of the National Indian Institute, "the result would be that the indigenous communities in Mexico will receive better attention to their demands and better protection of their land and rights." The proposed amendment, however, did not address the most pressing concern of all, namely, the tribe's right to cross the border without the interference of immigration authorities. And the biggest problem of all was that the bill as a whole was subsequently left to languish.[91]

In *It Is Not Our Fault*, the 2001 publication discussed earlier, the O'odham urged Congress to amend the 1952 Immigration and Nationality Act to include a subsection that granted U.S. citizenship to *any* enrolled tribal member, regardless of whether they resided north or south of the U.S.-Mexico border. The hope was that their tribal membership credentials could serve as "the legal equivalent of the federally-issued Certificate of Citizenship and/or the state-issued birth certificate for all intents and purposes."[92] The tribe distributed the publication to every senator and representative in Washington, but to no avail.[93] Again, it appeared that reforms in either the United States or Mexico would inevitably stop at the border. While the Kickapoo case marked a rare moment when the United States and Mexico collaborated in securing rights for a transnational indigenous group, the O'odham's difficulties remain unaddressed.

Still, the three groups discussed herein all exhibited a remarkable level of resourcefulness and tenacity as the political, economic, legal, and cultural implications of the U.S.-Mexico border became all the more apparent over the course of the twentieth century. As the United States and Mexico became ever more rigorous in protecting their borders, so too did these indigenous nations. And while the historians Andre Marak and Gary Van Valen argued in 2015 that the North American West "remained a place of shifting boundaries and allegiances" only up until the early twentieth century, these case studies suggest that at least in the U.S.-Mexico border region this process is actually ongoing.[94] Violent clashes in the interest of protecting the integrity of borders may be a thing of the past, but by the end of the twentieth century the determination to protect tribal sovereignty that had so often strained Indian-white relations proved stronger than ever. The fact that the Indians' definition of tribal sovereignty included the right to systematically sidestep or completely ignore immigration rules and regulations in not one but two powerful nation-states was bound to raise eyebrows. In the end, however, policy climates on both sides of the border at the time of their final push for status clarification often worked in their favor, as did the sympathies of well-connected individuals and organizations, at least as far as the Yaqui and Kickapoo cases are concerned. Thus, officials on both sides of the border ultimately had little choice but to grudgingly accept the reality of these transborder indigenous nations, and, again at least in the Yaqui and Kickapoo cases, award them the requisite rights. That the Tohono O'odham still struggle with their transnational orientation attests to the fact that officials on both sides of the border still have a way to go in addressing the legacy of a formal boundary created without regard for those they were walling in or walling out.

Epilogue

. . . .

It is not important that European languages and western civilization
limit the natural expression of the Indian within us and have caused the
disappearance of the Indian race in some countries; in the land itself, in the
same physical environment, as in our history, art, and tradition, the voice of
Native America will always speak.

—Inaugural issue of *Boletín Indigenista*, 1941

Kate nacion itom nokriamachi.
(There is no nation can defeat us)

—Yaqui rallying cry following their defeat under Cajeme, 1879

In 2007, a journalist from the *High Country News* visited the lands of the
Tohono O'odham to investigate reports of worsening conditions along the
U.S.-Mexico border. He was evidently surprised by what he found, observing: "On a warm Sunday afternoon in early January, no one from U.S. law
enforcement is checking documents as people move back and forth at a
crossing—really, just a steel cattle guard in a gap in the fence—known as
the San Miguel Gate. There are no signs of Mexican border officials keeping tabs on the gate. Tohono O'odham tribal police are nowhere to be
seen . . . Officially, only members of the Tohono O'odham Nation are allowed to pass through the San Miguel Gate. But no signs warn non-members
against crossing. The biggest obstacles to traversing the border at the San
Miguel Gate, it seems, are the six-inch gaps between the steel rails of the
cattle guard there."[1]

Although the San Miguel Gate appeared rather laxly guarded, which
seemingly contradicts reports of O'odham oppression at the hands of immigration authorities, appearances rarely tell the whole story. More recent
trends along the border have impacted the Tohono O'odham in a variety of
ways that are not always obvious. In 1996, for example, the U.S. government undertook Operation Gatekeeper and passed the Illegal Immigration
Reform and Immigrant Responsibility Act to more effectively regulate transborder traffic. However, both did little more than foster anti-immigrant

attitudes while ultimately failing to curb illegal immigration. If anything, border crossing became far more dangerous as a consequence of these efforts. Designed primarily to address the influx of immigrants across California's borders, Operation Gatekeeper sent a flood of human traffic into southern Arizona more generally and the isolated, sparsely populated O'odham reservation more specifically, thereby aggravating an already formidable problem facing the O'odham. The Illegal Immigration Reform and Immigrant Responsibility Act not only increased the risk involved in crossing; it also increased the economic cost of immigrating, both of which upped the odds of migrants not surviving the journey and/or being economically exploited by human smugglers. It also led to a decline in the standard of living among undocumented migrants. And as the anthropologist Laura Velasco Ortiz observed, the 9/11 terrorist attacks, coupled with Mexico's refusal to support the U.S.-led war in Iraq, "chilled the incipient negotiations on a new migration treaty" between the two nations. Since then, any negotiations over immigration reform have steadily degenerated into little more than innocuous discussions of how best to deport illegal migrants. As a consequence, she continues, "border controls under the new U.S. security and anti-terror policies forced many Mexican commuters who lacked legal documents or whose families had mixed documentation to move to U.S. soil permanently," and even legal commuters found crossing points more congested because of increasingly thorough inspections of migrants.[2]

The seventy-five-mile stretch of the O'odham reservation that abuts the U.S.-Mexico border has indeed become a hotbed of illicit activities in recent decades, drug trafficking being the most serious. Even some tribal members have been unable to pass up to the opportunity to profit from the enterprise. After all, the majority of tribal members remain impoverished, with a full 40 percent living below the poverty line. In fact, the O'odham are poor even compared to other Indian tribes. Per capita income for the year 2000 stood at $8,000, far below the $13,000 average for American Indians. The reservation's biggest employers are the string of casinos that, between the three, employ about 1,400 workers, only half of whom are O'odham. Casino revenue, however, has been stretched thin in the tribe's efforts to administer to the vast, isolated reservation. Complicating their financial situation is the fact that a sizable portion of the O'odham's annual budget goes toward cleaning up the estimated six tons of trash left behind by migrants, which is just one of many border-related expenses. Still, the casino revenue has enabled the tribe to build a new hospital, a nursing home, a community college, a slew of recreation centers, and, finally, a museum and cultural center. Recent beneficiaries of casino revenue include college-aged O'odham, whose education is incentivized by the tribe to help address the high dropout rate at the high school level, which currently stands at 48 percent. Given these challenges, then, it is hardly surprising that a minority has engaged in illegal activity. In 2003 and 2004, for example, law enforcement arrested more than one hundred O'odham, and even some tribal leaders have relatives in prison for drug-related convictions. The temptation can be hard to resist. Smuggling drugs (or illegal migrants for that matter) just once can earn an O'odham a quick $3,000 to $5,000. The only way to counteract this disturbing trend, according to some tribal members, is to shore up the reservation economy by offering easier access to education and more employment opportunities. "If these things are not done," one tribal member warned, "we will be lost as a people."[3]

Although the O'odham government has been proactive in addressing problems posed by the influx of illegal migrants and drug traffickers into tribal territory, results have been limited, and assistance from outside the nation has not always been forthcoming. As tribal chairperson Vivian Juan Saunders recently asserted, "Anywhere else this would be considered a crisis, but there is a double standard because we are Indians."[4] Thus, O'odham often get caught up in broader efforts to police the U.S.-Mexico border. The result has been what another O'odham described as a "climate of oppression" on O'odham lands, one in which immigration officials force O'odham to carry documents and subject them to frequent stops, searches, and even threats of deportation, a scenario that does not seem likely to change in the near future.[5]

As for the Yaquis, even at midcentury it was apparent that the border had come to represent not only a physical barrier but also a psychological one. While living among Sonoran Yaquis in the late 1940s and early 1950s, Edward Spicer observed that a good number of Yaquis along the river valley had at various times lived in and moved between Yaqui settlements in Arizona, with some even expressing, as mentioned earlier, "homesickness" for Tucson and Phoenix. However, they now found themselves cut off from their Arizona communities by an increasingly formidable boundary. Linkages between the two halves of the Yaqui whole were even then in the process of devolving into little more than the regular exchange of letters, while *physical* movement became, at most, "sporadic." Spicer noted a surprising trend, though, namely that "a new kind of contact has developed as more prosperous Yaquis from the United States have come as tourists to attend and observe the important ceremonies in Potam and the other villages."[6] As of the mid-twentieth century, Sonoran Yaquis seemed preoccupied primarily with economic development, their villages having gradually emerged as, in one scholar's words, "burgeoning outposts of commercial agriculture" boasting a "semiautonomous government" within the state. As they grew more confident economically and politically, they also became more aggressive in maintaining their cultural distinctiveness from the Mexican mainstream. In other words, although they had become an integral part of the regional and even national economy, they had also effectively maintained, as always, a physical and emotional distance from greater Mexico.[7]

More recently, the 32,000 Yaquis living within the Yaqui Zone have contended with NAFTA and the "opening" of the Mexican economy. Generally speaking, they have become more and more indebted and, as one scholar put it, "dependent on Mexican banks and beholden to the dictates of the market" as large corporate and privately owned farms have proliferated. Unemployment and underemployment have become the norm, while travelers through the region often cannot help but note, as one put it, the "crumbling walls of wattle-and-daub houses, their tarpaper roofs held down with rocks and bottle and soil, the dirt roads that wind away from the main thoroughfare, the conglomeration of cramped, dusty stores, rusted bicycles, and limping cars."[8]

Arizona's Yaquis, meanwhile, have had other concerns. They worked diligently in the years following recognition to draft a tribal constitution and formalize a tribal roll. As the group stabilized following seemingly constant leadership changes, Yaquis at New Pascua began attracting other Arizona Yaquis, so that by 1980 more than 4,000 tribal members participated in federally funded health, education, and social programs. The Yaquis too turned to gambling, opening the Casino of the Sun in the early 1990s. Casino revenue has allowed the tribe to administer to an ever-growing population that, by the end of that decade, hovered around 15,000. Finally, in 2001 the tribe honored the contributions of Anselmo Valencia, who some had likened to Moses, by attaching his name to a multimillion-dollar performing arts center.[9] As for transborder movement among the Yaquis, one scholar observed, "The right of Mexican Yaqui to cross the U.S.-Mexico border still depends on individual INS officials at the regional and border gate level, and, unfortunately, the mood that they are in on any particular day." But then again, the Yaquis' ability to cross the border even for ceremonial purposes has long depended on "whether the individual INS officer, or the supervisor on duty, was familiar with the Yaqui ceremonial occasion." In other words, whether or not a Yaqui will be granted transborder passage was, and remains, a bit of a crapshoot.[10]

In short, both the Yaquis and the Tohono O'odham face contemporary challenges that are rooted in both broader Arizona politics and, especially, national debates about immigration and the border. These debates began assuming a harsher tone in the 1970s; then, in the 1990s, as the historian Geraldo Cadava put it, the state began "peddl[ing] laws that sought to limit access by undocumented immigrants to government benefits, forbid citizens from offering them assistance, and make English the official language." Anti-immigrant "vigilante" groups became more vocal, visible, and influential. Then along came Arizona's Senate Bill 1070, which Cadava calls "the pinnacle of state-sponsored discrimination" and which was nicknamed the "show me your papers" law. Among other things, it empowered law enforcement to make arrests, without a warrant, in cases where suspected "illegal aliens" could not verify their immigration or citizenship status. Not all Arizonans were on board with the new trend. One law enforcement official referred to the law as "stupid," "racist," and "an embarrassment." Mexican officials, meanwhile, characterized it as a "violation of civil rights" and a "kind of apartheid." From the perspective of many, the intent of the law was to legalize racial profiling. And in the end, while the Supreme Court struck down most of the law, it upheld the provision empowering law enforcement to demand papers from those they suspect might be in the country illegally.[11]

While the O'odham's woes continue to mount and the Yaqui presence in both Sonora and Arizona continues to stabilize, much has changed in recent decades among the Kickapoos. Although Eagle Pass is now the center of Kickapoo tribal life, Nacimiento remains a seasonal hub, as well as their primary ceremonial center, to this day. Perhaps the most notable recent development was their controversial decision to engage in casino gambling. In fact, as the *Dallas Morning News* reported in 2002, "A once destitute, 850-member tribe that two decades ago lived under a bridge and shared water from a single spigot are forging ahead with a $47 million expansion of their 5-year-old Lucky Eagle Casino." The development plan included two hotels, an eighteen-hole golf course right alongside the Rio Grande, and new roads, so that future visitors would not have to endure the "bone-rattling three-mile drive over a rut-filled road off the main highway." "It will be an oasis in the desert," claimed tribal representative Isidro Garza.[12]

All did not go as planned, however. In 2006, federal prosecutors approved a plea bargain with Kickapoo casino managers following charges of corruption and tax evasion. For years, allegations of mismanagement of casino funds had swirled around the 125-acre reservation. The tumult appears to have begun in 2002, when Kickapoo Melina Anico began a letter-writing campaign to tribal leaders demanding an explanation as to why, given the availability of millions of dollars of casino revenue, elders residing in Nacimiento lacked even blankets and indoor plumbing. In October of that year, an overwhelming majority voted for a dramatic change in tribal leadership, ousting several members of the tribal council. Federal indictments soon followed, and seven former tribal leaders stood accused of stealing more than $900,000 in casino revenue. The tribe also soon realized it was $20 million in debt because of fraud and mismanagement. The new casino finally opened in 2004, accompanied by a massive surge in profits. The tribe is now using these profits to shore up other on-reservation economic endeavors, including their pecan orchards, to lessen their dependence on the casino. Still, their economic situation remains precarious. When asked what would become of the tribe if the casino were to close, one Kickapoo responded that many would "probably have to go back to migrant work to survive."[13]

The Kickapoos have also more recently struggled with substance abuse. They can appear, according to the journalist Jan Reid, "incapable of moderate social drinking." While alcohol consumption is forbidden on both Kickapoo reserves, alcohol-related problems still abound. However, the intoxicant that tribal elders find especially worrisome is commercially available spray paint. Reid wrote in the 1990s, "About 450 people are enrolled as legal members of the Texas Kickapoo tribe. At least eighty, most of them adults, are addicted to paint fumes." Tribal member Joe Hernandez struggled with spray paint addiction between the ages of twelve and thirteen, and described his hallucinations as being similar to "the flickering, jerky effect of dancers under a strobe light." When high, he could feel his blood pulsing through his veins and his heart nearly beating out of his chest. "You don't want to do nothing else," he said, continuing, "I wouldn't eat, and I kept getting caught by my parents. Even now when I smell paint, I still want to do it." One especially lurid story involving paint sniffing concerned a twenty-six-year-old Kickapoo woman who, in 1992, passed out on railroad tracks, only to be cut in half when a train came roaring through Eagle Pass.[14]

As these cases all demonstrate, then, the process of reconciling formal borders with a transnational orientation can be complicated, painful, and, above all, interminable. Reservation status has not always translated into tribal stability, federal recognition has not always delivered on the promise of tribal sovereignty, and the U.S.-Mexico border looms larger than ever in the collective imaginations of theses indigenous nations. In recent decades, indigenous peoples and pro-Indian politicians and intellectuals all over the globe have begun questioning the legitimacy of borders that were drawn without considering preexisting ethnic and spatial structures. The historians Michiel Baud and Willem van Schendel argue that the inspiration for these attitudes can be found along the U.S.-Canada border, where via the aforementioned Jay Treaty both governments have long recognized the right of indigenous groups to cross the boundary without state interference. They point to Latin America as a region where we are likely to see mounting challenges to the legitimacy of existing borders, as well as Africa, a place with famously permeable state borders where one can most clearly see the survival of "ancient networks of regional trade." Whether these networks have been maintained because of sheer practicality or as a form of protest against "a predatory postcolonial state," they will no doubt continue to problematize those borders that locals view as having been arbitrarily imposed on the landscape.[15]

Transnational indigenous groups have also begun grabbing headlines with increasing frequency of late, stirring up international controversies that have in some cases escalated to near-crisis proportions. For example, in 2009 *Indian Country Today* reported on the Kumeyaay Indians, many of whom had for decades moved on a regular basis between twelve reservations in southern California and four communities in northern Mexico. Like the O'odham, the Kumeyaays found themselves divided by the border drawn in the wake of the U.S.-Mexican War, and by the 1960s security along that boundary had become tighter than ever. Suddenly Kumeyaays wishing to enter the United States found that right more frequently denied. Keeping transborder channels open, then, has become, in the words of Viejas Band of Kumeyaay chairman Bobby L. Barrett, "a constant struggle." It has also become common for the Indians, according to Ron Christman, a Kumeyaay from the Santa Ysabel Reservation in San Diego County, to "sing Indian songs right there on the border" as a form of protest. The U.S. government responded to this crisis in the late 1990s by issuing what were called "laser visas" to the southern Kumeyaays, which the *Indian Country Today* article describes as a "multi-use travel credential." The article goes on to explain, "While the document doesn't give them dual citizenship or recognize them as part of a sovereign nation, it gets them across the border." Getting authorization for the visas, however, was not a simple affair. Northern Kumeyaays had to travel to Mexico, conduct a census, and help acquire passports for those tribal members who resided south of the boundary (documents that the laser visas require) before the U.S. government would agree to issue the roughly 1,900 visas requested by the tribe.[16] U.S. officials were also actively working with the Seneca Nation of New York and Southern Ontario, the Kootenai Tribe of Idaho, the Pascua Yaquis of Arizona, and twenty-five other Indian groups to develop and distribute border-crossing identification cards. One source estimated that North America's international borders affect about forty tribes, so the process of addressing their needs will likely require time, effort, and increasingly precious financial resources. But for the Seneca Nation, this move on the part of the U.S. government meant not only that the tribe's right to pass and repass the border would no longer be hindered; it also amounted to a long-overdue recognition of their sovereignty.[17]

Scholars are also increasingly realizing that formal borders have the tendency to encourage the formation of *entirely new* identities and organizations. One scholar, for example, characterized the Yaquis' transnational orientation as "a fundamental aspect of their identity."[18] Another agreed, observing that "narratives of movement" have helped define them in a contemporary sense, shaping "who they are today and how they envision their connection to [the Yaqui homeland]."[19] More recently, increasing globalization has been blamed for encouraging the creation of subnational identities that have even further undermined the nation-state. It has energized and emboldened those groups with long-standing claims to some form of autonomy, ultimately leading to the emergence of wholly new groups that are intent on capitalizing on the existence of formal borders. Their presence has been as predictable as it has been consequential. They have tended to, in a very real way, "unmake" these formal borders by exposing the limits of state power in border regions, revealing again and again, in the historian Rachel St. John's words, "the divide between the states' aspirations and their actual power." But questions remain. Have these subnational identities *actually* succeeded in weakening the states? Or have they done the opposite and heightened the repressive capabilities of the states? Focusing on dynamics in far northern Mexico, the anthropologist Carmen Martínez Novo argues that although national governments have not entirely succeeded in controlling the "production of identities" along their borders, they have "retained the ability to shape subjects to adapt to novel global situations." Thus, in the face of competing identities and claims to nationalism, larger, more powerful, and more omnipresent nation-states have very often put into place the means of keeping these in check, whether it be through surveillance, stepped-up policing, stricter immigration policies, the erection of physical barriers, or even violence. They have not, however,

managed to reconcile these efforts with the fact that borders have historically been sites where, again in St. John's words, "categories blurred and
power was compromised," which is a reality of border life that is not likely
to change.[20]

Yet the case studies examined herein suggest that if borderlanders have
been forced to "adapt to novel global situations," so too have the United
States and Mexico. In the face of competing claims to nationhood from indigenous sectors, claims that clearly were not going away, both nation-states
hammered out compromises that would acknowledge these claims while
also blunting their legal, political, and cultural force. In the end, each of
these abutting and even overlapping variables within the broader U.S.-
Mexico border region realized that stubborn recalcitrance would get one
only so far, and that in an increasingly interconnected world one must share
power in order to maintain power. In other words, the United States and
Mexico came to realize, however belatedly, what indigenous peoples had
long known: that resistance to transnationalism is futile. After all, the indigenous peoples in this story literally could not take a step without "going
transnational" in some form or fashion. As the historians Andrae Marak and
Gary Van Valen argue, the very fact that indigenous peoples gradually
forged nations within nations "automatically makes their lived experience
transnational." Simply leaving their reserves to work, hunt or gather, attend
religious ceremonies, or attend school, for example, meant crossing into a
different category of nationhood. Leaving their reserves meant being
subjected to different laws and assuming a different (or at least dual) citizenship status. It meant immersing oneself in a potentially disorienting
environment where conceptions of national belonging and symbols of national culture were rooted in a set of historical experiences that often felt
unfamiliar at best and oppositional at worst. And since these reserves were
owned and controlled by the nation-state, one could "go transnational"
without so much as leaving the reserve.[21]

As for the characterization of transnational players as "subnational," as
has been shown, North America's indigenous peoples have long employed
the rhetoric of nationhood even without official Mexican or U.S. government
sanction, and have often bristled at being reduced to a subset of some larger
national identity that is not their own. The assertion of these groups' nationhood, however, obviously stems from some deeper impulse, one that tran-
scends this relatively narrow construct. The fact that nations encompass a
number of different communities does not automatically unite those communities as a "people," at least not in a permanent sense. At the end of the

day, *inherent* sovereignty, at least among the groups discussed herein, has tended to be an outgrowth of a shared language and ceremonial cycle, a shared connection with a specific territory (whether adopted or "traditional"), and a common sacred history. And one could argue that it was this all-consuming and almost innate sense of peoplehood that gave rise to modern nationalism, indigenous or otherwise.[22] As O'odham Joe Velasco put it, "Down to my roots, down to my boots, I am Tohono O'odham." Some identities, it turns out, are nonnegotiable.[23]

However, while it is comforting to know that some things never change, it is also nice to see how *dramatically* things can change. A 2005 *Arizona Republic* article, for example, reported on a "lost" band of Kickapoo Indians living in, of all places, southern Arizona. The article stated: "Until recently, the group had almost no contact with its parent tribe in Oklahoma, and its presence has gone largely unnoticed by other tribal leaders in Arizona. But last year, with help from the Oklahoma tribe, the Arizona group purchased a building in Douglas, just north of the border, to serve as a tribal field office. The tribe plans to seek trust status for the building, a process that can take several years. If successful, the tribal land holding would make the Kickapoos . . . eligible to participate in state gambling compacts." The article concludes with a passing mention of a "splinter group" that "settled in lands in Texas and Mexico," and claims that at least a portion of those Kickapoos seeking some kind of "status" in Arizona "live in a tiny Mexican village called Tamichopa."[24] As formidable as the border has become, such transnational networks are not yet a thing of the past, suggesting that not only do other hidden histories likely await discovery, but that other indigenous nations likely await their due recognition.

Acknowledgments

This book came together in fits and starts over a rather long span of time. I have accrued countless debts in the process, not all of which I can acknowledge here without writing *another* book, and some of which I am confident would escape my memory if I were to try. I will therefore stick to the basics, with heartfelt apologies to those who do not deserve to be overlooked. The staffs at the following institutions were nothing but professional, courteous, and helpful: the Archivo Histórico de la Secretaría de las Relaciones Exteriores, the Archivo Histórico del Estado de Sonora, the Arizona State Museum Archives, the Benson Latin American Collection at the University of Texas at Austin, the Southwest Collection at Texas Tech University, the University of Arizona Library Special Collections, and the V. Garcia Library Archives. Many thanks to all of you.

I am also grateful to the Arts and Humanities Department at the University of Texas at Dallas for providing me with a paycheck, of course, but also a warm, collegial, and stimulating work environment. My fellow historians have made me especially proud to call the department home for the past decade. The University of North Carolina Press has been nothing but supportive (and patient) in helping steer this book toward publication. Ben Johnson, who I was fortunate enough to work with while a graduate student at Southern Methodist University, recommended I reach out to them, and I am glad he did. I join a roster of authors and scholars with whom I am both delighted and humbled to be associated, and working with their editorial staff has been a pleasure.

Andrae Marak and Jeff Shepherd reviewed this book at UNC's behest, and I cannot say enough about how helpful their feedback proved to be. It was gratifying to see this project taken so seriously by historians of their caliber, and the finished product benefited in innumerable ways from their insight, expertise, and apparently genuine interest. Ben Johnson, Samuel Brunk, and the late David Weber also had a hand in making this a better book. The research that forms this book's foundation was largely funded by the history departments at Southern Methodist University and Texas Tech University. A research trip to Mexico City was made possible by a historian (whose name was never revealed to me) who graciously forfeited book prize money awarded by SMU's Clements Center for Southwest Studies in order to help fund graduate student research. We need more people like that in the profession (and in the world, for that matter).

The Clements Center's various special events and manuscript workshops afforded me the opportunity to learn from and even rub shoulders with many of my heroes in the profession, which did a lot to keep me inspired and also to keep me current. Andrea Boardman and Ruth Ann Elmore were especially proactive in helping me remain in the Clements Center loop after I moved on from SMU. Jim Dudlo, José Ramírez, the late Constance Bishop, and I began our PhD journey at SMU together, and thanks in large part to them I loved every minute of it. Matt Babcock, who became an "honorary" member of our cohort a year later, also helped make my graduate experience a rich and memorable one.

Sherry Smith deserves her own separate acknowledgments section, but this will have to do. She took me on as a young master's student at the University of Texas at El Paso, and her mentorship made all the difference as I was trying (and mostly failing) to figure out what to do with my life. From there, she allowed me to ride her coattails to SMU, where I was fortunate enough to get to study with some of the best in the business. She has remained an unfailing advocate as I have tried to stay afloat in the profession, and her example as a scholar continues to inspire. Her contributions to this project can be seen on every page.

I have also been remarkably fortunate in the family department. Getting to this point would not have been possible without the generosity and selflessness of my grandparents Gerald and Amy Clark, my stepfather, Sam Pierce, and, especially, my father, Robert Schulze. All went out of their way to provide me with the opportunity to indulge my passion for learning, as uncertain as my career trajectory might have at times seemed. My grandfather Clinton Schulze did a lot to spark my curiosity about the world around me, and he is missed. My grandmother Julia has been yet another reliably supportive presence in my life. Thanks also to my brother Jason, sister-in-law Cindy, and niece Mia for their love and friendship, and to my friends at the Dubliner and the Cold Beer Company for tolerating my unconventional work habits.

My mother, Deborah Anita Pierce, passed away after a long illness while I was wrapping up this project, and I miss her dearly. This book would have made her enormously proud. With a heavy heart, I dedicate it to her memory. These days I have had to rely more than ever on the love and support of my wife, Samantha Mabry, and she has not failed to deliver. Her intelligence, creativity, compassion, and class astound even fifteen years later. I am so grateful for our little family.

Finally, I want to express my respect and admiration for the indigenous peoples whose past and present form the heart and soul of this book. I hope my efforts did justice to their collective histories and honored, in some small way, their cultural and political resilience and vitality. My most fervent hope for this book, though, is that it provides not only historical context for their contemporary predicaments, but also a nudge forward in addressing them, however slight that nudge might be.

Notes

Introduction

1. *Tucson Daily Citizen*, 25 May 1887.

2. Evelyn Hu-DeHart, "Yaqui Resistance to Mexican Expansion," in Kicza, *The Indian in Latin American History*, 142–43; Evans, *Bound in Twine*, 69.

3. Hu-DeHart, "Yaqui Resistance," 142–43.

4. Guidotti-Hernández, *Unspeakable Violence*, 185; Spicer, *Cycles of Conquest*, 67.

5. Ramón Corral, "Biografía de José María Leyva, Cajeme," in Corral, *Obras históricas*, 149–50; Guidotti-Hernández, *Unspeakable Violence*, 185, 189, 195.

6. Quoted in Spicer, *The Yaquis*, 159.

7. J. Trujillo (no title given), Sahuaripa, Sonora, to Secretary of State, Hermosillo, Sonora, 15 January 1887, tomo 22, expediente 7, #016470; R. Aragón (no title given), Moctezuma, Sonora, to Secretary of State, Hermosillo, Sonora, 25 April 1887, tomo 22, expediente 7, #016488, Archivo Histórico del Estado de Sonora, Hermosillo, Mexico.

8. Guidotti-Hernández, *Unspeakable Violence*, 185; Corral, *Obras históricas*, 190, translation found in Hu-DeHart, "Yaqui Resistance," 161. Ramón Corral was governor of the state of Sonora from 1887 until 1891, and later served as vice president under Porfirio Díaz, resigning his post at the outset of the Mexican Revolution and relocating to Paris. Throughout Sonora, he was known as a member of the so-called triumvirate, a group of governors (including Luis Torres and Rafael Izábel) who advocated aggressive modernization and economic growth, often at the expense of the state's indigenous population. See Evans, *Bound in Twine*, 69.

9. *Tucson Daily Citizen*, 25 May 1887; Hillary, "Cajeme," 136. Cajeme's legacy, perhaps not surprisingly, would prove to be as complicated as the man himself. As the historians Manuel Ferrer Muñoz and María Bono López point out, Cajeme's popularity "transcended the limits of the valley and spread to neighboring states, like Chihuahua, where at the beginning of the twentieth century the following corrido was still sung: "They say that Cajeme is dead, / but he isn't dead by any means. / He's gone to the Sierra Mojada / to see his ancestors." See Muñoz and Bono López, *Pueblos indígenas y estado nacional*, 357, author's translation. Cajeme was also one of the rare North American Indians to make international news. Paris's *Le Temps* and *Agence Hava*, after receiving word via telegram from New York, reported on Cajeme's execution, painting an almost celebratory portrait of him as the chief of the "savage" Yaqui tribe that had long terrorized the U.S.-Mexico borderlands. See Ramón Fernandez, Legación de los Estados Unidos Mexicanos en Francia, to Senior Secretary of Foreign

Relations, 27 April 1887, newspaper clippings enclosed, 27 April 1887, topográphica 17-21-117, Archivo Histórico de la Secretaría de las Relaciones Exteriores, Mexico City, Mexico. Some Yaquis, however, eschewed the hero worship, instead remembering Cajeme as a traitor who, in pursuit of glory and power, betrayed the best interests of the tribal whole. For example, a Yaqui who served under Cajeme recalled an episode whereby a group of Yaqui soldiers, at Cajeme's urging, departed a Yaqui camp to raid a Mexican camp. They had not gotten far when Cajeme, for reasons that are unknown, lit a bonfire, tipping off nearby Mexican soldiers that Yaquis were in the area. The soldiers subsequently swept the area, taking the lives of many women, children, and elders and imprisoning the rest. Cajeme, meanwhile, fled for Guaymas a free man, leaving more than a little resentment in his wake. See Kelley, *Yaqui Women*, 82–83. And when interrogated shortly before Cajeme's execution, two captured Yaquis claimed that the majority of the inhabitants of their pueblos had grown weary of fighting the Mexican military and only wanted peace. Thus, not all Yaquis rallied behind Cajeme and his vision of an independent Yaqui nation. See G. Monteverde, Guaymas, Sonora, to Secretary of State, Hermosillo, Sonora, 18 January 1886, tomo 21, expediente 5, #015809, Archivo Histórico del Estado de Sonora.

10. Spicer, *The Yaqui*, 160–61.

11. O. Martínez, *Troublesome Border*, 71–73.

12. Underhill, *Papago Woman*, 31–32.

13. Manuel and Neff, *Desert Indian Woman*, 189–91; Marak and Tuennerman, *At the Border of Empires*, 146.

14. In other words, they joined the ranks of other groups and individuals inhabiting the broader U.S.-Mexico border region that, as the historians Samuel Truett and Elliott Young recently put it, "history forgot." They explain, "Ever since the border was mapped in 1854, the borderlands have supported a complex web of historical relationships that transcended—even as they emerged in tandem with—the U.S. and Mexican nations." These stories, they observe, "are characterized most of all by their absence from mainstream Mexican and U.S. history." See Truett and Young, *Continental Crossroads*, 1–2.

15. See Ortiz, *Mixtec Transnational Identity*; Novo, *Who Defines Indigenous?*; Luna-Firebaugh, "The Border Crossed Us," 159–81; Hays, "Cross-Border Indigenous Nations," 40–42.

16. Baud and Van Schendel, "Toward a Comparative History of Borderlands," 233.

17. Ortiz, *Mixtec Transnational Identity*, 12.

18. Donald L. Fixico, "Ethics and Responsibilities in Writing American Indian History," in Mihesuah, *Natives and Academics*, 88–89.

19. Spicer, "Potam," 55.

20. Here I am essentially building on Brian DeLay's insights into how "Mexican, American, and indigenous politics came together in a forgotten nexus that reshaped North American boundaries for all of its peoples" while also showing that this process of negotiating boundaries actually continued well into the twentieth century. See DeLay, *War of a Thousand Deserts*, xviii.

21. Juliana Barr and Edward Countryman have observed that "a really good map of the colonial situation of the early western hemisphere would show a set of sometimes fluid, sometimes unbending fields of force, all of them dealing with the issue of space." I would argue that this conception of the Western Hemisphere still applies, as evidenced by the spatial distribution of both the peoples and spheres of power and influence in the histories contained herein. In fact, they later argue, "In some ways, the American hemisphere may be just as much a colonial space today as it was in 1700, considering as we might the Indian reservations still dotting the maps of Canada and the United States and the continued battles fought by independent Indians in Chiapas and Brazil." See Barr and Countryman, *Contested Spaces of Early America*, 2, 25.

22. Martínez, *Troublesome Border*, 8–10.

23. Ibid., 10–12, 18–22; DeLay, *War of a Thousand Deserts*, xv. It should be added that the dual nature of the U.S.-Mexico border would have a direct hand in influencing the historical trajectories of the indigenous groups discussed herein. While the eastern half of the border corresponded with a well-known geographic feature, the Rio Grande, the so-called desert border that stretches from El Paso to the Pacific Ocean is essentially a straight line connecting several geographically significant locations: El Paso, the Gila River, the intersection of the Colorado and Gila Rivers, and San Diego Bay. While at one point the border followed a section of the Gila River, the 1853 treaty moved it well to the south. As the historian Rachel St. John observed, "The Rio Grande had drawn people to its banks for trade, travel, and settlement long before it became a part of an international border, but on the site of the western border there had simply been no *there* there before the Treaty of Guadalupe." It would take some time for the western border region to gain widespread recognition as and assume the character and appearance of a political line of demarcation, and the gradual nature of this transition would play a key role in shaping the historical experiences of the Yaquis and, especially, the Tohono O'odham. St. John also pointed out that surveying parties, especially on the Mexican side, often struggled with funding issues in completing their assigned tasks. Ironically, one assistant engineer sent by Mexico to survey the Gila River was, as St. John puts it, "only able to complete his assignment by . . . securing assistance from Maricopa and Tohono O'odham Indians." The Tohono O'odham, then, had at least an indirect hand in the mapping of the U.S.-Mexico border. See St. John, *Line in the Sand*, 2, 25.

24. Chief John Horse to "General Augur," 12 December 1873, "Research Materials, 1873–1965," box 32, folder 12, Felipe and Dolores Latorre Papers, Benson Latin American Collection, University of Texas at Austin.

25. Ambassador M. Aspíroz, Washington, DC, to Secretaría de las Relaciones Exteriores, Mexico City, 28 February 1900, topográphica 15-8-118, Archivo Histórico de la Secretaría de las Relaciones Exteriores; St. John, *Line in the Sand*, 36–37.

26. Ron Robin, "The Exhaustion of Enclosures: A Critique of Internationalism," in Bender, *Rethinking American History in a Global Age*, 372.

27. Michael Kearney, "Mixtec Political Consciousness: From Passive to Active Resistance," in Nugent, *Rural Revolt in Mexico*, 144.

28. Carey and Marak, *Smugglers, Brothels, and Twine*, 2.

29. Ibid., 42, 45, 85–86, 119, 129, 142; Gerardo Rénique, "Race, Region, and Nation: Sonora's Anti-Chinese Racism and Mexico's Postrevolutionary Nationalism, 1920s–1930s," in Appelbaum, Macpherson, and Rosemblatt, *Race and Nation in Modern Latin America*, 213.

30. Anderson, *Imagined Communities*, 3, 6–7.

31. Shepherd, *We Are an Indian Nation*, 11; Barr, *Peace Came in the Form of a Woman*, 8–9.

32. Harvard Project, *The State of Native Nations*, 13.

33. Thomas C. Holt, "The First New Nations," in Appelbaum, Macpherson, and Rosemblatt, *Race and Nation in Modern Latin America*, x.

34. Edward H. Spicer, "The United States–Mexico Border and Cultural Alternatives: The Yaqui Case," paper presented at the UTEP Conference on Border Studies, June 1976, A-1191, pp. 1–9, 14, Edward H. Spicer Papers, Arizona State Museum Archives, Tucson; *The Oregonian*, 18 September 2006.

35. Spicer, "The United States–Mexico Border," 1–9, 14.

36. Deloria and Lytle, *The Nations Within*, 242; Holm, Pearson, and Chavis, "Peoplehood," 10.

37. Holm, Pearson, and Chavis, "Peoplehood," 12, 14–17; Shepherd, *We Are an Indian Nation*, 215. It should be pointed out that, as the historian Colin Woodward put it, "Americans . . . often confuse the terms *state* and *nation*, and are among the only people in the world who use *statehood* and *nationhood* interchangeably." Woodward goes on to try to differentiate between the two, concluding that "a *state* is a sovereign political entity like the United Kingdom, Kenya, Panama, or New Zealand, eligible for membership in the United Nations and inclusion on the maps produced by Rand McNally or the National Geographic Society. A *nation* is a group of people who share—or believe they share—a common culture, ethnic origin, language, historical experience, artifacts, and symbols. Some nations are presently stateless—the Kurdish, Palestinian, or Québécois nations, for instance. Some control and dominate their own *nation-state*, which they typically name for themselves, as in France, Germany, Japan, or Turkey. Conversely, there are plenty of states—some of them federated—that aren't dominated by a single nation, like Belgium, Switzerland, Malaysia, Canada, and, indeed, the United States." See Woodward, *American Nations*, 3.

38. Prucha, *The Great Father*, 75–77; (Signature illegible) to Augustin Muñoz, 7 May 1840, tomo 14, expediente 15, #10647, Archivo Historíco del Estado de Sonora. The author references the "nación Papago."

39. Barr and Countryman, *Contested Spaces of Early America*, 8.

40. Deloria and Lytle, *The Nations Within*, 14.

41. Salas, *In the Shadow of the Eagles*, 109.

Chapter One

1. J. Turner, *Barbarous Mexico*, 24. Originally published in book form in 1910, Turner's work was partially serialized in 1909 in *American Magazine*.

2. J. Turner, *Barbarous Mexico*, 7–8, 12–13, 15.

3. Ibid., 26–27.

4. Turner's influence on popular opinion north of the border regarding events, leaders, and institutions in Mexico should not be underestimated. *Barbarous Mexico*, according to one scholar, has since developed a reputation as "the *Uncle Tom's Cabin* of the [1910] Mexican Revolution." Initially an indictment of the Díaz regime, it ultimately became much more. Like Stowe's book, it ultimately helped foster and sustain a popular emphasis on universal human freedom even in the throes of civil war. See Sinclair Snow's introduction to the 1969 edition of *Barbarous Mexico*.

5. Gibson, *The Kickapoos*, x.

6. Winfrey and Day, *The Indian Papers of Texas and the Southwest*, 4:274.

7. Erikson, *Yaqui Homeland and Homeplace*, 41, 54.

8. Spicer, *The Yaquis*, 10, 13; and Spicer, *Cycles of Conquest*, 46; Miller, "The Yaquis Become American Indians," 184; Forbes, "Historical Survey," 341; Griffith, *Beliefs and Holy Places*, 94; Folsom, *The Yaquis and the Empire*, 74.

9. Folsom, *The Yaquis and the Empire*, 6, 73, 119; Shorter, *We Will Dance Our Truth*, 9.

10. Spicer, *The Yaquis*, 42–49; Weber, *Spanish Frontier in North America*, 242.

11. Spicer, *The Yaquis*, 129–30.

12. Evelyn Hu-DeHart, "Yaqui Resistance to Mexican Expansion," in Kicza, *The Indian in Latin American History*, 54–55; Miller, "The Yaquis Become American Indians," 184; Jack Forbes, "Historical Survey," 341; Edward H. Spicer, "The United States–Mexico Border and Cultural Alternatives: The Yaqui Case," paper presented at the UTEP Conference on Border Studies, June 1976, A-1191, p. 12, Edward H. Spicer Papers, Arizona State Museum Archives, Tucson.

13. Folsom, *The Yaquis and the Empire*, 209.

14. Chantal Crasmaussel, "The Forced Transfer of Indians in Nueva Vizcaya and Sinaloa: A Hispanic Method of Colonization," in Barr and Countryman, *Contested Spaces of Early America*, 204–5.

15. Folsom, *The Yaquis and the Empire*, 190–93.

16. Quoted in Hu-DeHart, "Yaqui Resistance," 141.

17. Ibid., 146–47.

18. Ibid., 146.

19. Ibid., 148, 151–52.

20. Ibid., 157–58; Miller, "The Yaquis Become American Indians," 184.

21. Spicer, *The Yaquis*, 158.

22. "The Yaqui Rising," *Salt Lake City News*, 4 March 1900; "Yaqui Chiefs Put to Death," *San Francisco Call*, 25 February 1905; Guidotti-Hernández, *Unspeakable Violence*, 208.

23. "Traits of the Yaquis," *Washington Post*, 11 March 1900.

24. *Arizona Daily Star*, 27 April 1902.

25. M. Azpíroz, Secretary of Foreign Relations, to the Mexican Ambassador, Washington, DC, 12 March 1900, topográphica 15-8-118, Archivo Histórico de la Secretaría de las Relaciones Exteriores, Mexico City, Mexico.

26. Guidotti-Hernández, *Unspeakable Violence*, 210.

27. Quoted in Evans, *Bound in Twine*, 71.

28. Kelley, *Yaqui Women*, 74–75, 83.

29. Spicer, *The Yaquis*, 160–61; Kelley, *Yaqui Women*, 89; Haake, *The State, Removal and Indigenous Peoples*, 135–36.

30. Hu-DeHart, *Yaqui Resistance*, 8–9; Spicer, "The United States–Mexico Border," 14; M. Encinas, Sahuaripa, Sonora, to Secretary of State, Hermosillo, Sonora, 26 October 1890, tomo 22, expediente 7, #016835, and M. Sánchez, Torim, Sonora, to "the State Governor, Hermosillo," 15 October 1890, tomo 22, expediente 7, #016844, Archivo Histórico Estado de Sonora, Hermosillo, Mexico.

31. "2/9/37 E. Lu. Ch.," A-534, Spicer Papers.

32. Guidotti-Hernández, *Unspeakable Violence*, 214–15.

33. A. Piña, Mexican Consul, to M. H. McCord, United States Marshall, Phoenix, Arizona, 18 October 1904; A. Piña to Secretaría de las Relaciones Exteriores, 27 October 1904; Frederick S. Nave, United States Attorney for the Territory of Arizona, to M. H. McCord, 16 November 1905; and John Hay, Department of State, to Don Manuel de Azpíroz, 12 December 1904, topográphica 15-12-56, Archivo Histórico de la Secretaría de las Relaciones Exteriores.

34. Guidotti-Hernández, *Unspeakable Violence*, 216.

35. Evans, *Bound in Twine*, 72, 82; Guidotti-Hernández, *Unspeakable Violence*, 217.

36. Hu-DeHart, *Yaqui Resistance*, 9; Beals, *Mexican Maze*, 185; Hall, *Alvaro Obregón*, 20. One must actually wonder why Obregón did not harbor any ill will toward the Yaquis, since, as Hall explains, the Indians attacked his father's ranch near the Río Mayo when Obregón was a child, stealing all of his cattle and burning his house to the ground (ibid.).

37. Spicer, *The Yaquis*, 227.

38. Jürgen Buchenau, *Plutarco Elías Calles and the Mexican Revolution*, 74.

39. *Arizona Republic*, 14 June 1916.

40. B. F. Yost to Secretary of State, Washington, DC, 19 July 1919, and 6 August 1919, 16-28-49, Archivo Histórico de la Secretaría de las Relaciones Exteriores; Spicer, "Potam," 14–15.

41. George Summerlin, Chargé d'Affaires, to Salvador Diego-Fernandez, Department of Foreign Relations, 21 June 1919, and Juan Ríos, El General Oficial Mayor Encargado del Despacho, to C. Official M. Encargado de la Secretaría de Relaciones Exteriores, 29 July 1919, topográphica 16-28-132, Archivo Histórico de la Secretaría de las Relaciones Exteriores.

42. Ambassador Henry Lane Wilson to Manuel Calero, Minister for Foreign Affairs, 28 December 1911, 16-8-139, Archivo Histórico de la Secretaría de las Relaciones Exteriores.

43. Dwyer, *Agrarian Dispute*, 128–30.

44. Spicer, *The Yaquis*, 236.

45. "Notes of Lucas Chávez, Yaqui informant," 15 May 1937, A-675, Spicer Papers; Kelley, *Yaqui Women*, 205, 220.

46. Savala, *Autobiography of a Yaqui Poet*, 6–8.

47. Kelley, *Yaqui Women*, 102–3, 123–24; Spicer, *The Yaquis*, 236–39; Alexandra Minna Stern, "Nationalism on the Line: Masculinity, Race, and the Creation of the U.S. Border Patrol, 1910–1940," in Truett and Young, *Continental Crossroad*, 300.

48. Spicer, "The United States–Mexico Border," 8.

49. Latorre and Latorre, *The Mexican Kickapoo Indians*, 3–4; Reid, *Close Calls*, 34.

50. Latorre and Latorre, *The Mexican Kickapoo Indians*, 4–6; Nunley, "The Mexican Kickapoo Indians," 2; Fabila, *La tribu Kikapoo de Coahuila*, 25; Dillingham, "The Oklahoma Kickapoo," 42.

51. Gibson, *The Kickapoos*, 50.

52. *Confirming the Citizenship Status of the Texas Band of Kickapoo Indians: Hearings*, 14.

53. Latorre and Latorre, *The Mexican Kickapoo Indians*, 6–8; Reid, *Close Calls*, 34; Harrison quoted in Gibson, *The Kickapoos*, 56.

54. Latorre and Latorre, *The Mexican Kickapoo Indians*, 8–11; Nunley, "The Mexican Kickapoo Indians," 20–21; and Alan Taylor, "Remaking Americans: Louisiana, Upper Canada, and Texas," in Barr and Countryman, *Contested Spaces*, 220.

55. Gibson, *The Kickapoos*, 201.

56. Winfrey and Day, *The Indian Papers of Texas and the Southwest*, 1:62, 69, 126, and 3:90.

57. Gibson, *The Kickapoos*, 201; Latorre and Latorre, *The Mexican Kickapoo Indians*, 11–16; DeLay, *War of a Thousand Deserts*, 297–98; E. John Gesick Jr., "Historical Essay," in Wright, *The Texas Kickapoos*, 13–14; James T. Matthews, "The Edwards Plateau and Permian Basin," in Carlson and Glasrud, *West Texas*, 64; "Ministerio de relaciones interiores y exteriores," no title or signature, 18 October 1850, tomo 15, expediente 2, #10843, Archivo Histórico Estado de Sonora.

58. Quoted in Kristin Hoganson, "Struggles for Peace and Space: Kickapoo Traces from the Midwest to Mexico," in Confer, Marak, and Tuennerman, *Transnational Indians*, 214.

59. Ibid.

60. Gibson, *The Kickapoos*, 201–2.

61. Quoted in Latorre and Latorre, *The Mexican Kickapoo Indians*, 21.

62. Gibson, *The Kickapoos*, 210, 214–15; Latorre and Latorre, *The Mexican Kickapoo Indians*, 22; rancher quoted 218. George T. Díaz, *Border Contraband: A History of Smuggling across the Rio Grande* (Austin: University of Texas Press, 2015), 6; Andreas, *Smuggler Nation*, 2; Sheridan quoted in Reid, *Close Calls*, 35.

63. John W. Foster, "Legation of the United States," to G. M. Lafragua, Minister of Foreign Affairs, 8 May 1875, topográphica 5-16-8736, Archivo Histórico de la Secretaría de las Relaciones Exteriores; "Removal of Kickapoos and Other Indians

from Texas and Mexico, Letter from the Secretary of the Interior," Executive Document no. 39, 43rd Congress, 1st session, 7 January 1874, Center for American History, University of Texas at Austin; Winfrey and Day, *The Indian Papers of Texas and the Southwest*, 4:87, 127–28.

64. Winfrey and Day, *The Indian Papers of Texas and the Southwest*, 4:273; Henry M. Atkinson, U.S. Special Indian Commissioner, to Edward P. Smith, Commissioner of Indian Affairs, 22 March 1875 and 27 March 1875, and John W. Foster to Juan D. Arias, Department of Foreign Affairs, 9 February 1876, 5-16-8736, Archivo Histórico de la Secretaría de las Relaciones Exteriores.

65. F. Paschal of Chihuahua to War Department, Washington, DC, telegram, no date given, and John W. Foster to S. L. Vallarta, Minister of Foreign Affairs, Mexico, 2 January 1878, topográphica 1-15-1678, Archivo Histórico de la Secretaría de las Relaciones Exteriores.

66. *Hearings before the Joint Commission of the Congress of the United States*, 63rd Congress, 2nd session, 17 and 27 April 1914 (Washington, DC: Government Printing Office, 1914), 1500, mostly testimony by Martin J. Bentley, Shawnee, OK.

67. Ibid., 1503.

68. Ibid., 1508.

69. American Embassy, Mexico (no name given), to Ignacio Mariscal, Minister for Foreign Affairs, Mexico, 5 June 1906, and C. F. Larrabee to Secretary of the Interior (no name given), 14 April 1905, topográphica 15-14-27, Archivo Histórico de la Secretaría de las Relaciones Exteriores.

70. Frank A. Thackery to Commissioner of Indian Affairs (no name given), 2 June 1906, topográphica 15-14-27, Archivo Histórico de la Secretaría de las Relaciones Exteriores.

71. *Affairs of the Kickapoo Indians: Hearing before the Subcommittee of the Committee on Indian Affairs*, 41, 107.

72. Reid, *Close Calls*, 35; Hays, "Cross-Border Indigenous Nations," 42.

73. Marak, "The Attempted Eradication of Mexican Kickapoo Culture," 26.

74. Castillo and Cowan, *It Is Not Our Fault*, 9.

75. Forbes, "Historical Survey," 336–38.

76. Jacoby, *Shadows at Dawn*, 20, 26.

77. Erickson, *Sharing the Desert*, 21, 24–25, 32; Meeks, *Border Citizens*, 20–21.

78. Underhill, *The Papago Indians of Arizona*, 63. The term "Papaguería" refers to that portion of the Sonoran Desert that lies in far southern Arizona and northern Sonora. See Lewis, *Neither Wolf nor Dog*, 120.

79. Underhill, *Papago Woman*, 31.

80. Forbes, "Historical Survey," 350, 358; *Arizona Daily Star*, 21 January 1916.

81. Erickson, *Sharing the Desert*, 75.

82. St. John, *Line in the Sand*, 31, 45, 49.

83. Quoted in Jacoby, *Shadows at Dawn*, 37–38.

84. R. A. Wilbur Papers, 1840–1882, AZ 565, University of Arizona Library Special Collections, Tucson.

85. St. John, *Line in the Sand*, 62; Jacoby, *Shadows at Dawn*, 198.

86. St. John, *Line in the Sand*, 74–75.

87. Manuel and Neff, *Desert Indian Woman*, 189–91; Erickson, *Sharing the Desert*, 83–84.

88. Erickson, *Sharing the Desert*, 91–93, 98; Lewis, *Neither Wolf nor Dog*, 139.

89. *Arizona Daily Citizen*, 8 April 1895, 1.

90. Lewis, *Neither Wolf nor Dog*, 148.

91. *Arizona Daily Star*, 5 August 1915.

92. *Tucson Citizen*, 21 January 1916; *Arizona Daily Star*, 21 January 1916; Lewis, *Neither Wolf nor Dog*, 148.

93. *Arizona Daily Star*, 23 January 1916; *Tucson Daily Citizen*, 18 February 1916.

94. Griffith, *Beliefs and Holy Places*, xix–xx, 14–15, 21, 29.

95. *Arizona Republican*, 3 February 1916; *Tucson Citizen*, 11 February 1916.

96. *Tucson Citizen*, 28 February 1916.

97. Erickson, *Sharing the Desert*, 107; Lewis, *Neither Wolf nor Dog*, 148.

98. Erickson, *Sharing the Desert*, 106.

99. Castillo and Cowan, *It Is Not Our Fault*, 52.

100. Erickson, *Sharing the Desert*, 112.

101. Ibid., 116.

102. St. John, *Line in the Sand*, 8.

103. Hoganson, "Struggles for Place and Space," 220.

Chapter Two

1. Though Paz's essay was first published in the *New Yorker* on September 17, 1979, it can also be found in later editions of Paz, *The Labyrinth of Solitude*, 362.

2. Paz, *The Labyrinth of Solitude*, 363.

3. Rodríguez O., "The Emancipation of America," 139.

4. Prucha, *The Great Father*, ix.

5. Haake, *The State, Removal and Indigenous Peoples*, 6.

6. Harvard Project, *The State of Native Nations*, 18.

7. Haake, *The State, Removal and Indigenous Peoples*, 13–15; Prucha, *The Great Father*, 70–72.

8. Haake, *The State, Removal and Indigenous Peoples*, 16.

9. Prucha, *The Great Father*, 224–28; Koppes, "From New Deal to Termination," 544–55.

10. Adams, *Education for Extinction*, 18–19; Wilkinson, *Blood Struggle*, 6. See also Trafzer, Keller, and Sisquoc, *Boarding School Blues*.

11. Wilkinson, *Blood Struggle*, 21.

12. Philp, *John Collier's Crusade for Indian Reform*, 117–20, 137–43, and Philp, "Termination," 165.

13. J. Wilson, *The Earth Shall Weep*, 356.

14. Harvard Project, *The State of Native Nations*, 19.

15. Philp, *Termination Revisited*, 151; and Philp, "Termination," 165. Incidentally, the BIA experimented with a policy that closely resembled termination on the Tohono O'odham reservation at midcentury. The so-called Papago Development Program called for an end to the U.S. government's supervision of the tribe and for the tribe's merger with the "general community." The program, however, failed to effect positive change on the reservation, at least not to the degree that would have allowed the tribe to stand alone without federal assistance. See Cadava, *Standing on Common Ground*, 83–84.

16. Hoxie, *A Final Promise*; and Philp, *Termination Revisited*, 168.

17. Deloria, *American Indian Policy in the Twentieth Century*, 28; and Philp, *Termination Revisited*, 174–75. For a comprehensive overview of American Indian activism, see Cobb and Fowler, *Beyond Red Power*.

18. Wilkinson, *Blood Struggle*, 352–53. For an overview of late twentieth-century federal Indian policy, see also Castile, *Taking Charge*.

19. Frye, *Indians into Mexicans*, 4.

20. Quoted in F. Turner, *The Dynamic of Mexican Nationalism*, 173.

21. Quoted in *Boletín Indigenista* 2, no. 2 (1942): 18–19.

22. León-Portilla, "Mexico," 68.

23. Stephen E. Lewis, "The Nation, Education, and the 'Indian Problem' in Mexico, 1920–1940," in Vaughan and Lewis, *The Eagle and the Virgin*, 178.

24. Haake, *The State, Removal and Indigenous Peoples*, 85.

25. Ibid., 86–87.

26. Ibid., 91.

27. David J. Weber, *The Spanish Frontier*, 306–8; Rubin, Smilde, and Junge, "Lived Religion and Lived Citizenship," 12, 20.

28. Haake, *The State, Removal and Indigenous Peoples*, 91–92.

29. Quoted in ibid., 94; Scott, *Seeing Like a State*, 5–7.

30. Luis Reyes García, "Comentarios sobre historia India," in Warman and Argueta, *Moviminetos indígenas contemporaneous en México*, 196.

31. Powell, "Mexican Intellectuals and the Indian Question," 19–22, 30.

32. Ibid., 26, 33.

33. Ibid., 34.

34. Ibid., 35–36.

35. Quoted in Buchenau, *Plutarco Elías Calles*, 64–65.

36. Weber, *The Spanish Frontier*, 203.

37. Marak, *From Many, One*, 15–16.

38. López, "The India Bonita Contest of 1921," 294–95.

39. Reyes García, "Comentarios," 170–74; Thomas C. Holt, "The First New Nations," in Appelbaum, Macpherson, and Rosemblatt, *Race and Nation in Modern Latin America*, xi.

40. *Boletín Indigenista* 8 (1948): 143.

41. *Boletín Indigenista* 2, no. 3 (1942): 25.

42. Dawson, *Indian and Nation*, xiii–xiv; Alexandra Minna Stern, "From Mestizo-philia to Biotypology: Racialization and Science in Mexico, 1920–1960," in Appel-baum, Macpherson, and Rosemblatt, *Race and Nation in Modern Latin America*, 196.

43. León-Portilla, "Mexico," 78–80.

44. *Boletín Indigenista* 1 (1941): 10.

45. *Boletín Indigenista* 8 (1948): 135–137; *Boletín Indigenista* 1 (1941): 2–3.

46. *Boletín Indigenista* 13 (1953): 127–29.

47. Ibid., 131.

48. Dawson, *Indian and Nation*, 93–94.

49. Quoted in ibid., 70.

50. Lewis, "The Nation, Education, and the 'Indian Problem,'" 191.

51. Marak and Tuennerman, *At the Border of Empires*, 18.

52. Haake, *The State, Removal and Indigenous Peoples*, 100.

53. Cadava, "Borderlands of Modernity and Abandonment," 376–77.

54. Marak and Tuennerman, *At the Border of Empires*, 1; Dawson, *Indian and Nation*, xvii.

55. Dawson, *Indian and Nation*, xxi, xxiii.

56. Ibid., 18–19, 79.

57. Ibid., 79, 82–83.

58. Haake, *The State, Removal and Indigenous Peoples*, 103–5.

Chapter Three

1. Moisés, Kelley, and Holden, *The Tall Candle*, 150–51. Portions of this chapter appeared in Jeff Schulze, "'The Year of the Yaqui': Texas Tech's Sonoran Expeditions," *Journal of the West* 48, no. 3 (Summer 2009). Copyright © 2009 by *Journal of the West*, an imprint of ABC-CLIO, LLC. All rights reserved. Reproduced with permission of ABC-CLIO, LLC, Santa Barbara, CA.

2. Frank M. Madden Jr., "Yaqui Expedition Diary," 13 March 1934, box 81, folder 20, William Curry Holden Papers Southwest Collection, Texas Tech University, Lubbock, TX.

3. *Lubbock Avalanche-Journal*, 21 April 1984; *Lubbock Morning Avalanche*, 20 February 1934; Madden, "Yaqui Expedition Diary," 13 March 1934.

4. Ruben Flores, *Backroads Pragmatists*, 177, 179, 187, 190–91.

5. A. Guy, "They Lived with the Yaquis"; *University Daily* (Lubbock, TX), 16 April 1984.

6. Flores, *Backroads Pragmatists*, 197.

7. Spicer, *Pascua*, 7, 17, 25.

8. Guidotti-Hernández, *Unspeakable Violence*, 210, 212; Matthews, "Yaqui Country," 8.

9. Moisés, Kelley, and Holden, *The Tall Candle*, 151–53.

10. Carl Coleman Seltzer, "Physical Characteristics of the Yaqui Indians," in Holden, "Studies of the Yaqui Indians of Sonora, Mexico," 92–97; Holden, "Studies of the Yaqui Indians of Sonora, Mexico," 11.

11. Madden, "Yaqui Expedition Diary," 27 March 1934.

12. Charles John Wagner, "Medical Practices of the Yaquis," in Holden, "Studies of the Yaqui Indians of Sonora, Mexico," 88, 90; *Lubbock Morning Avalanche*, 15 March 1934, 18 March 1934, and 22 March 1934; *Lubbock Avalanche-Journal*, 21 April 1934.

13. Moisés, Kelley, and Holden, *The Tall Candle*, 156–57.

14. Ramón Torry to "Mr. Dr. Holden," 27 May 1934, box 81, folder 13, William Curry Holden Papers.

15. William Curry Holden to Ramon Torry, 14 June 1934, box 81, folder 13, Holden Papers.

16. Ramon Torry to Dr. Holden, 28 April 1935, box 81, folder 13, Holden Papers.

17. W. C. Holden to Mr. Ramon Terry, 5 May 1935, box 81, folder 13, Holden Papers.

18. W. C. Holden to Mr. Ramon Beteta, 8 May 1935, box 81, folder 13, Holden Papers; Flores, *Backroads Pragmatists*, 202.

19. Ramón Beteta to Mr. W. C. Holden, 29 January 1938, box 81, folder 13, Holden Papers.

20. McGuire, *Politics and Ethnicity*, 21–22; Matthews, "Yaqui Country," 4–6.

21. Moisés, Kelley, and Holden, *The Tall Candle*, 193–94, 213, 227–28, 234.

22. "The Year of the Yaqui" program, "Yaqui" folder, Southwest Collection, Texas Tech University.

23. Ettinger, " 'We Sometimes Wonder What They Will Spring on Us Next,' " 160, 167, 174, 180; Limerick, *The Legacy of Conquest*, 222.

24. Martínez, *Troublesome Border*, 132–33.

25. Quoted in Spicer, *People of Pascua*, 205.

26. *Tucson Daily Citizen*, 31 July 1936, 1–2; Edward H. Spicer, "The United States–Mexico Border and Cultural Alternatives: The Yaqui Case," paper presented at the UTEP Conference on Border Studies, June 1976, A-1191, p. 15, Edward H. Spicer Papers, Arizona State Museum Archives, Tucson; Edward H. Spicer, "Pascua, 1936–37, University of Chicago Culture Contact Seminar; Field Reports to University of Chicago," A-669, p. 5, Spicer Papers.

27. *Tucson Daily Citizen*, 31 July 1936, 2; Holden, "Studies of the Yaqui Indians," 7. After reading the "shirt-tail" history following its translation from Yaqui to Spanish by "Generale" Flores, Holden was evidently unimpressed. He described it as "mostly a sketchy account of the tribal wars with the Mexicans since 1740."

28. J. F. Weadock to Enrique Liekens, "Residentes en el Extranjero," 23 May 1931, topográphica IV-341-35, Archivo Histórico de la Secretaría de las Relaciones Exteriores, Mexico City, Mexico.

29. *Tucson Daily Citizen*, 1 August 1936, 1. For more on the repatriation campaign, see Balderrama and Rodríguez, *Decade of Betrayal*.

30. Quoted in Spicer, *People of Pascua*, 178, 182.

31. Quoted in Dwyer, *Agrarian Dispute*, 131.

32. Dawson, *Indian and Nation*, 67.

33. Dwyer, *Agrarian Dispute*, 132.

34. Ibid., 86.

35. *Boletín Indigenista* 3 (1943): 41–43; Dwyer, *Agrarian Dispute*, 134.

36. Adrian A. Bantjes, *As If Jesus Walked on Earth*, 36.

37. Ibid., 37.

38. "Field Notes—Potam," "Mexican Major of 3rd Batallon [*sic*], Feb. 17, 1942," A-505, Spicer Papers.

39. Bantjes, *As If Jesus Walked on Earth*, 38.

40. Ibid., 125.

41. Ibid., 145–46; Dwyer, *Agrarian Dispute*, 134–35.

42. *Tucson Daily Citizen*, 23 September 1947; Spicer, "Potam," 55, 63.

43. Spicer, *Cycles of Conquest*, 335–41.

44. "Field Notes—Potam," "Paulino Valenzuela, March 5, 1942," A-505, Spicer Papers.

45. McGuire, *Politics and Ethnicity*, 21–22; Matthews, "Yaqui Country," 4–6; Bantjes, *As If Jesus Walked on Earth*, 144; Dwyer, *Agrarian Dispute*, 133.

46. Quoted in Dawson, *Indian and Nation*, 127; "Field Notes—Potam" "Potam Fariseo Captain, Feb. 18, 1942," A-505, Spicer Papers; Dwyer, *Agrarian Dispute*, 135.

47. Quoted in Bantjes, *As If Jesus Walked on Earth*, 147.

48. Ibid., 148.

49. *Boletín Indigenista* 12 (1952): 311–13.

50. León-Portilla, "Mexico," 72.

51. Bartell, "Directed Culture Change among the Sonoran Yaquis," 38–40.

52. Ibid., 32–35, 62.

53. Quoted in Erikson, *Yaqui Homeland and Homeplace*, 6.

54. Ibid., 39–40.

55. McGuire, *Politics and Ethnicity*, 38–39, 88–89, 121.

56. Ibid., 196; Meeks, *Border Citizens*, 86–87; Griffith, *Beliefs and Holy Places*, xiv, 94.

57. *Arizona Daily Star*, 29 August 1940.

58. Spicer, *People of Pascua*, 46.

59. Ibid., 44–45.

60. Ibid., 1–3, 16; Spicer, "Potam," 17; Fabila, *Las tribus Yaquis de Sonora*, 209.

61. Spicer, *People of Pascua*, 34–35.

62. *El Porvenir*, 20 January 1965; Martínez, *Troublesome Border*, 119.

63. Spicer, University of Chicago Culture Contact Seminar, 13.

64. Spicer, *People of Pascua*, 16–18, 38.

65. Ibid., xvi.

66. Ibid., 39–40.

67. Ibid., 37.

68. Field Notes, Pascua Yaquis, "10/10/36 E. T. A.," A-534, Spicer Papers; Meeks, *Border Citizens*, 11–12.

69. Spicer, *People of Pascua*, 42–43.

70. The Mexican government responded to Yaqui concerns such as these by establishing a "culture mission" near Vicam Viejo, which was in line with their plan to establish missions within all of Mexico's predominantly indigenous regions in an effort to fuse their cultures with a developing mainstream Mexican culture. Spicer visited the Vicam mission and found it to be relatively benign. He noted a series of murals painted "in the Diego Rivera tradition" that told the history of the Yaqui people. Spicer was surprised that one of the murals "elevated to a position of tremendous importance" Tetabiate, who directed the tribe's rebellion after Cajeme's execution. "Tete Biate [*sic*] dominates the whole cultural mission," Spicer stated, obviously aware of the irony. Spicer further noted that mostly mixed-blood Yaquis attended classes at the missions, and that full-blood Yaquis had yet to take to the mission idea. Still, Spicer witnessed some good being done at the mission. For instance, he saw a group of Yaquis disassemble then reassemble an old Model T engine, while others were learning to build and maintain agricultural equipment. Thus, while introducing Mexican cultural and economic influences, the mission, simultaneously, made at least a halfhearted effort at keeping Yaqui history and institutions alive. See *Arizona Daily Star*, 12 December 1939; *Tucson Daily Citizen*, 23 September 1947.

71. Molina, Salazar, and Kaczkurkin, *The Yaquis*, 8–9.

72. Spicer, "The United States–Mexico Border," 16.

73. Spicer, University of Chicago Culture Contact Seminar, 6.

74. Castile, "Yaquis, Edward H. Spicer, and Federal Indian Policy," 392; McGuire, "Ritual, Theater, and the Persistence of the Ethnic Group," 173, 176.

75. Erickson, *Yaqui Homeland and Homeplace*, 52–53.

76. Kelley, *Yaqui Women*, 251–52.

77. Ibid., 151–53.

78. McGuire, *Politics and Ethnicity*, 1–2.

79. *Lubbock Avalanche-Journal*, 21 April 1984.

80. Dan L. Flores, "A Journal of the 1984 Texas Tech University Yaqui Expedition," Dan L. Flores Papers, 1984–1985, wallet 1, pp. 1–5, Southwest Collection, Texas Tech University, Lubbock, TX.

81. Ibid., 9–14; Marilyn Bentz, "Beyond Ethics: Science, Friendship, and Privacy," in Biolsi and Zimmerman, *Indians and Anthropologists*, 120.

82. Flores, "Journal," 17–18.

83. Erikson, *Yaqui Homeland and Homeplace*, 8.

84. Ibid., 10, 39–40.

85. Anselmo Valencia, David G. Ramírez, and Justo Estrella to Neil Bruno, United States Immigration and Naturalization Service, 3 January 3 1985, and David G. Ramirez, "Affidavit," 26 December 1984, MS 325, folder 676/5, University of Arizona Archives, Tucson.

86. Andres M. Flores, Rebecca Flores, and Guadalupe Valenzuela, untitled affidavit, 28 December 1984, MS 325, folder 676/5, University of Arizona Archives.

87. Moisés, Kelley, and Holden, *The Tall Candle*, 123.

88. Matthews, "Yaqui Country," 8.

89. Meeks, *Border Citizens*, 229.

90. "Aug 2, 1940, Cayetano Lopez," A.S.C. # 2000-175, MS 5, folder 472, Spicer Papers.

91. Shorter, *We Will Dance Our Truth*, 288.

92. Folsom, *The Yaquis and the Empire*, 37; Thomas C. Holt, "The First New Nations," in Appelbaum, Macpherson, and Rosemblatt, *Race and Nation in Modern Latin America*, xii.

93. Spicer, *People of Pascua*, 48, 262.

Chapter Four

1. Edward H. Spicer to Wade Head, 4 December 1948, ASC# 2000-175, MS-5, box 7, Edward Spicer Papers, Arizona State Museum Archives, Tucson.

2. Marak, "The Attempted Eradication of Mexican Kickapoo Culture," 26.

3. Delores L. Latorre to Carl Hardin, 18 March 1966, box 10, folder 23, Felipe and Dolores Latorre Collection, Benson Latin American Collection, University of Texas at Austin; Felipe Latorre to Milton D. Swenson, 10 February 1970, box 10, folder 23, Latorre Collection; Felipe Latorre to Wilson E. Spier, 2 May 1966, box 10, folder 23, Latorre Collection.

4. Wilson E. Speir to General and Mrs. Felipe Latorre, 7 April 1966, box 10, folder 23, Latorre Papers.

5. Felipe Latorre to Wilson E. Speir, 2 May 1966, box 10, folder 23, Latorre Collection; Reid, *Close Calls*, 35.

6. Nunley, "The Mexican Kickapoo Indians," 60–62.

7. *Austin American Statesman*, 6 December 1985.

8. Frank X. Tolbert, "Tolbert's Texas," *Dallas Morning News*, 6 October 1966.

9. Pancho Jiménez to Mr. George Schuman, 8 January 1968, box 10, folder 7, Latorre Collection. My emphasis.

10. Dolores L. Latorre to Mr. C. S. Dawson, 22 February 1967, box 10, folder 5, Latorre Collection.

11. Fernando Jiménez to Mr. Dick Burr, 3 March 1969, box 10, folder 7, Latorre Collection.

12. Correspondence addressed only to "Dear friends," from the Latorres, 9 March 1969, box 10, folder 18, Latorre Collection.

13. Jesusita Valdes to Mr. C. S. Dawson, 19 February 1965, box 10, folder 14, Latorre Collection. Occasionally, the Latorres would see fit to interject a disclaimer in their letters to employers, such as, "We are in no way work contractors or agents and can assume no responsibility for the actions of the Kickapoo. We are anthropologists writing a book on their customs and history and just incidentally help them with their

many problems which face any illiterate group." See Felipe Latorre to Mr. George Schuman, 7 June 1968, box 10, folder 7, Latorre Collection. At other times, their interjections suggest a familiarity with these same employers. "Howdy!" begins the postscript of one letter. "We are still here working hard on the manuscript. Hope all of you are well and happy. Still remembering the fine experience of meeting you." See John Mohawk to Mr. Dick W. Burr, 5 December 1969, box 10, folder 5, Latorre Collection.

14. Margarito Treviño to Mr. S. C. Carranza, 3 March 1969, box 10, folder 12, Latorre Collection.

15. Pancho Valdes to Mr. Jay Bernardi, 26 March 1965, box 10, folder 15, Latorre Collection.

16. John Mohawk to Mrs. Dick W. Burr, 5 December 1969, box 10, folder 5, Latorre Collection; Melecio Jimenez Sr. to Mr. Earl Christensen, 15 March 1970, box 10, folder 7; John Mohawk to Mr. Dick W. Burr, 18 March 1966, box 10, folder 5, Latorre Collection.

17. Kiehtahmookwa (Cecilia Jiménez) to Mr. Jim Katakyaha, 8 April 1968, box 10, folder 7, Latorre Collection.

18. *Mexico City Collegian*, 20 April 1954.

19. See, for example, Winfrey and Day, *The Indian Papers of Texas and the Southwest*, 3:270 and 5:186, 205.

20. *Mexico City Collegian*, 20 April 1954.

21. *International News-Guide*, 26 February 1948.

22. "Travel and Transportation," 18 January 1965, box 28, folder 20, Latorre Collection.

23. *Confirming the Citizenship Status of the Texas Band of Kickapoo Indians: Hearings*, 159–60.

24. *Granting Federal Recognition to the Texas Band of Kickapoo Indians*, 7–8.

25. Osburn, "Problems and Solutions Regarding Indigenous Peoples," 479–81.

26. *San Antonio News*, 15 April 1973.

27. Frank X. Tolbert, "Tolbert's Texas," *Dallas Morning News*, 5 April 1961.

28. *Confirming the Citizenship Status of the Texas Band of Kickapoo Indians: Hearings*, 163; Latorre and Latorre, *The Mexican Kickapoo Indians*, 108, 110, 117.

29. Miguel León-Portilla, "Mexico," 20, 71.

30. Ibid., 71–72.

31. Reid, *Close Calls*, 43.

32. Ibid.

33. Marak, "The Attempted Eradication of Mexican Kickapoo Culture," 26–27.

34. *Confirming the Citizenship Status of the Texas Band of Kickapoo Indians: Hearings*, 148.

35. Ibid., 149.

36. Ibid., 160–61, 163; Latorre and Latorre, *The Mexican Kickapoo Indians*, 132.

37. Reid, *Close Calls*, 36, 40.

38. *Clarifying the Citizenship Status of the Members of the Texas Band of Kickapoo Indians,"* 6, 19.

39. *San Antonio News*, 15 April 1973; *El Sol de México*, 28 January 1966.

40. Felipe Latorre to Mr. James Wahpepah, 8 April 1968; Felipe Latorre to Mr. Gordon Wahpepah, 9 February 1966, box 10, folder 24; Dolores Latorre to Mrs. Ernestine Green, 29 March 1968, box 10, folder 19, Latorre Collection; "Oklahoma Kickapoos," journal entries, no date, box 28, folder 8, Latorre Collection.

41. Dolores L. Latorre to Mr. C. T. Slack, ACSW, Social Worker, United States Department of the Interior, 24 April 1967, box 10, folder 1, Latorre Collection.

42. "Oklahoma Kickapoos," journal entries, 7 February 1966, box 28, folder 8, Latorre Collection.

43. Dolores L. Latorre to Dr. William Shirley Fulton, 16 March 1962, box 28, folder 10, Latorre Collection.

44. Pancho Minacoa to Mr. Tom Bentley, 28 January 1968, box 10, folder 15, Latorre Collection; "Oklahoma Kickapoos," journal entries, 19 September 1965, box 28, folder 8, Latorre Collection.

45. Maxine Jamison to Palo Trevino, 8 January 1968, box 10, folder 12, Latorre Collection.

46. C. T. Slack to Mrs. Latorre, 2 March 1967, box 10, folder 1, Latorre Collection.

47. *Houston Chronicle*, 28 November 1986.

48. *Austin American-Statesman*, 6 December 1985.

49. Reid, *Close Calls*, 41–43.

50. Ibid., 43.

51. Ibid., 45; Latorre and Latorre, *The Mexican Kickapoo Indians*, 260.

52. *Austin American-Statesman*, 3 July 1977; also quoted in Latorre and Latorre, *The Mexican Kickapoo Indians*, 14.

53. *Austin American-Statesman*, 3 July 1977; *Houston Chronicle*, 25 November 1962; Frank X. Tolbert, "Tolbert's Texas," *Dallas Morning News*, 5 January 1966; *Houston Chronicle*, 28 November 1986; Latorre Collection, Series 3, Photographs, folder 9.5. The photograph of the Kickapoo young men is dated circa 1962 and the caption reads, "Kickapoo Youths Wearing Their Hair in Imitation of the Beatles [sic]".

54. *San Antonio Express*, 13 May 1964; *Dallas Morning News*, 8 May 1977; *Austin American-Statesman*, 29 April 1977.

55. *Forum* (Austin, TX), 30 March 1973; Nunley, "The Mexican Kickapoo Indians," 50–52.

56. *Confirming the Citizenship Status of the Texas Band of Kickapoo Indians: Hearings*, 12.

57. *Heraldo de Aragon*, 4 March 1979.

58. *Confirming the Citizenship Status of the Texas Band of Kickapoo Indians: Hearings*, 7, 10, 12–13, 22.

59. *Austin American-Statesman*, 20 April 1977.

Chapter Five

1. "Open Letter to the Public and T.O.N. Officials," 13 August 1990, folder "O'odham in Mexico," V. Garcia Library Archives, Sells, Arizona.

2. Ibid.; Hays, "Cross-Border Indigenous Nations," 41.

3. *Tucson Citizen*, 16 March 1982.

4. C. Wilson, "Migration, Change, and Variation," 53.

5. Quoted in Cadava, "Borderlands of Modernity and Abandonment," 379.

6. Dobyns, *Papagos in the Cotton Fields*, 12.

7. Josiah Moore to Ms. Ruth Ann Meyers, District Director, Immigration and Naturalization Services, 4 February 1987, Morris K. Udall Papers, MSN 325, box 675, folder 13, University of Arizona Library Special Collections, Tucson; St. John, *Line in the Sand*, 25.

8. Waddell, *Papago Indians at Work*, 17–18.

9. Marak, *From Many, One*, 108–9; Marak and Tuennerman, *At the Border of Empires*, 103.

10. Ibid., 68.

11. "The Off-Reservation Papagos: Program and Proceedings of the Arizona Commission of Indian Affairs: Held in Sells, Arizona, December 7, 1957," pp. 9, 14, 18, Special Collections, University of Arizona at Tucson.

12. Spicer, *Cycles of Conquest*, 469.

13. Underhill, *Papago Woman*, 77–82.

14. "The Off-Reservation Papagos," 42.

15. Blaine, *Papagos and Politics*, 75–76.

16. Ibid., 77. For an examination of New Deal–era stock reduction, see O'Neill, *Working the Navajo Way*, 22–29. She describes Navajo stock reduction as implemented through the Bureau of Indian Affairs as just another in a long succession of assaults on Navajo subsistence, one that proved to be a "devastating blow" to the Navajo economy. Further, scientists and "well-meaning reformers" failed to grasp the social and cultural significance of sheep in Navajo culture, which made the program doubly hard to bear.

17. Meeks, *Border Citizens*, 128–129.

18. Ibid., 134.

19. Marak, *From Many, One*, 105–8; Meeks, *Border Citizens*, 136.

20. Quoted in Marak, *From Many, One*, 115.

21. Ibid., 112–13.

22. Ibid., 142; Cadava, "Borderlands of Modernity and Abandonment," 373–75.

23. Marak, *From Many, One*, 130–31.

24. *Arizona Daily Star*, 20 December 1947.

25. *Hearing before a Subcommittee of the Committee on Interior and Insular Affairs, United States Senate*, 82nd Congress, 1st session, on S. 107, a Bill to Promote the Rehabilitation of the Papago Tribe of Indians and a Better Utilization of the Resources of the Papago Tribe, and for Other Purposes, July 16, 1951 (Washington, DC: Government Printing Office, 1951, 3.

26. Ibid., 11.

27. Ibid., 18, 22.

28. Prucha, *The Great Father*, 1077.

29. Spicer, *Cycles of Conquest*, 145.

30. Waddell, *Papago Indians at Work*, 18–19.

31. Dobyns, *Papagos in the Cotton Fields*, 2–19, 24, 42, 67.

32. Cadava, *Standing on Common Ground*, 1, 4.

33. "The Off-Reservation Papagos," 14, 50, 57.

34. Waddell, *Papago Indians at Work*, 144.

35. Area Plans Division, "Provisional Overall Economic Development Plan, Papago Reservation, 1962," no author given, University of Arizona Special Collections, Tucson, 12; Edwards, "Diary of an Internship," 21.

36. McGee, *Trails to Tiburón*, 46–47, 55.

37. Ibid., 69–71.

38. Griffith, *Beliefs and Holy Places*, 31–33, 38.

39. Ibid., 43.

40. Ibid., xi–xiv; McGee, *Trails to Tiburón*, 88–89, 93–94.

41. *Arizona Daily Star*, 3 October 1947.

42. Griffith, *Beliefs and Holy Places*, 32.

43. Dobyns, *Report on Investigations on the Papago Reservation*, 17.

44. Griffith, *Beliefs and Holy Places*, 47–48.

45. Ibid., 70.

46. Salvador López, interview with R. D. Jones, 24 September and 24 October 1963, San Pedro village, RG 8, Bureau of Ethnic Research Archives, Arizona State Museum Archives, Tucson.

47. Marak and Tuennerman, *At the Border of Empires*, 1, 136–37, 139, 141.

48. Ramón Yocupicio to "the Mayor, Altar, Sonora," 5 February 1937, translated by Daniel S. Matson, instructor in anthropology, University of Arizona, Arizona State Museum Archives, A-261.

49. Brigadier General José Tafolla Caballero to the Constitutional President of the Republic, 2 September 1938, University of Arizona, Arizona State Museum Archives, A-261.

50. Alonso Fernandez F., Assistant Head of the Department of Assistance and Public Works, to José Ventura Bustamante, Governor of the Papago Tribe, Altar, Sonora, 25 July 1945, University of Arizona, Arizona State Museum Archives, A-261.

51. "Memorandum, Government of the State of Sonora, Hermosillo," 28 August 1945, Governor Abelardo L. Rodriguez to Rodolfo Shiels Martínez, General Agent of the Secretary of Agriculture in the State, 24 October 1945, University of Arizona, Arizona State Museum Archives, A-261.

52. Healy, *Historia general de Sonora*, 308.

53. "Minutes of Meeting at Sells Agency, Saturday, May 15, 1943, 10 a.m.," topográphica III-2465-13, Archivo Histórico de la Secretaría de las Relaciones Exteriores, Mexico City, Mexico.

54. *Boletín Indigenista* 3 (1943): 105–7.

55. "Memorandum, Indios Papagos," 2 June 1943, Mexico City, topográphica III-2465-13, Archivo Histórico de la Secretaría de las Relaciones Exteriores.

56. Castillo and Cowan, *It Is Not Our Fault*, 75.

57. "Provisional Overall Economic Development Plan," 8–9.

58. Spicer, *Cycles of Conquest*, 145.

59. Cadava, *Standing on Common Ground*, 127.

60. Marak and Tuennerman, *At the Border of Empires*, 127.

61. Meeks, *Border Citizens*, 221–22. The power of the O'odham tribal council, however, should not be overstated. As one historian explained, "Not all members of the tribe saw the tribal council as their highest authority. Many instead placed greater stock in the decision-making powers of village councils." See Cadava, *Standing on Common Ground*, 87.

62. Meeks, *Border Citizens*, 226–28.

63. *San Antonio Express*, 24 June 1977.

64. Ibid.

65. *Tucson Citizen*, 17 August 1989.

66. Castillo and Cowan, *It Is Not Our Fault*, 9–10, 18, 28.

67. Josiah Moore to Ms. Ruth Ann Meyers, 4 February 1987; Luna-Firebaugh, "The Border Crossed Us," 159.

68. Castillo and Cowan, *It Is Not Our Fault*, 33, 52–55, 59–60.

69. Ibid., 34, 36, 70; Griffith, *Beliefs and Holy Places*, 176.

70. Castillo and Cowan, 90.

71. John Dougherty, "One Nation, under Fire," *High Country News*, 19 February 2007, 12.

72. Cadava, *Standing on Common Ground*, 239–40.

73. Ibid., 181.

74. Ibid., 84; Marak and Tuennerman, *At the Border of Empires*, 146.

75. Underhill, *Papago Woman*, 96.

76. Griffith, *Beliefs and Holy Places*, 66.

77. Hays, "Cross-Border Indigenous Nations," 40–41.

78. Lucero, "Friction, Conversion, and Contention," 172–73, 181.

Chapter Six

1. A. Turney Smith to Morris Udall, 11 August 1964, and S. Leonard Scheff to Morris Udall, 30 March 1963, Morris K. Udall Papers, box 13, folder 165, University of Arizona Library Special Collections, Tucson.

2. "Correspondence, notes, newspaper clippings, 1930–1947," handwritten notes, A-467, Edward H. Spicer Papers, Arizona State Museum Archives, Tucson.

3. Rosamond Spicer, "Living in Pascua: Looking Back Fifty Years," in E. Spicer, *People of Pascua*, xxvii–xxxiv.

4. White, *The Middle Ground*, 53.

5. Harring, *Crow Dog's Case*, 7.

6. Ibid., 7, 20–21.

7. Ibid., 4, 12.

8. Ibid., 15.

9. Quinn, "Federal Acknowledgment of American Indian Tribes," 333.

10. Wilkinson, *American Indians, Time, and the Law*, 63–64.

11. Dobbs v. U.S., 33 Ct. Cl. 308, 315–316 (1898).

12. Quinn, "Federal Acknowledgment," 352.

13. Quoted in ibid.

14. *Sixty-First Annual Report of the Commissioner of Indian Affairs to the Secretary of the Interior* (Washington, DC.: Government Printing Office, 1892), 31.

15. United States v. Sandoval, 231 U.S. 28, 46 (1913).

16. Act of June 18, 1934, chap. 576, 48 Stat. 984.

17. Quinn, "Federal Acknowledgement," 356–57.

18. Cohen, *Handbook of Federal Indian Law*, 270.

19. Ibid., 271.

20. Philp, "Termination: A Legacy of the New Deal," 165.

21. Quinn, "Federal Acknowledgment," 362–63.

22. 25 CFR 83.7 (1982), originally promulgated as 25 CFR 54 (1978).

23. Greenbaum, "In Search of Lost Tribes," 364–65.

24. Miller, *Forgotten Tribes*, 3, 19.

25. Greenbaum, "In Search of Lost Tribes," 361–62, 364.

26. Ibid., 365.

27. Harmon, *Indians in the Making*, 3.

28. Greenbaum, "Lost Tribes," 361.

29. Miller, *Forgotten Tribes*, 9, 11.

30. Greenbaum, "Lost Tribes," 365.

31. Miller, *Forgotten Tribes*, 75.

32. Klopotek, *Recognition Odysseys*, 4, 9, 18.

33. As of the end of the 1990s, the BIA had recognized fourteen tribes, declined to recognize thirteen, was in the process of recognizing one additional tribe, and had just announced the rejection of six more petitions. See Miller, *Forgotten Tribes*, 54.

34. Miller, *Forgotten Tribes*, 15; Truett, *Fugitive Landscapes*, 6–8.

35. Robert A. Roessel Jr. to Morris Udall, 10 October 1962, Roger C. Wolf to Senators Paul J. Fannin and Barry Goldwater, 9 January 1976, and Mrs. Ray A. Johnston to Morris Udall, 1 February 1963, Morris K. Udall Papers, box 13, folder 165.

36. *Confirming the Citizenship Status of the Texas Band of Kickapoo Indians: Hearings*, 20.

37. *New York Post*, 2 February 1970.

38. Los Animados, c/o Sam Tapia, to Morris K. Udall, 25 February 1970, Udall Papers, MS 325, box 24, folder 546.

39. Miller, *Forgotten Tribes*, 88.

40. *Arizona Daily Star*, 29 January 1963; *Tucson Daily Citizen*, 30 January 1963; Miller, *Forgotten Tribes*, 88–89.

41. Miller, *Forgotten Tribes*, 89, 95–96.

42. *Arizona Daily Star*, 20 February 1963; *Arizona Daily Star*, 28 September 1966.

43. Quoted in Miller, *Forgotten Tribes*, 92.

44. Ibid., 92–93.

45. *Tucson Daily Citizen*, 20 September 1966; *Arizona Daily Star*, 16 April 1967; *Arizona Daily Star*, 26 September 1975.

46. Miller, *Forgotten Tribes*, 99–100.

47. Quoted in ibid., 105, 107–8.

48. *Arizona Daily Star*, 26 September 1975; *Arizona Daily Star*, 23 November 1975.

49. *Tucson Daily Citizen*, 19 November 1975; *Arizona Daily Star*, 23 November 1975.

50. *Arizona Daily Star*, 12 August 1976.

51. *Tucson Daily Citizen*, 8 January 1977.

52. *Arizona Daily Star*, 27 May 1977.

53. *Tucson Citizen*, 10 February 1978.

54. *Trust Status for the Pascua Yaqui Indians of Arizona: Hearing*, 2.

55. Ibid., 12.

56. *Arizona Daily Star*, 20 March 1978.

57. *Trust Status for the Pascua Yaqui Indians of Arizona: Hearing*, 5.

58. Ibid., 7.

59. Public Law 95–375 (92 Stat. 712).

60. Miller, *Forgotten Tribes*, 79.

61. Ibid., 119, 122.

62. *Tucson Citizen*, 24 June 1978.

63. *Arizona Daily Star*, 3 May 1993; *Arizona Daily Star*, 7 April 1994.

64. *Heraldo de Aragon*, 4 March 1979.

65. J. Ortiz, "Tribus Mexicans se Extinguen," *Revista Jueves de Excelsior*, 17 July 1969.

66. *Confirming the Citizenship Status of the Texas Band of Kickapoo Indians: Hearings*, 7, 10, 12–13, 22.

67. *Austin American-Statesman*, 20 April 1977. For more on the Tiguas, see Schulze, "The Rediscovery of the Tiguas," 14–39.

68. Nunley, "The Mexican Kickapoo Indians," 57–58.

69. *Confirming the Citizenship Status of the Texas Band of Kickapoo Indians: Hearings*, 25–26.

70. Ibid., 24.

71. Ibid., 7, 10, 12–13, 22.

72. Ibid., 18–19.

73. Ibid., 201–2.

74. Ibid., 22–23, 38.

75. Ibid., 37, 48,49, 51.

76. Ibid., 68–69, 74–75.

77. James A. McLeod, "Testimony before the House Interior and Insular Affairs Committee," 30 October 1981, in *Confirming the Citizenship Status of the Texas Band of Kickapoo Indians: Hearings*, 105–9.

78. *Houston Post*, 22 November 1985.

79. John MacCormack, "Let the Chips Fall," *Dallas Observer*, 12–18 April 2001, 31.

80. Hays, "Cross-Border Indigenous Nations," 42.

81. Shepherd, *We Are an Indian Nation*, 119.

82. Underhill, *Papago Woman*, 94.

83. Erickson, *Sharing the Desert*, 148–51; Underhill, *Social Organization of the Papago Indians*, 70, 78; Lucero, "Friction, Conversion, and Contention," 173; Marak and Tuennerman, *At the Border of Empires*, 7.

84. Underhill, *The Papago Indians of Arizona*, 34, 65.

85. Castillo and Cowan, *It Is Not Our Fault*, 12–13.

86. *Tucson Citizen*, 17 July 1989.

87. Ibid.; Marak and Tuennerman, *At the Border of Empires*, 132–33.

88. *Tucson Citizen*, 17 July 1989.

89. Harvard Project, *The State of Native Nations*, 84.

90. *Tucson Citizen*, 17 August 1989.

91. *Tucson Citizen*, 20 October 1989.

92. Castillo and Cowan, *It Is Not Our Fault*, 13.

93. As mentioned, the tribe contends that the September 11 attacks interrupted the momentum their citizenship drive had gained over the years, since, as one tribal member communicated to me, the U.S. government had bigger problems.

94. Marak and Van Valen, "Introduction," *Transnational Indians of the North American West*, 4.

Epilogue

1. John Dougherty, "One Nation, under Fire," *High Country News*, 19 February 2007, 8.

2. Ortiz, *Mixtec Transnational Identity*, 195–96.

3. Dougherty, "One Nation, under Fire," 10, 13; *Washington Post*, 15 September 2006, A01.

4. *Los Angeles Times*, 21 March 2004.

5. Brenda Norrell, "Civil Rights Commission Hears Indigenous Peoples at Mexican Border," *Indian Country Today*, 29 September 2004.

6. Spicer, "Potam," 17.

7. McGuire, *Politics and Ethnicity*, 158, 162–64.

8. Erikson, *Yaqui Homeland and Homeplace*, 7–8, 10.

9. Miller, *Forgotten Tribes*, 122.

10. Luna-Firebaugh, "The Border Crossed Us," 173–74.

11. Cadava, *Standing on Common Ground*, 8.

12. *Dallas Morning News*, 31 March 2002, 35A.

13. *Southwest Texas LIVE!*, 17 November 2006.

14. Reid, *Close Calls*, 33, 39.

15. Baud and Van Schendel, "Toward a Comparative History of Borderlands," 238–40.

16. *Indian Country Today* (no author given), www.indiancountrytoday.com /global/53941672.html (accessed 12 October 2009).

17. Mickey McCarther, "Indian Tribe to Develop Enhanced Border-Crossing ID," *Homeland Security Today*, www.hstoday.us, 14 September 2009 (accessed 12 October 2009); *Indian Country Today* (no author given), www.indiancountrytoday.com /national/southwest/59054837.html (accessed 12 October 2009).

18. Shorter, *We Will Dance Our Truth*, 9.

19. Erikson, *Yaqui Homeland and Homeplace*, 54.

20. Novo, *Who Defines Indigenous?*, 3–4; St. John, *Line in the Sand*, 5, 14.

21. Marak and Van Valen, "Introduction," *Transnational Indians of the North American West*, 10–11.

22. Holm, Pearson, and Chavis, "Peoplehood," 16–17.

23. Castillo and Cowan, *It Is Not Our Fault*, 64.

24. "'Lost' Tribe Seeks Status," *Arizona Republic*, 8 March 2005.

Bibliography

Primary Sources

Archives Utilized

Archivo Histórico de la Secretaría de las Relaciones Exteriores, Mexico City, Mexico

Archivo Histórico del Estado de Sonora, Hermosillo, Mexico

Dan L. Flores Papers, Southwest Collection, Texas Tech University, Lubbock

Edward H. Spicer Papers, Arizona State Museum Archives, Tucson

Felipe and Dolores Latorre Papers, Benson Latin American Collection, University of Texas at Austin

Morris K. Udall Papers, University of Arizona Library Special Collections, Tucson

R. A. Wilbur Papers, University of Arizona Library Special Collections, Tucson

V. Garcia Library Archives, Sells, AZ

William Curry Holden Papers, Southwest Collection, Texas Tech University, Lubbock

Congressional Testimony

Affairs of the Kickapoo Indians: Hearing before the Subcommittee of the Committee on Indian Affairs. 60th Congress, 1st session, vol. 1, 8 February–11 November 1907, Washington, DC.

"Clarifying the Citizenship Status of the Members of the Texas Band of Kickapoo Indians; Providing for a Reservation for the Texas Band of Kickapoo; Providing to Members of the Texas Band of Kickapoo Those Services and Benefits Furnished to American Indian Tribes and Individuals; and for Other Purposes." House of Representatives, 97th Congress, 2nd session, 23 September 1982, Washington, DC.

Confirming the Citizenship Status of the Texas Band of Kickapoo Indians: Hearings before the Committee on Interior and Insular Affairs. House of Representatives, 97th Congress, 1st and 2nd sessions, on H.R. 4496, 30 October 1981 and 5 August 1982, Washington, DC.

Granting Federal Recognition to the Texas Band of Kickapoo Indians. Select Committee on Indian Affairs, 97th Congress, 2nd session, 15 December 1982, Washington, DC.

Pascua Yaqui Tribe Extension of Benefits: Hearing before the Committee on Indian Affairs. United States Senate, 103rd Congress, 2nd session, Washington, DC: Government Printing Office, 1994.

"Removal of Kickapoos and Other Indians from Texas and Mexico, Letter from the Secretary of the Interior." Executive Document no. 39, 43rd Congress, 1st session, 7 January 1874, Washington, DC.

Trust Status for the Pascua Yaqui Indians of Arizona: Hearing before the United States Senate Select Committee on Indian Affairs. 95th Congress, 1st session, 27 September 1977, Washington, DC.

Newspaper Articles (Grouped by Tribe)

YAQUIS

Arizona Daily Star, 27 April 1902
Arizona Daily Star, 12 December 1939
Arizona Daily Star, 29 August 1940
Arizona Daily Star, 29 January 1963
Arizona Daily Star, 20 February 1963
Arizona Daily Star, 28 September 1966
Arizona Daily Star, 16 April 1967
Arizona Daily Star, 26 September 1975
Arizona Daily Star, 23 November 1975
Arizona Daily Star, 12 August 1976
Arizona Daily Star, 27 May 1977
Arizona Daily Star, 20 March 1978
Arizona Daily Star, 3 May 1993
Arizona Daily Star, 7 April 1994
Arizona Republic, 14 June 1916
El Porvenir, 20 January 1965
Lubbock Avalanche-Journal, 21 April 1934
Lubbock Avalanche-Journal, 21 April 1984
Lubbock Morning Avalanche, 20 February 1934
Lubbock Morning Avalanche, 15 March 1934
Lubbock Morning Avalanche, 18 March 1934
Lubbock Morning Avalanche, 22 March 1934
New York Post, 2 February 1970
Salt Lake City News, "The Yaqui Rising," 4 March 1900
San Francisco Call, "Yaqui Chiefs Put to Death," 25 February 1905
Tucson Citizen, 10 February 1978
Tucson Citizen, 24 June 1978
Tucson Daily Citizen, 25 May 1887
Tucson Daily Citizen, 31 July 1936
Tucson Daily Citizen, 1 August 1936
Tucson Daily Citizen, 23 September 1947
Tucson Daily Citizen, 30 January 1963
Tucson Daily Citizen, 20 September 1966
Tucson Daily Citizen, 19 November 1975

Tucson Daily Citizen, 8 January 1977
University Daily (Lubbock, TX), 16 April 1984
Washington Post, "Traits of the Yaquis," 11 March 1900

KICKAPOOS

Arizona Republic, 8 March 2005
Austin American-Statesman, 20 April 1977
Austin American-Statesman, 29 April 1977
Austin American-Statesman, 3 July 1977
Austin American Statesman, 6 December 1985
Dallas Morning News, "Tolbert's Texas," by Frank X. Tolbert, 5 April 1961
Dallas Morning News, "Tolbert's Texas," by Frank X. Tolbert, 5 January 1966
Dallas Morning News, "Tolbert's Texas," by Frank X. Tolbert, 6 October 1966
Dallas Morning News, 8 May 1977
Dallas Morning News, 31 March 2002
Dallas Observer, 12–18 April 2001
El Sol de México, 28 January 1966
Forum (Austin, TX), 30 March 1973
Heraldo de Aragon, 4 March 1979
Houston Chronicle, 25 November 1962
Houston Chronicle, 28 November 1986
Houston Post, 22 November 1985
International News-Guide, 26 February 1948
Mexico City Collegian, 20 April 1954
Revista Jueves de Excelsior, 17 July 1969
San Antonio Express, 13 May 1964
San Antonio News, 15 April 1973
Southwest Texas LIVE!, 17 November 2006

TOHONO O'ODHAM

Arizona Daily Citizen, 8 April 1895, page 1
Arizona Daily Star, 5 August 1915
Arizona Daily Star, 21 January 1916
Arizona Daily Star, 23 January 1916
Arizona Daily Star, 3 October 1947
Arizona Daily Star, 20 December 1947
Arizona Republican, 3 February 1916
High Country News, 19 February 2007
Indian Country Today, 29 September 2004
Los Angeles Times, 21 March 2004
San Antonio Express, 24 June 1977
Tucson Citizen, 21 January 1916
Tucson Citizen, 11 February 1916

Tucson Citizen, 28 February 1916

Tucson Citizen, 16 March 1982

Tucson Citizen, 17 July 1989

Tucson Citizen, 17 August 1989

Tucson Citizen, 20 October 1989

Tucson Daily Citizen, 18 February 1916

Washington Post, 15 September 2006, page A01

Miscellaneous

Boletín Indigenista

The Oregonian, 18 September 2006

Published Primary Sources

Beals, Carleton. *Mexican Maze.* Philadelphia: J. B. Lippincott, 1931.

Castillo, Guadalupe, and Margo Cowan, eds. *It Is Not Our Fault: The Case for Amending Present Nationality Law to Make All Members of the Tohono O'odham Nation United States Citizens, Now and Forever.* Sells, AZ: Tohono O'odham Nation, 2001.

Dobyns, Henry F. *Papagos in the Cotton Fields.* Self-published, 1950. Southwest Collection, Texas Tech University, Lubbock, TX.

———. *Report on Investigations on the Papago Reservation.* Ithaca, NY: Cornell University Department of Sociology-Anthropology, 1949.

Edwards, Betsy. "Diary of an Internship with the Papago Indian Agency Bureau of Indian Affairs." Master's thesis, University of Arizona, Tucson, 1964.

Guy, Charles A. "They Lived with the Yaquis." *West Texas Today* 15, no. 3 (May 1934): 35–41.

Holden, William Curry, ed. "Studies of the Yaqui Indians of Sonora, Mexico." Special issue, *Texas Technological College Bulletin* 12, no. 1 (January 1936).

Matthews, John. "Yaqui Country." *Grain Producers News* 28, no. 10 (October 1978): 4–8.

McGee, W. J. *Trails to Tiburón: The 1894 and 1895 Field Diaries of W. J. McGee.* Transcribed by Hazel McFeely Fontana, annotated by Bernard L. Fontana. Tucson: University of Arizona Press, 2000.

Moisés, Rosalio, Jane Holden Kelley, and William Curry Holden, *A Yaqui Life: The Personal Chronicle of a Yaqui Indian.* Lincoln: University of Nebraska Press, 1971.

Reid, Jan. *Close Calls: Jan Reid's Texas.* College Station: Texas A&M Press, 2000.

Savala, Refugio, with Kathleen M. Sands, ed. *The Autobiography of a Yaqui Poet.* Tucson: University of Arizona Press, 1980.

Turner, John Kenneth. *Barbarous Mexico.* Austin: University of Texas Press, 1969. Originally published in book form in 1910.

Winfrey, Dorman H., and James M. Day, eds. *The Indian Papers of Texas and the Southwest.* Vols. 1–5. Austin: Texas State Historical Association, 1995.

Secondary Sources

Adams, David Wallace. *Education for Extinction: American Indians and the Boarding School Experience, 1875–1928*. Lawrence: University Press of Kansas, 1995.

Anderson, Benedict. *Imagined Communities: Reflections on the Origins and Spread of Nationalism*. Rev. ed. New York: Verso, 1996.

Andreas, Peter. *Smuggler Nation: How Illicit Trade Made America*. New York: Oxford University Press, 2013.

Appelbaum, Nancy C., Anne S. Macpherson, and Karin Alejandra Rosemblatt. *Race and Nation in Modern Latin America*. Chapel Hill: University of North Carolina Press, 2003.

Balderrama, Francisco E., and Raymond Rodríguez. *Decade of Betrayal: Mexican Repatriation in the 1930s*. Albuquerque: University of New Mexico Press, 1995.

Bantjes, Adrian A. *As If Jesus Walked on Earth: Cardenismo, Sonora, and the Mexican Revolution*. Wilmington, DE: Scholarly Resources, 1998.

Barkan, Elliott. "America in the Hand, Homeland in the Heart: Transnational and Translocal Immigrant Experiences in the American West." *Western Historical Quarterly* 35 (Autumn 2004): 331–54.

Barr, Juliana. *Peace Came in the Form of a Woman: Indians and Spaniards in the Texas Borderlands*. Chapel Hill: University of North Carolina Press, 2007.

Barr, Juliana, and Edward Countryman, eds. *Contested Spaces of Early America*. Philadelphia: University of Pennsylvania Press, 2014.

Bartell, Gilbert Duke. "Directed Culture Change among the Sonoran Yaquis." Ph.D. Dissertation, Tucson, University of Arizona, 1964.

Baud, Michiel, and Willem Van Schendel. "Toward a Comparative History of Borderlands." *Journal of World History* 8, no. 2 (1997): 211–42.

Bender, Thomas, ed., *Rethinking American History in a Global Age*. Berkeley: University of California Press, 2002.

Blaine, Peter. *Papagos and Politics*. Tucson: Arizona Historical Society, 1981.

Bonfil Batalla, Guillermo. *México Profundo: Reclaiming a Civilization*. Austin: University of Texas Press, 1996.

Buchenau, Jürgen. *Plutarco Elías Calles and the Mexican Revolution*. Lanham, MD: Rowman and Littlefield, 2007.

Cadava, Geraldo L. "Borderlands of Modernity and Abandonment: The Lines within Ambos Nogales and the Tohono O'odham Nation." *Journal of American History* 98, no. 2 (September 2011): 362–83.

———. *Standing on Common Ground: The Making of a Sunbelt Borderland*. Cambridge, MA: Harvard University Press, 2016.

Carey, Elaine, and Andre M. Marak, eds. *Smugglers, Brothels, and Twine: Historical Perspectives on Contraband and Vice in North America's Borderlands*. Tucson: University of Arizona Press, 2011.

Carlson Paul H., and Bruce A. Glasrud, eds. *West Texas: A History of the Giant Side of Texas*. Norman: University of Oklahoma Press, 2014.

Castile, George Pierre. *Taking Charge: Native American Self-Determination and Federal Indian Policy, 1975–1993.* Tucson: University of Arizona Press, 2006.

——. "Yaquis, Edward H. Spicer, and Federal Indian Policy: From Immigrants to Native Americans." *Journal of the Southwest* 44, no. 4 (Winter 2002): 383–486.

Cobb, Daniel M., and Loretta Fowler, eds. *Beyond Red Power: American Indian Politics and Activism since 1900.* Santa Fe: School for Advanced Research Press, 2007.

Cohen, Felix. *Handbook of Federal Indian Law.* Washington, DC: U.S. Government Printing Office, 1942.

Confer, Clarissa, Andrae Marak, and Laura Tuennerman, eds. *Transnational Indians in the North American West.* College Station: Texas A&M Press, 2015.

Cook, Curtis, and Juan D. Lindau. *Aboriginal Rights and Self-Government: The Canadian and Mexican Experience in North American Perspective.* Montreal: McGill–Queen's University Press, 2000.

Corral, Ramón. *Obras históricas.* Hermosillo, Mexico: Biblioteca sonorense de geografía e historia, 1959.

Crumrine, N. Ross, and Phil C. Weigand, eds. *Ejidos and Regions of Refuge in Northwestern Mexico.* Tucson: University of Arizona Press, 1987.

Dawson, Alexander S. *Indian and Nation in Revolutionary Mexico.* Tucson: University of Arizona Press, 2004.

DeLay, Brian. *War of a Thousand Deserts: Indian Raids and the U.S.-Mexican War.* New Haven, CT: Yale University Press, 2008.

Delgado, Grace. "In the Age of Exclusion: Race, Region and Chinese Identity in the Making of the Arizona-Sonora Borderlands, 1863–1943." PhD diss., University of California, Los Angeles, 2000.

Deloria, Vine, Jr., ed. *American Indian Policy in the Twentieth Century.* Norman: University of Oklahoma Press, 1985.

Deloria, Vine, Jr., and Clifford Lytle. *The Nations Within: The Past and Future of American Indian Sovereignty.* New York: Pantheon Books, 1984.

Díaz, George T. *Border Contraband: A History of Smuggling across the Rio Grande.* Austin: University of Texas Press, 2015.

Dillingham, Betty Ann Wilder. "The Oklahoma Kickapoo." PhD diss., University of Michigan, 1963.

Dobyns, Henry F. *The Papago People.* Phoenix: Indian Tribal Series, 1972.

Dwyer, John J. *The Agrarian Dispute: The Expropriation of American-Owned Rural Land in Postrevolutionary Mexico.* Durham, NC: Duke University Press, 2008.

Erickson, Winston P. *Sharing the Desert: The Tohono O'odham in History.* Tucson: University of Arizona Press, 1994. Official textbook of the Tohono O'odham Nation.

Erikson, Kirstin C. *Yaqui Homeland and Homeplace: The Everyday Production of Ethnic Identity.* Tucson: University of Arizona Press, 2008.

Ettinger, Patrick. "'We Sometimes Wonder What They Will Spring On Us Next': Immigrants and Border Enforcement in the American West." *Western Historical Quarterly* 37, no. 2 (Summer 2006): 159–81.

Evans, Sterling. *Bound in Twine: The History and Ecology of the Henequen-Wheat Complex for Mexico and the Canadian Plains, 1880–1950.* College Station: Texas A&M Press, 2007.

Fabila, Alfonso. *Las tribus Yaquis de Sonora: Su cultura y anhelada autodeterminacion.* Mexico City: Departamento de Asuntos Indigenas, 1940.

——. *La tribu Kickapoo de Coahuila.* Enciclopedia Popular No. 50. Mexico City: Secretaria de Educacion Publica, 1945.

Flores, Ruben. *Backroads Pragmatists: Mexico's Melting Pot and Civil Rights in the United States.* Philadelphia: University of Pennsylvania Press, 2014.

Folsom, Rafael Brewster. *The Yaquis and the Empire: Violence, Spanish Imperial Power, and Native Resilience in Colonial Mexico.* New Haven, CT: Yale University Press, 2014.

Fontana, Bernard L. *Of Earth and Little Rain: The Papago Indians.* Flagstaff, AZ: Northland Press, 1981.

Forbes, Jack. "Historical Survey of the Indians of Sonora, 1821–1910." *Ethnohistory* 4, no. 4 (1957): 335–68.

Friedlander, Judith. *Being Indian in Hueyapan: A Study of Forced Identity in Contemporary Mexico.* New York: St. Martin's Press, 1975.

Frye, David. *Indians into Mexicans: History and Identity in a Mexican Town.* Austin: University of Texas Press, 1996.

Gibson, A. M. *The Kickapoos: Lords of the Middle Border.* Norman: University of Oklahoma Press, 1963.

Greenbaum, Susan D. "In Search of Lost Tribes: Anthropology and the Federal Acknowledgment Process." *Human Organization* 44 (1985): 361–67.

Griffith, James S. *Beliefs and Holy Places: A Spiritual Geography of the Pimería Alta.* Tucson: University of Arizona Press, 1992.

Guidotti-Hernández, Nicole M. *Unspeakable Violence: Remapping U.S. and Mexican National Imaginaries.* Durham, NC: Duke University Press, 2011.

Haake, Claudia. *The State, Removal and Indigenous Peoples in the United States and Mexico, 1620–2000.* New York: Routledge, 2007.

Hall, Linda B. *Alvaro Obregón: Power and Revolution in Mexico, 1911–1920.* College Station: Texas A&M University Press, 1981.

Harmon, Alexandra. *Indians in the Making: Ethnic Relations and Indian Identities around Puget Sound.* Berkeley: University of California Press, 1998.

Harring, Sidney L. *Crow Dog's Case: American Indian Sovereignty, Tribal Law, and United States Law in the Nineteenth Century.* New York: Cambridge University Press, 1994.

Harvard Project on American Indian Economic Development. *The State of Native Nations: Conditions under U.S. Policies of Self-Determination.* New York: Oxford University Press, 2008.

Hatfield, Shelley Bowen. *Chasing Shadows: Apaches and Yaquis along the United States–Mexico Border, 1876–1911.* Albuquerque: University of New Mexico Press, 1998.

Hays, Rachel. "Cross-Border Indigenous Nations: A History." *Race Poverty, and the Environment* 6, no. 4, and 7, no. 1 (Summer/Fall 1996): 40–42.

Healy, Ernesto Camou. *Historia general de Sonora, 1929–1984*. Hermosillo, Mexico: Gobierno del Estado de Sonora, 1985.

Hillary, Frank M. "Cajeme and the Mexico of His Time." *Journal of Arizona History* 8, no. 2 (Summer 1967): 120–36.

Holm, Tom, J. Diane Pearson, and Ben Chavis. "Peoplehood: A Model for the Extension of Sovereignty in American Indian Studies." *Wicazo Sa Review* 18, no. 1 (Spring 2003): 7–24.

Hoxie, Frederick E. *A Final Promise: The Campaign to Assimilate the Indians, 1880–1920*. New edition. Lincoln: University of Nebraska Press, 2001.

Hu-DeHart, Evelyn. *Missionaries, Miners, and Indians: Spanish Contact with the Yaqui Nation of Northwestern New Spain, 1533–1820*. Tucson: University of Arizona Press, 1981.

———. *Yaqui Resistance and Survival: The Struggle for Land and Autonomy, 1821–1910*. Madison: University of Wisconsin Press, 1984.

Jacoby, Karl. *Shadows at Dawn: A Borderlands Massacre and the Violence of History*. New York: Penguin Press, 2008.

Kelley, Jane Holden. *Yaqui Women: Contemporary Life Histories*. Lincoln: University of Nebraska Press, 1978.

Kicza, John E., ed. *The Indian in Latin American History: Resistance, Resilience, and Acculturation*. Wilmington, DE: Scholarly Resources 1993.

Klopotek, Brian. *Recognition Odysseys: Indigeneity, Race, and Federal Tribal Recognition Policy in Three Louisiana Indian Communities*. Durham, NC: Duke University Press, 2011.

Koppes, Clayton R. "From New Deal to Termination: Liberalism and Indian Policy, 1933–1953." *Pacific Historical Review* 46 (1977): 543–66.

Latorre, Felipe A., and Dolores L. Latorre. *The Mexican Kickapoo Indians*. Austin: University of Texas Press, 1976.

León-Portilla, Miguel. "Mexico." *Indianist Yearbook* (Mexico City) 22 (1962): 65–82.

Levitt, Peggy. "Transnational Migration: Taking Stock and Future Directions." *Global Networks* 1 (July 2001): 195–216.

Lewis, David Rich. *Neither Wolf nor Dog: American Indians, Environment, and Agrarian Change*. New York: Oxford University Press, 1994.

Limerick, Patricia Nelson. *The Legacy of Conquest: The Unbroken Past of the American West*. New York: W. W. Norton, 1987.

López, Rick A. "The India Bonita Contest of 1921 and the Ethnicization of Mexican National Culture." *Hispanic American Historical Review* 82, no. 2 (May 2002): 291–328.

Lucero, José Antonio. "Friction, Conversion, and Contention: Prophetic Politics in the Tohono O'odham Borderlands." Special issue, *Latin American Research Review* 49 (2014): 168–84.

Luna-Firebaugh, Eileen M. "The Border Crossed Us: Border Crossing Issues of the Indigenous Peoples of the Americas." *Wicazo Sa Review* 17, no. 1 (Spring 2002): 159–81.

Manuel, Frances, and Deborah Neff. *Desert Indian Woman: Stories and Dreams.* Tucson: University of Arizona Press, 2001.

Marak, Andrae M. "The Attempted Eradication of Mexican Kickapoo Culture." *World History Bulletin* 30, no. 2 (Fall 2014): 26–27.

———. *From Many, One: Indians, Peasants, Border, and Education in Callista, Mexico, 1924–1935.* Calgary: University of Calgary Press, 2009.

Marak, Andrae M., and Laura Tuennerman. *At the Border of Empires: The Tohono O'odham, Gender, and Assimilation, 1880–1934.* Tucson: University of Arizona Press, 2013.

Martínez, Oscar J. *Troublesome Border.* Tucson: University of Arizona Press, 1988.

McGuire, Thomas R. *Politics and Ethnicity on the Río Yaqui: Potam Revisited.* Tucson: University of Arizona Press, 1986.

———. "Ritual, Theater, and the Persistence of the Ethnic Group: Interpreting Semana Santa." *Journal of the Southwest* 31, no. 2 (Summer 1989): 159–75.

Meeks, Eric V. *Border Citizens: The Making of Indians, Mexicans, and Anglos in Arizona.* Austin: University of Texas Press, 2007.

Mihesuah, Devon A., ed. *Natives and Academics: Researching and Writing about American Indians.* Lincoln: University of Nebraska Press, 1998.

Miller, Mark Edwin. *Forgotten Tribes: Unrecognized Indians and the Federal Acknowledgment Process.* Lincoln: University of Nebraska Press, 2004.

———. "The Yaquis Become American Indians: The Process of Federal Tribal Recognition." *Journal of Arizona History* 35, no. 2 (1994): 183–204.

Moisés, Rosalio, Jane Holden Kelley, and William Curry Holden. *The Tall Candle: The Personal Chronicle of a Yaqui Indian.* Lincoln: University of Nebraska Press, 1971.

Molina, Felipe S., Octaviana Salazar, and Mimi V. Kaczkurkin, *The Yaquis: A People and Their Place.* Tucson: Arizona Humanities Council, 1983.

Muñoz, Manuel Ferrer, and María Bono López. *Pueblos indígenas y estado nacional en el siglo XIX.* Mexico City: Universidad Autónoma de México, 1998.

Novo, Carmen Martínez. *Who Defines Indigenous? Identities, Development, Intellectuals, and the State in Northern Mexico.* New Brunswick, NJ: Rutgers University Press, 2006.

Nugent, Daniel, ed. *Rural Revolt in Mexico: U.S. Intervention and the Domain of Subaltern Politics.* Durham, NC: Duke University Press, 1998.

Nunley, Mary Christopher. "The Mexican Kickapoo Indians: Avoidance of Acculturation through a Migratory Adaptation." PhD diss., Southern Methodist University, 1986.

O'Neill, Colleen. *Working the Navajo Way: Labor and Culture in the Twentieth Century.* Lawrence: University Press of Kansas, 2005.

Ortiz, Laura Velasco. *Mixtec Transnational Identity.* Tucson: University of Arizona Press, 2005. Originally published as *El regreso de la comunidad: Migración indígena y agentes étnicos; Los mixtecos en la frontera México-Estados Unidos* (Mexico City: El Colegio de México, 2002).

Osburn, Richard. "Problems and Solutions regarding Indigenous Peoples Split by International Borders." *American Indian Law Review* 24, no. 2 (1999/2000): 471–85.

Paz, Octavio. *The Labyrinth of Solitude*. New York: Grove Press, 1985.

Philp, Kenneth R. *John Collier's Crusade for Indian Reform, 1920–1954*. Tucson: University of Arizona Press, 1977.

———. "Termination: A Legacy of the New Deal." *Western Historical Quarterly* 14 (1983): 165–80.

———. *Termination Revisited*. Lincoln: University of Nebraska Press, 1999.

Powell, T. G. "Mexican Intellectuals and the Indian Question, 1876–1911." *Hispanic American Historical Review* 48, no. 1 (February 1968): 19–36.

Prucha, Francis Paul. *The Great Father: The United States Government and the American Indians*. Abridged ed. Lincoln: University of Nebraska Press, 1984.

Quinn, William, Jr. "Federal Acknowledgment of American Indian Tribes: The Historical Development of a Legal Concept." *Journal of Legal History* 34, no. 4 (1990): 331–64.

Rodríguez O., Jaime E. "The Emancipation of America." *American Historical Review* 105 (2000): 131–52.

Rubin, Jeffrey W., David Smilde, and Benjamin Junge. "Lived Religion and Lived Citizenship in Latin America's Zones of Crisis." Special issue, *Latin American Research Review* 49 (2014): 7–26.

Salas, Miguel Tinker. *In the Shadow of the Eagles: Sonora and the Transformation of the Border during the Porfiriato*. Berkeley: University of California Press, 1997.

Schulze, Jeffrey M. "The Rediscovery of the Tiguas: Federal Recognition and Indianness in the Twentieth Century." *Southwestern Historical Quarterly* 105, no. 1 (July 2001): 15–39.

Scott, James C. *Seeing Like a State: How Certain Schemes to Improve the Human Condition Have Failed*. New Haven, CT: Yale University Press, 1998.

Shepherd, Jeffrey P. *We Are an Indian Nation: A History of the Hualapai People*. Tucson: University of Arizona Press, 2010.

Shorter, David Delgado. *We Will Dance Our Truth: Yaqui History in Yoeme Performances*. Lincoln: University of Nebraska Press, 2009.

Spicer, Edward H. *Cycles of Conquest: The Impact of Spain, Mexico, and the United States on the Indians of the Southwest, 1533–1960*. Tucson: University of Arizona Press, 1962.

———. *Pascua: A Yaqui Village in Arizona*. Tucson: University of Arizona Press, 1967. Originally published in 1940.

———. *People of Pascua*. Tucson: University of Arizona Press, 1988.

———. *Potam, a Yaqui Village in Sonora*. Menasha, WI: American Anthropological Association, 1954.

———. *The Yaquis: A Cultural History.* Tucson: University of Arizona Press, 1980.

St. John, Rachel. *Line in the Sand: A History of the Western U.S.-Mexico Border.* Princeton, NJ: Princeton University Press, 2012.

Trafzer, Clifford E., Jean A. Keller, and Lorene Sisquoc. *Boarding School Blues: Revisiting American Indian Educational Experiences.* Lincoln: University of Nebraska Press, 2006.

Truett, Samuel. *Fugitive Landscapes: The Forgotten History of the U.S.-Mexico Borderlands.* New Haven, CT: Yale University Press, 2006.

Truett, Samuel, and Elliott Young, eds. *Continental Crossroads: Remapping U.S.-Mexican Borderlands History.* Durham, NC: Duke University Press, 2004.

Turner, Frederick C. *The Dynamic of Mexican Nationalism.* Chapel Hill: University of North Carolina Press, 1968.

Underhill, Ruth M. *The Papago Indians of Arizona and Their Pima Relatives.* Washington, DC: U.S. Department of the Interior, Branch of Education, 1941.

———. *Papago Woman.* Prospect Heights, IL: Waveland Press, 1985.

———. *Social Organization of the Papago Indians.* New York: AMS Press, 1969.

Vaughan, Mary Kay, and Stephen E. Lewis, eds. *The Eagle and the Virgin: Nation and Cultural Revolution in Mexico, 1920–1940.* Durham, NC: Duke University Press, 2006.

Waddell, Jack O. *Papago Indians at Work.* Tucson: University of Arizona Press, 1969.

Warman, Arturo, and Arturo Argueta, coordinators. *Moviminetos indígenas contemporaneous en México.* Mexico City: Miguel Angel Porrua Grupo Editorial.

Weber, David J. *The Spanish Frontier in North America.* New Haven, CT: Yale University Press, 1992.

White, Richard. *The Middle Ground: Indians, Empires, and the Great Lakes Region, 1650–1815.* New York: Cambridge University Press, 1991.

Wilkinson, Charles F. *American Indians, Time, and the Law: Native Societies in a Modern Constitutional Democracy.* New Haven, CT: Yale University Press, 1987.

———. *Blood Struggle: The Rise of Modern Indian Nations.* New York: W. W. Norton, 2005.

Wilson, Charles Roderick. "Migration, Change, and Variation: A Papago Case." PhD diss., University of Colorado, 1972.

Wilson, James. *The Earth Shall Weep.* New York: Atlantic Monthly Press, 1998.

Womack, John, Jr. *Rebellion in Chiapas: An Historical Reader.* New York: New Press, 1999.

Woodward, Colin. *American Nations: A History of the Eleven Rival Regional Cultures of North America.* New York: Viking, 2011.

Wright, Bill. *The Texas Kickapoos: Keepers of Tradition.* El Paso: Texas Western Press, 1996.

Index

109; geographic orientation, Kickapoos, 5, 7, 77–78, 110–11, 165, 188; geographic orientation, Tohono O'odham, 7, 57, 77–78, 157, 161, 194, 197, 203; geographic orientation, Yaquis, 7, 30, 35, 77–78, 82, 86, 101, 109, 165, 203; claims to indigenous nationhood, 8–9, 17, 152, 188, 190, 197, 204; networks in the border region, 11–12, 30, 57, 78, 134, 146, 157, 188, 207

Treaty of Greenville, 37, 117

Treaty of Guadalupe Hidalgo, 10, 135

Treaty of Paris, 36

Treviño, Margarito, 114

Trevino, Palo, 125

Tribe, definition, 167–71

Triqui Indians, 6, 14

Tuberculosis, 158

Tucson, 21 (map); Yaqui presence, 20, 30, 34, 81, 97, 99–100, 106–108, 163, 177–83, 200; Tohono O'odham presence, 30, 49–50, 53–54, 133, 137–39, 142, 145, 153–54, 160

Tucson Daily Citizen, 1, 3

Turkey, 6, 214n37

Turner, John Kenneth, 19–20, 22, 29

"Two village" system, 135–36

Udall, Morris K., 163, 175–79, 184

Udall, Stewart, 178

Ulloa, Antonio de, 36

Underhill, Ruth, 161, 193

United Nations, 155, 196, 214n37

United Nations Commission on the Rights of Indigenous People, 196

United States: early history, 9–11, 38–39; and filibusters, 49–50; and the Jay Treaty, 116–17; as refuge, 4, 18, 27, 29, 33–35, 52, 74, 81, 106, 132; and border protection, 5–6, 18, 29–30, 106–108, 204–205; and Indian policy, 8, 40–45, 50–52, 54, 58–65, 143, 165,

192–95; and federal recognition, 16, 166–75; and Kickapoo recognition, 185–92; and Yaqui recognition, 175–85; and migrant labor, 34, 99, 111–15; and immigration policy, 89, 97–98, 101, 110, 115, 118–19, 148; *See also* Arizona; Texas

U.S.-Canada border, 6, 117, 175, 188, 204–205. *See also* Cree, Rocky Boy; Seneca Nation

U.S. Customs and Border Enforcement, 157

U.S. Department of Housing and Urban Development (HUD), 186

U.S. Immigration and Naturalization Service (INS), 106–107, 111, 201

U.S.-Mexican War, 10, 39, 62, 204

U.S.-Mexico border: early history, 9–10, 213n23; as a contested space, 9, 11, 47, 56, 155, 162, 175, 197, 206; as survival strategy, 2, 6–7, 35, 40, 57, 115, 166, 177; and identity construction, 8; contemporary conditions, 158–60, 199–201

U.S. State Department, 10, 28, 31

United States v. Sandoval (1913), 170

U.S. War Department, 43, 61

Universal Declaration of Human Rights, 194–95

Utah, 112, 114

Valdes, Jesusita, 114

Valdes, Pancho, 114

Valencia, Anselmo, 178–81, 183

Valencia, Francisco, 81

Valenzuela, Antonia, 103

Valenzuela, Guadalupe, 107

Valenzuela, Paulino, 93

Velasco, Alejandro, 159

Velasco, Francisco, 159

Velasco, Joe, 207

Vicam, 21 (map), 33, 84, 93, 106–107, 224n70. *See also* Eight Yaqui towns

CPSIA information can be obtained
at www.ICGtesting.com
Printed in the USA
LVOW12s0930180418

573922LV00002B/207/P